How Language Began

Human language is not the same as human speech. We use gestures and signs to communicate alongside, or instead of, speaking. Yet gestures and speech are processed in the same areas of the human brain, and the study of how both have evolved is central to research on the origins of human communication. Written by one of the pioneers of the field, this is the first book to explain how speech and gesture evolved together into a system that all humans possess. Nearly all theorizing about the origins of language either ignores gesture, views it as an add-on, or supposes that language began in gesture and was later replaced by speech. David McNeill challenges the popular "gesture-first" theory that language first emerged in a gesture-only form, and proposes a ground-breaking theory of the evolution of language which explains how speech and gesture became unified.

DAVID MCNEILL is Professor Emeritus in the Departments of Psychology and Linguistics at the University of Chicago. His publications include *Hand and Mind* (1992), *Gesture and Thought* (2005), and *Language and Gesture* (Cambridge, 2000).

Approaches to the Evolution of Language

The evolution of human language is a rapidly growing area of study and research, undertaken from a wide range of perspectives. This new series provides a forum for the very best contributions to this fascinating subject. Taking an interdisciplinary approach, the series as a whole encourages a productive dialogue between those working in linguistics, biology, psychology, anthropology and cognitive science.

Published titles
Language Evolution and Syntactic Theory Anna R. Kinsella
The Evolution of Human Language: Biolinguistic Perspectives
    Richard K. Larson, Viviane Depréz and Hiroko Yamakido
How Language Began: Gesture and Speech in Human Evolution
    David McNeill

How Language Began

Gesture and Speech in Human Evolution

DAVID MCNEILL

CAMBRIDGE
UNIVERSITY PRESS

CAMBRIDGE UNIVERSITY PRESS
Cambridge, New York, Melbourne, Madrid, Cape Town,
Singapore, São Paulo, Delhi, Mexico City

Cambridge University Press
The Edinburgh Building, Cambridge CB2 8RU, UK

Published in the United States of America by Cambridge University Press, New York

www.cambridge.org
Information on this title: www.cambridge.org/9781107605497

First published 2012

Printed and bound in the United Kingdom by the MPG Books Group

A catalog record for this publication is available from the British Library

Library of Congress Cataloging in Publication data

McNeill, David.
    How language began : gesture and speech in human evolution / David McNeill.
        pages ;   cm
    Includes bibliographical references and index.
    ISBN 978-1-107-02121-1 (hardback : alkaline paper)
    1. Language and languages – Origin.   2. Speech and gesture.   I. Title.
    P116.M455   2012
    401 – dc23   2012021835

ISBN 978-1-107-02121-1 Hardback
ISBN 978-1-107-60549-7 Paperback

For Our Lucky Charm

Contents

Figures

Tables

Preface – Out on a limb

This is my third book to focus on the nexus of gesture and language. Together, the three amount to a kind of unintended trilogy, what has turned out to be a sustained examination and ultimate explanation of a certain phenomenon. The first, *Hand and Mind* (1992), introduced what was then a newly discovered world of gesture, not the stand-alones (known as emblems) that have been acknowledged for millennia, but those over-looked but omnipresent gestures that wed themselves to speech itself. The second, *Gesture and Thought* (2005), developed an explanation of this wedding, the growth point. Now I tackle the origin of the growth point in evolution. By this third volume I am aware of having run far out on a limb. Out on a limb because in crafting the book I have followed a line of argument to its logical limit, or as close to a limit as I can get. The line is that language is more than the lexicosyntactic forms that one sees in written texts and the analyses of linguistics. It is also imagery. This imagery is in gesture, and is inseparable from language. The hypothesis of a growth point encompasses this idea. Taking seriously that language includes gesture as an integral component changes the look of everything. We see language in a new way, as a dynamic "language-as-action-and-being" phenomenon, not replacing but joining the traditional static (synchronic) "language-as-object" conception that has guided linguistics for more than a century.

One idea is more than one note, and in pursuing it I have discovered that it touches a wide range of other topics in language, children's development, brain, mind, and society. In this way, a great breadth of phenomena is linked. I cover, besides gesture and its binding power with speech, a specific mechanism for the origin of language, and the scenarios in which it could have arisen; an alternative, the "gesture-first" hypothesis, which fails both by predicting what did not evolve and not predicting what did evolve; the "equiprimordiality" of speech and gesture instead; a thought–language–hand brain link present in all humans but revealed directly in deafferentation cases where gestures occur normally but practical actions are impossible; phylogenetic echoes in ontogenesis of *two* language origins, one of which is extinct (which extinction is also echoed in ontogenesis); new forms of action of the hands and vocal tract orchestrated by significances other than the actions themselves; the origin of syntax, while biological, to make these new actions shareable and portable in encounters with others in socio-culturally maintained templates (constructions); psychological sources of linguistic diversity; parallels and non-parallels to human language in chimpanzee and other primates; the remarkable, still-emerging discoveries in comparative genetics of the two or three kinds of humans known to have existed and how they may have differed in linguistic capacities; how consciousness and memory were reshaped by the origin of language; gestures during musical performances and the possibility of gestures hidden in written prose on the page; the loss of language at points of vulnerability left over from the origin; and the unlikelihood of language evolving in any species that lacks hands.

Acknowledgments

For comments on the manuscript, I am grateful to Carolin Kirchhof, Liesbet Quaeghebeur, Kazuki Sekine, Randall L. B. McNeill, Frank Bechter, Jana Bressem, and above all Elena Levy, with whom years ago I started the serious study of speech and gesture and who has read and commented on the manuscript more than once. I have done my best to incorporate everything these responsive fellow gesture-world inhabitants have suggested.

My colleague, Susan Duncan, has played a huge role in the development of the growth point concept, and her many contributions are recognized throughout the text.

Many of the ideas developed here were first explored with my colleagues, Bennett Bertenthal, Jonathan Cole, Susan Duncan, and Shaun Gallagher (see McNeill *et al.* 2005, 2008).

I wish to acknowledge Michael Arbib for his spirited defense of "gesture-first" made in his editor's review of our McNeill *et al.* paper in *Interaction Studies* (2008), which has helped shape the discussion in Chapter 3.

Bencie Woll provided excellent feedback especially concerning Chapter 2, which is far more digestible as a result, and also for the precious Henry Sweet reference, quoted in Table 3.1.

Nobuhiro Furuyama made very helpful comments about the "supplantation" arguments of Chapter 3.

Sarah Thomason made saving comments about the "Psycho-Babel" section of Chapter 3.

Steve McCafferty's comments helped jell the discussion of metaphoricity in Chapter 4.

The title and subtitle emerged in interactions with Cambridge University Press.

I wish to thank both Susan and Elena for seeing that what started as notes had undergone a metamorphosis into this book.

For a second time Nobuko McNeill has inspired chapters with her amusing, pithy, clear-headed and invariably thought-provoking and (often) thought-shaking remarks.

I thank my family, Nobuko, Cheryl and Randall, for their patience, laughter, encouragement, and suggestions as they combated my wavering determination to see this project through, and provided ideas that figure in several chapters.

The work tapped in writing this book has been supported over the years by research grants from NSF, NIH, the Video Analysis and Content Extraction (VACE) project (with Francis Quek and Mary Harper), The Spencer Foundation, and The Samuel Beck Memorial Fund of the University of Chicago.

I have lectured on the topics in this book at two International Society for Gesture Studies Conferences, in Austin and in Evanston, at the Chicago Linguistics Society, at the German Semiotics Society in Dresden, at the two *ORAGEs* (in Besançon and Aix-en-Provence), and at universities and research institutes in Denmark, France, Germany, Italy, Japan, Sweden, and the US.

1 | Introduction – gesture and the origin of language

It's like seeing someone's thought.
        – Mitsuko Iriye, historian, on learning to code gestures
        (in the 1980s)

1.1 THE ORIGIN OF LANGUAGE

The origin of language, a prodigal topic, has recently returned to respectability after a long exile.[1] Discoveries in linguistics, brain science, primate studies, children's development, and elsewhere have inspired new interest after the infamous nineteenth-century ban (actually, bans) on the topic – both the Société de Linguistique de Paris in 1865 and the Philological Society of London in 1873 prohibiting all contributions on the topic (London promising that any such would be tossed directly into the wastebasket; all of this described in Kendon 1991). The topic can be approached from many angles. Most common seems to be the comparative – differences and resemblances between humans and other primates. A related approach is to consider the brain mechanisms underlying communicative vocalizations and/or gesture. These have been recorded directly in some primate species and can be compared to humans on performance measures thought to depend on similar brain mechanisms. Or a linguistic angle – the key features of human language and whether anything can be said of how they came to be and whether other animal species show plausible counterparts. Approaches are combined in comparing human language to vocalizations, gestures, and/or the instructed sign language use of, say, orangutans or chimps. I will take a third approach, gestures, which also has its devotees, but I shall diverge from other approaches in crucial ways. I am not endorsing a popular current theory, appearing over and over in a veritable avalanche of recent books – what I dub "gesture-first." Despite the theory's name, the primatologist, neuroscientist, developmental psychologist, anthropologist, sign-language linguist, regular linguist, computer scientist, etc. proponents of gesture-first seemingly lack any serious acquaintance with gesture other than (it appears) its folk culture portrayals (so they do not recognize a key point of this book:

that language is misconstrued if it is not seen as a unity of language and gesture).

Gesture-first holds that the initial form of language lacked speech – it was a pantomimic or a sign language. I show that gesture-first (to put it delicately) is unlikely to be true because it is unable to capture the connections of speech and gesture that we, living counter-examples, display: it "predicts" what did not evolve (that gesture withered or was marginalized when speech arose) and does not predict what did evolve (that gesture is an integral part of speaking). A theory that says what didn't happen did, and what did happen didn't, can't generally be true, to say the least. That so many have adopted it I explain by the above-mentioned folk (and fabricated) beliefs about gestures.

The origins question homes in on what makes us human; how we diverge from other animal species, including our near neighbors, the Great Apes; it exposes in a fundamental way what comprises the gift of language. The approach here will ultimately synthesize various approaches to the question that modern authors have pioneered, not out of an urge to be all-encompassing but because these approaches will find a place in this approach's own inner logic.

The origin of language brought forth not only language but also new forms of action, new modes of thought, and new structures in the human brain. And these changes in action, thought, and brain are the sources of much else without which history, culture, and the human story could not have unfolded as they have. I hope by the end to clarify this story, how it began in unexpected ways, and on what it depends at a foundational level.

1.1.1 How this book differs

The approach here is to uncover the kind of mind that made the origin of language possible; and correspondingly, the kind of mind that language, once started, modified and extended. Other approaches emphasize the external aspects of the origin – communication, structure, parallels to other animal communication, all of which are valid but do not attempt to uncover the mindset of the creatures in which language came to be. My guiding idea and fundamental divergence is the following, proffered as an insight into the human mindset for language in general: Gestures are components of speech, not accompaniments but actually integral parts of it. Much evidence supports this idea, but its full implications have not always been recognized. The *growth point* (GP) hypothesis is designed to explicate this integral linkage. It is presented briefly here, more fully with an example below, and explained in detail in Chapter 2.

Gestures offer one kind of symbol, language a different kind, and the two kinds of semiosis ("semiosis" and "semiotic" refer to the nature of symbols) are unified in GPs; in a GP symbols of these two different orders combine. A key insight is that speech on the one hand and gesture on the other, when combined in a GP, bring semiotically opposite modes of thinking together at the same time. A GP thus forms a single mental package or idea unit out of semiotically unlike components.

This "unity of opposites," as I will call it, creates a new form of human cognition that animates language and gives it a dynamic dimension. The semiotic opposition in a GP is intrinsically unstable; it seeks a resting place. The instability and the processes initiated to stabilize or resolve it, which I call "unpacking the GP," propel thought and speech forward, hence provide a dynamic dimension of language. All of these features of language were built in by how language began.

1.2 WHAT IS "GESTURE"?

1.2.1 Definitions of "gesture"

Gesture plays a central role in the arguments of this book. It is taken seriously and I need to explain what I mean when I refer to it. I cannot deny that the word is problematic. A journalist's cliché portrays a gesture as trivial, irrelevant, and slightly contemptible. It uses "gesture" to label something that a public figure, a politician or a magnate, has done as ungenuine and feckless; as sterile, futile, pointless, unfruitful, and untruthful, made for show and not effect. The cliché is worse than irrelevant. It positively obstructs understanding. Given the word's ragged appearance I would have preferred not to use it at all but there is no avoiding it; a suitable alternative simply does not exist in our language. I once concocted a term, "temaniosis," made from a Japanese root for "imitation in the hand"[2] and a Greek suffix for "of or relating to, of the nature of," which I thought would get close to the sense of "gesture" that I am using – but discovered that it is a combination so broad linguistically, exact though it is, that it offends some readers' sensibilities. And in any case it is vain to invent a word that will not gain general currency, and I judged there was little hope of that.

Adam Kendon (2004) placed gestures in the category of "actions that have the features of manifest deliberate expressiveness." I adopt this definition but with one qualification and one proviso. The qualification is that gesture cannot be deliberate; as we regard them "gestures" are unwitting and automatic, and anything but deliberate. (Kendon may have meant by "deliberate" non-accidental, and with this I agree; but the word also conveys, "done for a purpose," and with that I do not agree.) The proviso concerns "action." In the sense that we intend (gesture as a special or what I later call a "new" kind of action) movements are orchestrated by significances created by the speaker him- or herself, not movements to attain external goals (goals lead to practical actions, not gestures). So our definition, based on Kendon's but excising "deliberate" and specifying the kind of action (and far from tripping off the tongue), is this:

A gesture is an unwitting, non-goal-directed action orchestrated by speaker-created significances, having features of manifest expressiveness.

Very often I use "gesture" still more restrictively to mean all of the above, plus:

A gesture is a manifestly expressive action that enacts imagery (not necessarily by the hands or hands alone) and is generated as part of the process of speaking.

1.3 THE GESTURE CONTINUUM

The remainder of this chapter is organized around Figure 1.1, The Gesture Continuum, a continuum of manifest expressiveness modes, all differing but all termed "gestures," annotated to show where these definitions and other important concepts apply. Later, I give examples of the Continuum and describe in detail certain features of it, especially the gesticulation pole – the focus of this book. The Gesture Continuum plays an important role as well in sorting out different explanations of the beginning of language, as Chapter 3 explains.

To begin, as the Continuum shows, the word "gesture" is problematic not only because of the ragged aspects but also because it is seriously ambiguous. It covers very different phenomena. The gestures of concern to us are integral components of speech, not substitutes, accompaniments or ornaments. Such gestures appear at one end of the Continuum, called by Kendon (1988b) "gesticulations."[3] These gestures are synchronous and co-expressive with speech, not redundant; and not signs, salutes, or what are called emblems (see below). They are by far the most frequent – in descriptive speech about 90% of utterances are accompanied by them

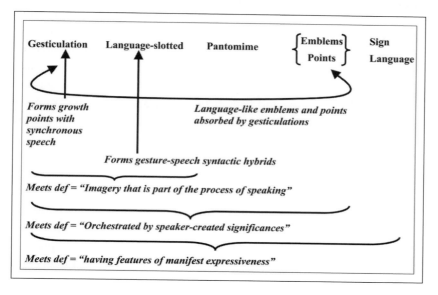

Figure 1.1 The Gesture Continuum annotated.

(Nobe 2000) and they occur in similar form and numbers across many languages.

1.3.1 Dimensions

Underlying the Continuum are three dimensions – how necessary speech is to the gesture; how language-like is the gesture; and how conventionalized is its form, so as one goes from gesticulation to sign the relationship of gesture to speech changes:

- The obligatory presence of speech decreases.
- Language-like properties increase.
- Socially regulated conventional signs replace self-generated form-meaning pairs.

1.3.2 Semiotic packages

We see the changes in how the positions along the Continuum form their own characteristic semiotic packages. At the gesticulation end (our concern) a *dual semiotic* prevails, imagery and linguistic encoding of the same underlying idea in one package, the GP. At the language-slotted point a gesture is absorbed into its sentence, changing the relationship to language by losing co-expressivity and becoming *a constituent of the sentence itself*. At pantomime the semiosis is *reenactment*, and at the emblem/pointing point a gesture is *partly encoded* in itself. Finally, at the sign language pole gesture is *fully encoded* (cf. Klima and Bellugi 1979, Bechter 2009). The examples below illustrate these semiotic packages.

1.3.3 Timing

Also characteristic of each position is a different speech–gesture temporal arrangement (difficult to indicate in a linear layout). At the gesticulation end, the significant part of the gesture – the "stroke" – and its co-expressive speech are synchronous; at the language-slotted position, gesture slots into a vacancy in the sentence; at the pantomime and emblem/point position, gesture and speech have loose temporal relationships and speech may be completely absent. Sign language, finally, is freestanding and without speech.

1.3.4 Examples (from the most to the least language-like)

An example of an American Sign Language (ASL) *sign* is TREE – the dominant arm extended upward at the elbow, the fingers extended outward (a "5-hand") and the hand rotating back and forth at the wrist. The subordinate hand is extended flat and prone under the dominant hand elbow. The sign obviously depicts a schematic tree – trunk, leaves fluttering in the wind and the ground – but the iconicity is conventionalized and must include these specific features. A signer does not make up a new sign for each occasion. Arika Okrent (pers. comm.) calls it "non-specific," in that it is used equally for all kinds of trees and tree shapes, not just those with long bare trunks and fluttering leaves. This too is part of its conventionalization. Sign Languages such as American Sign Language of the deaf and others around the world are socioculturally maintained linguistic codes that have arisen where vocal/auditory communication is impossible. The most established are full language systems in their own right. While iconicity is present it too is conventionalized. The ASL sign is an iconic depiction, but it is a *standardized* selection of iconic features that other sign languages, also with signs that are iconic and regulated, may not use at all (Danish Sign Language traces an outline of a tree).

The *emblem* is the sort of gesture that appears in atlases and dictionaries of the "gesture language" of some nationality or other. And emblems indeed show systematic language-like constraints. There are differences between well-formed and not-well-formed ways of making them. Placing the middle finger on the thumb results in a gesture with some kind of precision meaning but it is not recognizable as the "OK" sign, where forefinger and thumb are in contact and the rest of the fingers spread out (see Figure 1.4). The "OK" gesture, like a word, is constrained to assume a certain "phonological" shape. Emblems also have culturally fixed meanings or functions (for the "OK" sign approval) and exclude or hide otherwise plausible meanings (such as precision). Yet, the constraints are limited and don't by any stretch amount to a full language. There is no way to reliably reverse "OK," for example. Forming it and waving it back and forth laterally (another emblem that, on its own, signals negation) might convey "not OK" but it also might equally be seen as the opposite – waving the hand to call attention to the sign, or to suggest that many different things are OK – a flexibility that is basically not linguistic in character. I will later place *pointing* with the emblems (§1.3.2).

Pantomime is an object- or action-simulation performed without speech, a dumb show (to cite the *OED*). It is a movement, often complex and sequential, that does not accompany speech but also is not part of a gesture code. If there is speech, the pantomime tends to appear during a brief pause or oppositely may extend well before, during and after the utterance; in other words, it is loosely timed or not timed at all with speech. A simple example is, in silence, moving the hand forward from the hip with pinched fingers and turning it, to depict taking a key out of the pocket and opening a lock. The same pantomime can be performed with speech (e.g., "there's only one thing to do"), and while speech and pantomime coincide they have no organic connection, quite unlike gesticulations. Pantomimes figure prominently in the discussion of gesture-first in Chapter 3.

Language-slotted gestures may look like pantomimes or gesticulations (the least language-like pole) but the distinguishing quality is how they combine with speech. They occupy a grammatical slot, become part of the syntax of the sentence, and acquire what Saussure (1959) called "syntag-matic" linguistic value (the value a word gains in combination with other words: how for example a noun becomes a "direct object" when combined with a verb, a value it does not have alone). An example is "the place was all [gesture suggesting uproar]," in which the uproar gesture has the syntagmatic value of a predicate adjective.

Gesticulation, in contrast to language-slotted gestures, is co-produced with speech. These gestures do not replace words in grammatical slots. In the

[/ and it **goe**s <u>dOWn</u>]

Both hands mirroring each other in tense spread C-shapes, palms toward center, move down from upper central periphery to lower central periphery; square brackets indicate a gesture phrase; boldface a stroke, underlining a hold, in which the shape and position of the stroke is maintained, and font size prosodic peaks; see Chapter 2 §2.2.1.1.2 for full details of notation.

Figure 1.2 A speech-synchronized gesticulation.

narrations that provide most of the cases studied in this book, gesticulations are by far the most frequent type, occurring as often as one per second. Beats, iconics and metaphorics (all explained later) are at this gesticulation pole of the Continuum – in all cases, gesture and co-expressive speech are synchronized, gestures lack the language-like properties of recurrence and combination, and are unconstrained by conventional rules of gesture form.

Not only hand movements but the space in which the gesture occurs also can be called gesticulation. Where to make a gesture is in itself gestural and carries significance. For example, Figure 1.2 uses space iconically, the locus and direction of the gesture carrying information about the layout of the event being depicted (other gesture spaces are more metaphoric – putting one discourse theme in the left space and a contrasting theme in the right space, for example, which depicts in one layout the two themes and that they contrast).

1.4 DETAILS OF SELECTED POINTS

1.4.1 The emblem

An emblem is characterized by four related properties:

- First, an emblem is like a word of spoken language in that it is repeatable, listable, and reportable. However, unlike spoken language words, emblems do not combine into larger units ("the" + "ball" forms a new unit, a noun phrase; that phrase plus "hit" forms another unit, a verb phrase, "hit the ball"; and that phrase plus "Ludwig" forms yet another unit, a sentence) and each of the new combinations is still a unit of the language: emblems do not have this combinatoric, hierarchic, recurrent property. One emblem, say "OK," followed by another emblem, say "no" (hand, palm forward, waving back and forth), may in some contexts look like "not OK," but the two emblems have not formed a larger emblem unit. It is, rather, still two emblems, first one, then another focused on it.

- Second and related, emblems have standards of good form. The "OK" sign must be made with the tips of the forefinger and thumb in contact, the other fingers more or less extended straight out. If some other finger makes contact it may be seen as a gesture of precision but it is not the "OK" sign. Whatever the historical origin of "OK," it must meet this form standard. I consider adherence to well-formedness as one half the hallmark of an emblem, such that violations result in rejecting the gesture, even though it is meaningful as a metaphor (precision in this instance). The other half-hallmark is having culturally specified functions (here approbation), another area that is standardized. The two hallmarks correspond to what Hockett and Altmann (1968) called "duality of patterning" – both signifier form (forefinger and thumb touching) and signified content (approbation) are "patterned" (regulated) linguistically and culturally.

- The third property, in keeping with these hallmarks, is that emblems are culturally defined and maintained. Kendon's 2004 book, *Gesture*, describes the Neapolitan gesture culture in detail. Every culture has a vocabulary of emblems, usually not nearly so developed as the Neapolitan, but everywhere emblems are culturally maintained symbolic forms with specified functions – again "OK" is a convenient example. Many emblems in North America seem to have Italian or even ancient Roman sources – "OK" is one, and there are less polite others (the favorite of the road-enraged, the "finger," is said to be Roman, Morris, *et al.* 1979; whether ancient Romans used it as such is not known but it is conceivable).

- The fourth property, having to do with sources, is that many emblems can be seen to be codified versions of metaphoric gestures (these being spontaneous gesticulations that present non-spatial, non-form meanings in terms of form and space) or metonymic gestures that present meanings in terms of something else that occurs with or causes the conveyed meaning. As "raw" forms these metaphoric or metonymic gestures appear in discourse on their own. An emblem is often (I suspect always) a culturally specified version of such a metaphor or metonym, with form and meaning constrained by standards (Ishino 2007 has studied metonymy in Japanese gestures). For example, again using "OK," finger tip–finger tip contact as a metaphor of precision in the emblem takes only a certain form (forefinger/thumb contact) and a meaning (approbation). The metaphor source is seen in that the approbation is of a certain kind, that for something "just right"; furthermore, a different metaphor source is in "thumbs-up," a different approbation emblem, not the precision of "just-right" but the general metaphor of better is higher, "up on top," this the spatial locus the upturned thumb depicts iconically). This link of approbation to precision and on-top is not only in emblems but also appears in spoken forms, "precisely – that's it!" and "came out on top" (of an exam or contest).

1.4.2 Pointing

Traditionally the point does not have its own spot on the Gesture Continuum and, indeed, it is not obvious where to put it. Almost every complex gesticulation implies some deixis. The downward thrust of Figure 1.2 indicated the location of the pipe, its position relative to the character and the bowling ball. This deixis was accomplished not with a dedicated point but was built into the gesticulation itself. A dedicated, stand-alone point on the other hand has properties that make it like an emblem. First, points also have form standards – the extended index finger is standard in North American and Northern European culture; a flat hand is standard in some British Isle uses (Kendon 2004); and lip points are standard in Laos (Enfield 2001; see Figure 1.3). All have in common an iconic vector from the zero point, or "origo," to some target of the point.

Another similarity, less obvious, is how points and emblems relate to speech. While points and demonstrative pronouns ("this," "that" etc.) can synchronize (Levelt, Richardson and La Heij 1982), and thus appear to be like gesticulations, in fact the timing is different from that of gesticulation and more like that of an emblem. The similarity appears when gesture and speech are asynchronous. For both points and emblems asynchronies are meaningful, and are so in both directions. Asynchronous gesticulations, on the other hand, are merely slovenly and are not meaningful. Say "that" and then point; or point and then say "that"; or say and point simultaneously – each combination is meaningful and different (the meanings seem

Figure 1.3 Jahai (Laos) lip point. From Enfield (2001).
Used with permission of John Benjamins Publishing
Company, Amsterdam/Philadelphia.
www.benjamins.com.

metapragmatic – indicating how speech and gesture are being used prag-matically). The same asynchronies and differences appear with emblems, e.g., do the same experiment, with "okay" and the OK emblem. In contrast, duplicate the experiment with the "falling hollowness" gesture of Figure 1.2, either synchronized with speech ("goes down") or not, and the meaning is the same until the asynchrony grows so great that the gesture and speech lose unity and seem to be repetitions. So for several reasons, pointing joins the emblem slot, and resides far from gesticulation as one of the most language-like of the non-Sign Language gestures.

1.4.3 Gesticulation

Finally, the gesticulation pole: the properties here will figure in arguments throughout book. Gesticulation contains clues to how language began – its global and synthetic semiosis, its co-expressivity with the opposite semiosis of speech, and its synchrony with speech at this point of co-expressivity – and our aim is to explain its origin in human evolution.

1.4.3.1 Semiotic opposites and co-expressivity

In Figure 1.2 the gesture showed, in one symbolic form, a moving entity (the bowling ball), its path (downward), and a landmark, the pipe, through which it passed, all in a single package. The effect is a uniquely gestural way of packaging meaning – something like "falling hollowness" (a bundle of semantic parts, according to Talmy 2000, that does not occur as a single word in any language but here spontaneously occurred as a single gesture). The two semiotic modes, imagery in gesture and codification in speech, formed this package of the idea.

The speaker's hands, furthermore, in their tension ("tense spread C-shapes"), also included the idea of the bowling ball as the point of energy in the episode, for which, again, there is no speech equivalent (although in this instance the speaker could have formed one).

The gesture was thus *synthetic* – synthesized several elements of meaning that would be separated in speech. The hands are simultaneously the ball, the shape of the pipe, and the downward motion of the ball, the point of energy and include meanings (like "downward moving hollowness") that never occur as single words in speech.

Furthermore, the gesture was *global* – the elements of the gesture (the handshape, the location, the direction, the tension) are meaningful only as parts of the whole. They are not meaningful in themselves – the meaning determination was from whole to part, not part to whole. "Global" doesn't mean that only the whole is meaningful; it is that the parts of the whole gain meaning from the whole. None of these meanings were attached to the hand properties before this immediate gesture but, within it, they have the meanings described.

In speech, everything is the reverse – analytic, segmented, and combinatoric. Rather than synthesis, speech componentializes the event: a directed path ("down") plus the idea of the ball ("it") as separate semantic components. This analytic separation requires that direction and entity then be combined to obtain the composite meaning of the whole. Rather than whole to part, the direction is part to whole. In speech the words "and it goes down," the intransitive construction, the metapragmatic function of the "and" (signaling that more is to come, and here it is), all conventional forms of English with their own meanings, broke the meaning of the whole into segments and then recomposed it, parts-to-whole, by combining the separately meaningful segments according to a grammatical plan which distributed the bits over the full surface of the construction ("and + it + goes + down").

At the gesticulation pole, accordingly, gesture and speech need not convey the same content but even if they do, they are *semiotic* opposites. While opposed as semiotic modes, speech and gesture are "co-expressive," meaning that each symbol, in its own way, expresses the same idea, possibly in different aspects. Moreover, speech and gesture synchronize at the point where they are co-expressive (holds enforce this). This fact – semiotically opposite symbols synchronizing where they are co-expressive – is fundamental to our method: it means that at points of co-expressivity, in GPs, ideas are cast simultaneously in opposite semiotic modes. From this fact an entire dynamic dimension of language arises. This *dual semiosis* is an important clue to what evolved at the origin of language.

1.4.3.2 The binding of opposites

A final point is the binding of gestures and speech when they participate in the formation of cognitive units, a binding so strong that efforts to separate them fail – either speech and gesture remain together or they are jointly interfered with; in either case the speech–gesture bond is unbroken. The following are experimental observations of tight binding:

- Delayed auditory feedback – the experience of hearing your own voice played back after a short delay – produces major speech disturbances but does not break the speech-gesture synchrony (McNeill 1992).
- Stuttering and gesture are incompatible. The onset of a gesture inoculates against stuttering and, conversely, once a gesture is going the onset of stuttering stops the gesture immediately (Mayberry and Jaques 2000).
- People blind from birth, who have never seen gestures and have no benefit from experiencing them in others, gesture and do so even to other blind people who they know are blind (Iverson and Goldin-Meadow 1997).
- People born without limbs "gesture," that is, have the neurological feeling they gesture, with full significance, as they speak (Ramachandran and Blakeslee 1998; see interpretation in McNeill 2005)
- Memory loss interrupts speech and gesture jointly; it is not that gesture is a "gap-filler" when speech fails (McNeill 2005).
- Conversely, gestures tend to protect memory from interference (Goldin-Meadow *et al.* 2001; also Chapter 4, §1.9.2).
- When speech and gesture contain content belonging to different conceptions (a "mismatch") gesture trumps speech, the content of which is lost (Goldin-Meadow and Sandhofer 1999); in other words, the transmission of *speech* information (orchestrated by gesture imagery) insists on speech–gesture co-expressivity.

A way to explain the superglue-like adhesiveness of speech and gesture these findings reveal is that they are bound together by the requirements of idea unit formation. Thought-in-speech takes place simultaneously in imagery and language form, and they cannot be separated. To think while speaking is to be active in both semiotic modes at once. We return to this dual semiotic form of cognition in Chapter 2 and its evolution in Chapter 3, where we will see that it was a condition for the beginning of language.

1.4.3.3 Metaphors

Spontaneous metaphoric/metonymic gestures while they have a kinship with emblems, lack gesture standards of their own, qua gestures. The metaphor/metonym itself is the regulator of the gesture's form and function. The only constraints are that, as a form, the gesture depicts the "vehicle" of its metaphor/metonym, and has a meaning that relates in some way to its "referent" ("vehicle" and "referent" from Richards 1936). A metaphoric gesture widespread in many languages is the palm up, open hand, for "hold-ing" a discursive "object," a gestural version of the "conduit" metaphor that was first identified linguistically by Reddy (1979) and extended by Lakoff and Johnson (1980). In the linguistic conduit, the concept of meaning itself is presented as a substance in the hand, e.g., "she handed him the answer." The gesture version iconically depicts this vehicle but otherwise has no standard of its own (the name "conduit" comes from another aspect of the metaphor – objects being sent along a conduit, as in "it got across/through"). Chapter 4 has extensive further discussion of emblems and their link to metaphor.

1.4.3.4 The beat

One other gesture type merits mention, and with it we finish our survey. The beat is also a gesture at the gesticulation pole – as such, it lacks language-like properties, is nonconventional, and is strongly dependent on co-expressive speech. It is unique among gestures in having almost purely a discourse meaning. Beats can be seen as miniaturized versions of other gestures, even when the other gesture is concurrent – a sort of double exposure, a conception based on Tuite 1993, who argued that every gesture contains a rhythmical pulse, a beat, on which iconicity and metaphoricity build; here, we say that every beat is a distillation or miniaturization of a more complex or larger gesture. It is called the "beat" after the musical beat or the idea of beating a surface of some kind – the hand(s) moving up and down or back and forth in short strokes. This rhythmicity of beats is said to be the beat's *raison d'être* but it may actually be effect rather than cause. The function of the beat's double exposure (concurrent or successive) is like that of yellow highlighter – the beat emphasizes that something else, speech or gestures other than the beat itself, is important in some larger context. It is this expansion to context the beat signals. This function explains why beats coincide with prosodic emphasis, since prosody performs a similar function; that is the true co-expressivity of the beat: prosodic highlighting. Thus beats move with the speech rhythm but this rhythm is not the source; rather, both beat and rhythm have a shared source in contextual highlighting. Bressem (2010) has tracked different handshapes and orientations of beats with shadings of this function.

The beat's formal simplicity belies its semiotic complexity. Of gestures, beats stand among the more semiotically complex. One can see the complexity in the at least four kinds of beat that capture different relationships to the larger context:

1. Beats alone highlight that content (otherwise not imaged) is new in the context. An example (from a narration of a film, Hitchcock's *Blackmail*) is enumerating the features of a newly introduced character in the story: "his **gir**lfriend, **Al**ice, Alice Wh**i**te," with a beat accompanying each increment of new (non-repeated) information – her functional role, first name, and last name. The stress peaks, indicated with enlarged font, perform the same function. The beats are co-expressive with this prosody marking. Together they add extra effort and this highlights the increments of content.

2. Beats following another gesture. An example is "the weight came down (with a large downward iconic gesture) and he got clobbered (a beat)." The beat, a miniaturized version of the first gesture, synchronizes with a stress peak but its function is not to tap out this rhythm but to indicate the point in speech that relates to the first gesture semantically (the result of the weight's falling).

3. Beats in advance of another gesture – the reverse of (2). Such a sequence indicates a shift of discourse level, from the metalevel (about the structure of the discourse) with the beat, to a descriptive level (the content of the discourse) with the following full gesture; the beat is a miniaturized anticipation of the larger gesture. For example, "so the next thing he does (metanarrative with a beat) is go in the front door" (narrative with an iconic gesture for motion). The beat indicates a structural feature of the story – its temporal sequence – to which the iconic gesture for entering that follows relates.

Finally, (4) a beat superimposed on an ongoing representational gesture. The beat signals that the gesture (and its concomitant speech) has a significance beyond itself in the larger context. It is the all-purpose highlighter in which the other cases (enumeration, semantic linkage, discourse level shift) all may occur, and is a "double flash" of the gesture on which it is riding.

To summarize, the beat in all its manifestations relates the moment of its occurrence to some other occurrence. Beats only exist in relation to things other than themselves.

The beat, miniscule as it is, also absorbs emblems. Beats coinciding with emblems like "OK" enable them to time exactly with co-expressive speech in the manner of a beat, as when someone says, "it **wa**s the p**er**fect t**i**me to g**O**," an "OK" sign superimposed, beatlike, on each stressed syllable, which has absorbed the emblem (the overall effect seems ironic).

1.4.4 Absorption and layering

The arrow in Figure 1.1 linking emblems/points to gesticulation reflects that the latter can absorb the former and bring them, standards and all, into the gesticulation's semiotic opposition to speech. In this way, the emblem/point borrows the gesticulation's timing. In return, the gesticulation imbibes the standards and prescribed functions of the emblem or point. The arrow in Figure 1.1 also runs from gesticulation back to the emblem/points slot, reflecting these two-way influences.

The Gesture Continuum changes along the three dimensions with which it was introduced: (1) the obligatory presence of speech declines; (2) language-like properties increase; and (3) socially regulated conventional signs replace self-generated form–meaning pairs. However, the changes are not smooth – there are "bumps." The best way to see them is in terms of the temporal alignments of gestures with speech. Timing has unique properties at each of the Gesture Continuum slots: gesticulations synchronize with their co-expressive speech; language-slotted gestures with a vacant linguistic constituent, for instance a vanished predicate adjective; pantomimes and emblems have no fixed temporal relationships with speech, and may appear without it; and sign languages are speech-free.

Consider again the "OK" sign, now a real occurrence by the then CIT CEO, Jeffrey Peek, in 2006 (Figure 1.4 from the *WSJ*, July 22, 2009). The gesture seems to have signified that some content or other that had already been identified with the gesture locus is "OK" (we don't have the accompanying speech). This gesticulation-like use of space with a non-spatial

Figure 1.4 Canonical "OK." From the WSJ. "OK" sign absorbed into (likely) metaphoric space.

meaning (using space as metaphor) and the emblem are layered within one gesture. By this process, the emblem takes on the temporal properties of gesticulation and synchronizes with the speech with which it is now (thanks to absorption) co-expressive. Blending emblems/points and gesticulations enriches both sides; awakening the metaphors hidden inside the emblem (Müller 2008) and the gesticulation acquiring some of the emblem's cultural anchor, and so linking itself to conventions without being conventionalized itself.

Pointing, like an emblem, is also readily absorbed into gesticulation. However, pantomime is not. When it co-occurs with speech the timing is irregular; it precedes or follows and, even when co-occurring with speech, is never synchronized with co-expressive speech as required to form a growth point. The only integration with speech is as a "gap-filler" (in Susan Duncan's phrase), speech ceasing, the pantomime sliding into the gap; in other words, it appears at the language-slotted position of the Continuum, not at the gesticulation one ("the parents were [pantomime of confusion]"). This has considerable significance for the evolutionary viewpoint to be laid out in Chapter 3. Because of how language originated, pantomime was rejected in the new emerging form. This rejection we see now in the way pantomime bounces along the Continuum ending up, not as a gesticulation, but as a grammatical constituent; not as a partner but as a kind of slot-filler.[4]

1.5 SUMMARIZING GESTURE

The focus of this book is the gesticulation pole. Here we find GPs and the semiotic oppositions of imagery and language forms, the origins of which we aim to elucidate.[5]

2 | What evolved (in part) – the growth point

2.1 THE TWO-DIMENSIONS FRAMEWORK

Why do we gesture? Many would say that it brings emphasis, energy, and ornamentation to speech (which is assumed to be the core of what is taking place); in short, gesture is an "add-on."[1] However, evidence is against this. While gestures enhance materialization, a topic we consider in Chapter 4, the core is gesture and speech *together*. They are bound more tightly than saying the gesture is an "add-on" or "ornament" implies. They are united as a matter of thought itself. Even if for some reason a gesture is not externalized (social inappropriateness, physical difficulty, etc.), the imagery it embodies can still be present, hidden but part of the speech process (it may even surface in some other part of the body, the feet for example).

To answer to the question, Why do we gesture?, this chapter says that it is an integral part of thinking in language; that combined with speech it creates a dynamic dimension on which thought and speech come alive. Observing the gesture and the co-expressive speech it synchronizes with, we witness the ongoing imagery–language dialectic of which the GP is the unit.

Chapter 1 introduced the growth point as the unit of this imagery-language dialectic. Now we flesh it out with a fuller picture of what evolved and what it does. Table 2.1 summarizes the semiotic contrasts bundled in GPs. It shows that, in the GP, ideas are simultaneously cast in two ways. These oppositions create the dialectic and are the engine driving language and thought forward in online thinking and speaking. A GP is the nexus at which the static and dynamic intersect – two dimensions of language that will be given equal weight. In combining the dynamic and static, the GP becomes the minimal unit of the dynamic dimension itself.

It is called a growth point because it is meant to be the initial pulse of thinking-for-(and while)-speaking, from which a dynamic process of organization emerges. The linguistic component categorizes the imagery component. Linguistic categorization is important since it brings imagery into the system of language. Imagery is equally important, since it grounds

Table 2.1 Semiotic oppositions within GPs

Imagery side	Language side
Global: meanings of parts dependent on whole.	*Compositional*: meaning of whole dependent on parts.
Synthetic: distinguishable meanings in single image.	*Analytic*: distinguishable meanings in separate linguistic forms.
Idiosyncratic: forms created on the fly.	*Conventional*: forms regulated by standards.
Additive: when images combine, there is new detail, no new syntagmatic value.	*Combinatoric*: when parts combine, there is new syntagmatic value.

the linguistic categories in a visuospatial frame. The imagery is visuoactional, not photographic. The gesture provides the GP with the property of "chunking," a hallmark of expert performance (cf. Chase and Ericsson 1981), whereby a chunk of linguistic output (not necessarily a grammatical chunk) is organized around the presentation of an image. Synchronized speech and gesture is the key to this theoretical GP unit.

2.1.1 The dimensions

Speaking is more than uttering speech sounds with meaning; more deeply it is also "inhabiting" language (a term from Merleau-Ponty 1962). The GP is a hypothesis of how this multilayered inhabitance takes place. The dimensions that cross in the GP have classically been called "linguistic" and "psychological" but better (and less proprietary) terms are *static* and *dynamic*. Some phenomena are accessible or prominent on one dimension, others on the other, but the dynamic and static dimensions cannot be isolated: they intersect and interact. The dimensions are structured on different principles and draw on different methods of description and analysis (the field of linguistics specializing on the static dimension). Yet, both are dimensions of language, and to explain the origin of language we must understand how they work together.

- The static dimension is classically accessed through the synchronic method. Language in this method is viewed as a totality at a single theoretical instant. Saussure (1959) argued that only in this way, with the whole of language laid out panoramically, could the contrasts be discerned that define *langue* (the "systematic" aspects of a given language) and the linguistic values of words and larger constituents that contrasts generate (two kinds of values – the "syntagmatic" and the "paradigmatic," defined below). "In language," Saussure said, "there are only differences" (he offered words to illustrate the concept but it applies to phrases and full sentences as well). To use Saussure's example, in English sheep on the hoof vs. sheep cooked contrast lexically, "sheep" vs. "mutton." French has no lexical contrast at this point – both states are "mouton." The words in the two languages therefore translate each other in one sense, but have different values, necessarily so because value is difference, and "sheep" and "mouton," despite translating each other, differ in their internal-to-*langue* contrasts). Difference and linguistic value are the foundation of the static dimension ("static" does not mean "stasis" – we are not speaking of moments of repose between bursts of activity: every linguistic event can be regarded statically or dynamically or, as here, both).

In a rather trenchant remark, Roman Jakobson wrote that "[t]he poetic function projects the principle of equivalence from the axis of selection into the axis of combination" (Jakobson 1960, p. 358), where the "axis of selection" is the **paradigmatic** dimension – contrasts established when a linguistic form is selected from a set of alternatives ("sheep'" and "mutton" are thus on an axis of selection), and the "axis of combination" is the **syntagmatic** dimension on which combined words generate new values and units ("hit" and "ball" combined into "hit the ball," a new unit, generate the syntagmatic value of a direct object). By poetic function, Jakobson means a process whereby syntagmatic sequences come to have paradigmatic values.[2]

- The *dynamic* dimension could be termed the "activity" of language but I am calling it (again invoking Merleau-Ponty) "inhabiting" language with one's being, thought, and action. This terminology has the advantage of alluding to both *langue*, the static system synchronically revealed, and to whatever animates it, the dynamic dimension. A historical figure associated with language so regarded dynamically is Vygotsky (1987). On the dynamic dimension, units come and go, emerge and disperse in real time. It crosses at 90 degrees the abstractions from time and the unmoving totality of synchronic *langue*.
- Chomsky's (1965) concept of *competence* aligns with Saussurian *langue*, the system of language, but with the difference that "competence" attributes the system of language to the individual as a personal property whereas *langue* is what Saussure called a "social fact," a socially constituted set of norms. These definitions are not contradictory but take different perspectives onto the same static sets of linguistic forms.

Parole and "performance," the other terms from Saussure and Chomsky, respectively, are each defined in relation to their own static counterparts. The formula is *langage* minus *langue* = *parole* (where *langage* is the semiotic totality of language). So *parole* is the "non-systematic" part (i.e., what remains after subtracting the systematic part or *langue*) of *langage*. "Performance" taps a different metaphor. It is the "use" of competence (the static totality of language in a personal knowledge base) subjected to the shortcomings of memory, attention, etc. that are irrelevant to competence. "Use" indeed belongs on the dynamic dimension but is not the same as "inhabiting" language with one's imagery and thought. Performance (the technical concept) is the attempt to deploy competence. Inhabitance (our concept) is not "deploying" – an inappropriate manipulative metaphor – but "living in" and "through" language. An imagery–language dialectic is neither "subtraction" nor "use." It is a positive process of its own that requires *langue*/competence (as one pole of the dialectic) but does not derive from it. Linguistic form (regarded either as *langue* or competence) and imagery are both necessary and are equally part of the dialectic.

2.1.2 The dialectic

A GP is a minimal unit of imagery–language dialectic in that:

- A conflict or opposition exists between the semiotic modes of imagery and linguistic categorization when they embody the same underlying idea.
- The combination is unstable.
- The dialectic accordingly seeks stability, change to find a resolution.
- Change is achieved by "unpacking" the growth point into a syntactic construction or approximation thereto, providing a stable stopping point that completes the process of growth (a new cycle able to start immediately). The construction renders the GP as a socially constituted entity of *langue*, the gesture-imagery providing the framework within which the unpacking works, and the GP as a whole evoking and guiding it.

The imagery–language dialectic is thus a model of the animation of language both in its embodiment of conflict and in the changes it evokes. Moreover, it also embodies the immediate context of speaking (of which more below). Because of this imagery–language dialectic gesture is an integral part of language in the sense of *langage*, "the semiotic totality of language in general," and works through its semiotic opposition to *langue* – the system of differences and linguistic values. (The seeming contradiction when we say that imagery "opposes" language, and also when we say that imagery is "part" of language, is illusory: different senses of the word "language" are involved, *langue* for "opposes" and *langage* for "part of." It would be tedious to always use the French terms, and I rely on the context to indicate the sense and mostly speak just of "language.")

2.1.2.1 How "dialectic" compares to "parole" and "performance"

The tags address different phenomena:

- "*Parole*": lack of linguistic system.
- "Performance": using and filtering the system.
- "The dialectic": inhabiting it.

These do not refer to each other and I see no coherent way to combine them. The first and second separate the action of speaking from the systematic aspects of language, the better to reveal the synchronic system, but in so doing cannot see that language itself is two-dimensional, an intersection of static and dynamic. The third has the merit that it combines them. The dynamic dimension arises only in interaction with the static. So our choice is for inhabitance, based on the conviction that language has a dynamic dimension, and that the static is brought to life on it by engagement with imagery, thought, and context.

I should be clear that the dialectic project cannot be identified with any one synchronic realization.[3] The choice of a static dimension description (or descriptions) for the GP is based solely on the ability of the static approach to throw light on how the static and dynamic dimensions intersect. Because of its general sympathy to the gesture approach, I rely mostly on cognitive grammar, but it, no less than others, is synchronic in character. Its unique approach lies in finding cognitive templates built into the system of language but this still has a static focus (as some have acknowledged, cf. Langacker 2000).

2.2 GP PROPERTIES

2.2.1 Empirical base

The GP is an empirical concept. It is a *hypothesis* concerning observed speech–gesture-context in observable data. Growth points are inferred from the totality of communicative events, with special focus on speech–gesture synchrony and co-expressivity.

A given GP, regarded as a hypothesis, is justified to the extent that speech and gesture are (a) synchronized, (b) co-expressive, (c) jointly form a "psychological predicate," and (d) present the same idea in opposite semiotic modes ("synchrony," "co-expressiveness," and "psychological predicate" will become clear in the following discussion). With careful observation these criteria can be tested for applicability, as illustrated with multiple examples below and elaborated in Chapter 6.

Our next step is to explain how we have collected our gesture samples and notate on the page what we observe.

2.2.1.1 The storytelling method

The gestures in Figures 1.2, 2.1 and other examples in this book were collected in a standardized manner: a participant is shown an approximately eight-minute long animated Tweety and Sylvester cartoon ("Canary Row," Warner Brothers, 1950). For readers unfamiliar with the genre, Tweety is a pear-shaped, pugilistic canary belonging to an elderly, far from retiring character named Granny. Sylvester is an enterprising cat, endlessly pursuing Tweety with culinary goals, whose lot is frustration and disaster. The genre was familiar to our narrators but the specific cartoon, Canary Row, was new to them. The cartoon consists of eight episodes, all with the same pursuit–catastrophe theme and often amusing surface variation. It was originally selected (McNeill and Levy 1982) to be shown to children but adults also find it engaging. One participant (the "speaker"), chosen at random, was shown the cartoon in its entirety. Immediately after viewing it the speaker recounted the story to a second participant "as accurately and completely as possible, as your listener will have to retell the story based on your narration" (or words to this effect). The second participant was a genuine listener, not one of the experimenters (usually a friend or spouse). The performance was audio-video recorded with the speaker in full camera view and at least the front half of the listener as well (using a single camera, the best recording position is diagonally to the front and side, at head level with respect to the speaker and turned slightly down to take in the entire seated person). The instructions emphasized that the aim of the experiment was to study storytelling; there was no mention of gesture.

2.2.1.1.1 Advantages and limits

The storytelling method, while not conversational (although the listener reacts and asks questions), is a natural form of discourse. There are no constraints or guides for what the speaker does, apart from "telling the story in full." Narrations typically run 5 or 6 minutes, almost as long as the cartoon itself, and may include more than 100 gesture events, an ample collection of entirely spontaneous, continuous, free, and "natural" behavior.

An advantage of the cartoon (as well as routes and living-spaces) as a gesture and speech stimulus is that while it gives the speaker freedom we, the observers, know the source of the story. This enables us to avoid a logical circularity that plagues other naturalistic observations, where often only speech provides the clue to what a gesture may be about. We use what is said by the speaker (or listener on occasion) to identify the events that are being talked about, but we also have our own knowledge of the event and can tell what the gesture is depicting from that knowledge as well. This is important since it gives us the basis to identify the gesture's own aspects of the event and not be limited to replications of the content of speech. Without this ability we cannot distinguish the co-expressiveness of speech and gesture (where they cover the same idea unit but not necessarily the same aspects) from redundancy (where they automatically have the same content).

2.2.1.1.2 Typological conventions

Most notation conventions we use are illustrated in the transcription of Figure 1.2:

[/ and it **goe**s dOWn]

What Kendon (1980) called the gesture *phrase* – one complete "manifestly expressive action" – is enclosed within the "[" and "]" brackets. In any gesture phrase are up to five distinguishable *phases*. Not all phases need be present, but a *stroke*, the image-bearing phase, marked in boldface, is obligatory; without a stroke a gesture is not said to have occurred. Figure 1.2 had one stroke during "goes." The *preparation* phase is the hand getting into position to make the stroke and is indicated by the span from the left bracket to the start of the boldface stroke (if the stroke begins immediately, there is no span and the boldface starts at the bracket). The preparation is the first indication that a gesture is coming into being (there is no other reason for the speaker's hands in Figure 1.2 to have shot up to head level). *Holds* are cessations of movement, and are either *prestroke*, the hand frozen and awaiting the stroke, or *poststroke*, the hand frozen in the position and handshape of the stroke even though movement has ceased. Holds of either kind are indicated with underlining (there was a poststroke hold over "down" in Figure 1.2). Prestroke and poststroke holds have different meanings (Kita 1990), prestrokes suggesting that the stroke-to-come is already tied to a particular linguistic segment which, because of grammatical or other constraints, has not yet appeared in the flow of speech; poststrokes that the stroke, even though its movement has ceased, is still relevant to the ongoing speech. The holds, pre- and poststroke, ensure speech–gesture synchrony at points of meaningful co-expressiveness. *Retraction* is from the end of the stroke or the poststroke hold to the right bracket (in Figure 1.2 retraction was immediate after "down"). The end of retraction signals that the gesture phrase and whatever psychic unit is linked to it have ended; the beginning of retraction signals that the stroke (whether extended or not) is itself spent. Prosodic emphasis in speech is not always indicated in the transcriptions but when it is, it is shown with enlarged font (as in "d**OW**n"). Slashes indicate silent pauses (multiple if the pause is elongated); the preparation phase in Figure 1.2 began during a pause (this is not always the case); crosshatches indicate audible breath pauses; asterisks ∗ indicate self-interruptions.[4]

2.2.2 Minimal unit

A GP is what Vygotsky (1987) termed a "minimal psychological unit" – the smallest package that retains the quality of a whole, in this case the whole of a gesture-language unit.

> By a unit we mean a product of analysis which, in distinction from elements, possesses all the basic properties of a whole. Further, these properties must be a living portion of the unified whole which cannot be broken down further ... (Vygotsky, *Thinking and Speech* [Russian 1934 version, p. 9], quoted by Zinchenko 1985, p. 97).

Vygotsky thus contrasts units to "elements," the latter the result of reducing the GP (in this case) to subpersonal events that do not preserve an imagery–language unity (subpersonal events, as they are termed by Quaeghebeur and Reynaert 2010, are word retrievals, true/false judgments and many others that figure in experimental studies, because they are relatively easy to measure and in computer models, because they can be handled algorithmically: *none are Vygotskian units*).

2.2.3 Examples of GPs

The semiotic oppositions fueling GPs are best demonstrated with concrete examples. This section and the next present some important observations.

Figure 2.1 "Rising hollowness" gesture with: "he goe[ss **up thrOUgh** the pipe] this time". Used with permission of University of Chicago Press. Computer art in this and later illustrations by Fey Parrill.

2.2.3.1 Stimulus

In the stimulus, Sylvester enters a drainpipe at street level and starts to climb it – on the inside. Figure 2.1 shows a speaker recounting this start of the bowling ball episode. It took place right before the bowling ball's downward motion that a different speaker highlighted in Figure 1.2. Tweety sees this attempt to climb the pipe unobserved and drops the eponymous bowling ball into the top. Sylvester and ball meet midway; he swallows it and, with the bowling ball inside (some say under) him, shoots back out of the pipe, rolls bowling-ball-like down a street, and into a bowling alley. We lose sight of him but a second later hear bowling pins being knocked over.

2.2.4 Co-expressiveness and contrast

In the stroke phase of Figure 2.1 the speaker raised her hand upward, palm facing up and fingers and thumb spread apart in a kind of upward moving open basket shape, as illustrated (the clip caught the moment she is saying the vowel of "through" with prosodic emphasis).

Speech and gesture are co-expressive but semiotically non-redundant in that each has its own means of packaging the shared idea of Sylvester's upness and interiority.

How do the semiotic frameworks differ?

Co-expressively with "up" the speaker's hand rose upward; co-expressively with "through" her fingers spread outward to create an interior space. The upward movement and the opening of the hand took place concurrently, not sequentially, and these movements occurred synchronously with "up through," the linguistic package that carries the same meanings. The contrastive emphasis on "through," highlighting interiority, is matched by the added complexity of the gesture, the spreading of the upturned fingers. What makes speech and gesture co-expressive is this joint realization of the idea of upward motion by a figure (Sylvester) and interiority.

Speech on the other hand divides the event into semantic units – a directed path ("up"), plus the idea of interiority ("through"). Analytic segregation further requires that direction and interiority be combined, to obtain the composite meaning of the whole. In gesture, this composite meaning is fused into one symbol and the semantic units are simultaneous – there is no combination (meaning determination moves from the whole to the parts, not from the parts to the whole). Thus, speech and gesture, at the moment of their synchronization, were co-expressive but semiotically opposites, and this sets the stage for packaging one thing (the conception of the cat's climbing up inside the pipe) in two forms – analytic/combinatoric and global/synthetic.

By "image" I do not mean a photo or pictogram. I mean a semiosis that is "global" and "synthetic." The "rising hollowness" gesture shows both properties.

- By 'global', I mean that the gesture's *parts* (= the hands/fingers/trajectory/space/orientation/movement details) have meanings dependent upon the meaning of the gesture *as a whole*. The parts do not have their own meanings, and the meaning of the whole is not composed out of the parts; rather; significance flows downward, from whole to parts. Thus we understand that the hand as a rising whole is Sylvester ascending; the fingers are the pipe; and the spreading of the fingers is the idea of hollowness.

The linguistic semiotic is the opposite. The meaning of the whole (the sentence or other smaller unit) is composed out of parts, which must then have their own meanings – "goes" for motion, "up" for path, and "through" for interiority; and in addition, "this time" for contrast to a preceding attempt where Sylvester climbed the pipe on its outside.

- By 'synthetic', I mean that meanings are synthesized into one symbolic form (the rising hollowness hand). In the companion speech, the gesture's meaning may be analytic separated into elements that spread over the surface of the sentence ("goes" + "up").

To summarize, the speakers in Figure 2.1 and Figure 1.2 illustrate global and synthetic gesture properties combined with analytic and combinatoric speech properties, and these were simultaneous. The gestures do not admit any decomposition. There are no subunits with independent meanings, no repeatable significances for the outspread fingers and upward palm of Figure 2.1. Only upward motion has independent meaning. It means upward, but this is all, and it is not enough to generate the meaning of the gesture whole. And even this upward meaning acquires significance as a part of the whole (it means rising *hollowness*, which comes from the whole, not from upward simple). The gesture is not composed out of parts: the parts are composed out of it. Also, the gesture is more a unified whole than just the combination of up and through. I have tried to convey this unity with the expression "rising hollowness" but whatever phrase we use the gesture has interiority, entity, and upward motion in one undecomposable symbolic form. The gesture synthesized ideas that in speech required separation – the figure in motion, the direction, and the idea of interiority were unified in the gesture while the same ideas were distributed into "he," "goes up," and "thrOUgh" in speech.

A third semiotic contrast is *combinatoric potential*; linguistic forms possess it, gesture imagery does not, and both exist within the GP (this is illustrated in Figure 2.2).

- When linguistic forms combine, new syntagmatic values emerge as part of the combination. Even a single word has the property (hence the phrase is combinatoric *potential*). Syntagmatic value (a component of linguistic value) belongs to a combination qua a combination. The simple example cited earlier is the direct object. In "toss the ball" the direct object property emerges, but "ball," by itself, is not a direct object. Note that the syntagmatic value of direct object presupposes that verb and noun form a larger unit of the sentence, here a verb phrase.

When gestures combine, in contrast, they add imagery but do not create syntagmatic values and do not create a new gesture on a higher level, with constituent gestures. There is only a more detailed version of one gesture, the parts of which retain the global-synthetic properties of gestures in general.

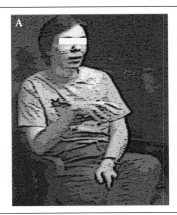 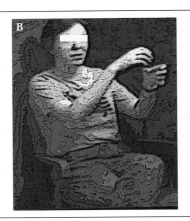

Figure 2.2 Illustrating gesture combinations. "Down the pipe" at different levels of detail. The hallmark is that a gesture combination provides new detail but not new syntagmatic value, on both scores unlike a linguistic combination (in a transitive verb phrase, "hit the ball," there is no new detail – both the act and the object are what they are independently – but there is a new value, where "ball" becomes a direct object).

Panel A, the speaker's initial description, one hand showing Tweety's "hand" shaped over the bowling ball as it is thrust into a drainpipe; the downward thrust occurred three times:

Speaker. [and throws **a bow**ling ball] [down in **the**∗] [the **thing**]

Panel B, the second description after the listener requested clarification, an elaborated gesture together with an expanded verbal description (the downward thrust now occurring six times in probably distinct GPs):

Listener. where does he throw the bowling ball?

Speaker. [**it's one of those**∗] [**the**] [**gu**][tter **pi**pes] [**an'** he t][hrows the ball into the top]

In B, the left hand adds pictorial detail but the value is intrinsic to the imagery and does not arise from the left hand–right hand combination, unlike the way that a direct object arises when a noun is combined with a transitive verb in a verb phrase.

Figure 2.2 shows gestures at two levels of detail depicting the bowling ball being dropped into the top of the drainpipe. The left panel is the initial gesture when the speaker first described the episode; the right panel is her elaboration after the listener requested clarification. The two-handed gesture in the right panel is, to be sure, a "combination" of hands but it is not a syntagmatic combination. The meanings of the hands are determined globally: that the gesture as a whole means something like *it's a gutter pipe, he drops a bowling ball into it*, and this global meaning determines the meanings of the parts; the "pipe" hand has value, not because of its combination with the "ball" hand, but from its role in the imagery as a whole. There is no new meaning emerging out of the combination as such, the way that "direct object" emerges out of the combination of verb and noun in a verb phrase, and there is not a higher gesture with the pipe and hand gestures as constituent sub-gestures; there is one gesture with enhanced detail for the whole. The gesture is also synthetic in capturing as a single expression all that, in speech, required a complex phrase (italicized above).[5]

Simultaneously speech is creating syntagmatic values ("ball" is direct object, "gutter pipe" is particularized in a nominal phrase); hence there is the further semiotic opposition involving combinatoric potential and its lack within GPs (and this applies to all GPs, since all language forms have this potential). The lack of syntagmatic value is not because gestures are unable to create them. Syntagmatic values appear in gestures when speech is suppressed and gesture is the sole means of communication. Under these conditions original, *sui generis* syntagmatic values can appear (some to be shown in Chapter 3). But when the gesture opposes linguistic form in a GP, it remains global-synthetic.

Speech and gesture differ obviously in how they distribute information in time. In speech, ideas are separated and arranged sequentially; in gesture, they are instantaneous in the sense that the meaning of the gesture is not parceled out over time (even though the gesture may take time to occur, its full meaning is immediately present). In Figure 2.1, upward motion and interiority were distributed across time in the words "up" and "through" but were concentrated in a single gesture in which were both upness and interiority.

The upshot is that the synchrony of gestures and speech puts different semiotic modes together at the same moment in the speaker's cognitive experience. This is the key to the dialectic. The modes are opposites in all the multiple ways listed in Table 2.1 – global meaning versus analytic meaning; idiosyncratic and created on the fly versus prespecified form–meaning pairings; idiosyncratic imagery versus forms regulated by conventions.

The gesture depicts, in a single symbol, the path of motion (upward), the moving figure (the cat), and the interiority of the path, a meaning we can describe as "upward moving hollowness" (like the "downward moving hollowness" in Figure 1.2, once again a semantic package in gesture that according to Talmy 2000 no language compacts into a single word).

Gestures and synchronous speech are thus *co-expressive* but *not redundant*: they express the same idea each in its own way – often each its own aspects of it. A co-expressive gesture is not a "mismatch" or a "supplement," in which speech and gesture present distinct meanings, but provides the ever-present semiotic opposition to the linguistically encoded meaning and together they fuel thought and speech.[6]

To illustrate how the dynamic dimension is energized this way, this section has explicated the semiotic contrasts between the "rising hollowness" gesture and the "up through" linguistic encoding. Co-expressiveness is the condition for speech–gesture synchrony; co-expressive speech and gesture synchronize by holding one idea in two semiotic modes. The modes then coincide. It is not necessary to a GP that speech and gesture carry the same aspects of the idea, only that they co-express the same idea and contrast in semiotic mode.

2.2.4.1 However, synchrony is NOT fundamental

Having emphasized the importance of speech–gesture synchrony, I now have to complicate matters and refine this dictum. For the dialectic, the critical factor is the combination of unlike semiotic modes. Synchrony is the *product* (not the condition) of this combination, a product of thinking with speech and gesture together when the two modes are brought into direct contact. However if gesture and speech do not precisely synchronize for some external reason (such as mechanical delay) a GP can still form. But then the evidence is less certain, and at some point speech–gesture asynchrony grows so large it signals that some other process has probably intervened. The line for this is far from clear. As a matter of data purity, requiring close speech–gesture synchrony filters out ambiguous data. The ultimate criterion is whether a single idea is embodied in two unlike semiotic modes (with or without different aspects of the idea in each mode) and that this combination creates instability. The combination and instability lead to change, to dynamism and this is not undone when, for mechanical reasons or others, there is an asynchrony. To put a figure to it, the time limit on GP asynchrony is probably around 1~2 s, this being the range of immediate attentional focus.

2.3 CONTEXT

Another source of dynamic dimension change is the incorporation of the changing, constantly updated, itself dynamic, immediate context of speaking; it is not that a GP "consults" the context or the context "sets parameters" for it; the GP *incorporates* it. GP and context are dependent on each other; they are mutually constitutive. These considerations are subsumed under the Vygotskian concept of a psychological predicate.

2.3.1 The psychological predicate

In a psychological (as opposed to a grammatical) predicate, newsworthy[7] content is *differentiated from a context*. One of Vygotsky's examples is a crashing clock (1987, p. 250): There is a crash in the next room – someone asks: "what fell?" (the answer: "the clock"), or: "what happened to the clock?" ("it fell"). Depending on the context – here crystallized in the questions – the newsworthy reply (the psychological predicate) highlights different elements.

This logic also applies to the GP. In forming a GP, the speaker shapes the background in a certain way, in order to highlight an intended differentiation within it, much as the questioner about the falling clock shaped the context of the replies.

A psychological predicate:

1. Marks a significant departure in the immediate context; and
2. Implies this context as background.

Regarding the GP as a psychological predicate suggests that the mechanism of GP formation is differentiation of a newsworthy point of focus from a background.

Such differentiation is validated by the very close temporal connection of gesture (strokes) with the peaks of acoustic output in speech, which also highlight newsworthiness. Nobe (1996) has documented this connection instrumentally:

The robust synchrony between gesture strokes and the peaks of acoustic aspects suggests that the information the gesture stroke carries has an intrinsic relationship with the accompanying speech information prominently pronounced with these peaks. The manifestation of the salient information seems to be realized through the synchronization of these two modalities. (p. 35)

I use the terms a *field of meaningful oppositions* and a *significant (newsworthy) contrast* to refer respectively to the background and the differentiation of a psychological predicate within it. A GP idea unit is both a point of differentiation *and* the context it differentiates. The background is itself a part of thought and is dynamically adjustable by the speaker, to make the differentiation meaningful. All of this is meant to be a dynamic, continuously updated process in which new fields of oppositions are formed and new psychological predicates are differentiated in ongoing cycles of thinking for speaking. A method for identifying fields of oppositions from data is described later in §2.5.1 ("The catchment").

2.3.1.1 What is "a meaning"?

In a GP one meaning is indissolubly a point of differentiation and a field of meaningful oppositions; the GP is both, as the first differentiates the second, and cannot exist without it.[8] Merely intending a meaning is not enough. The field of meaningful oppositions must also be included. "Context" is often a nebulous something that "guides" or "constrains" meaning (cf. Duranti and Goodwin 1992), but for our purposes the "context" of any given idea unit is the more focused idea of the background from which a psychological predicate is differentiated.

"One meaning" on the dynamic dimension is thus *two things* – a field of meaningful oppositions *and*, inseparably, a significant contrast within it. A significant contrast is impossible without the context it differentiates. This conception thus differs from familiar "one-thing" conceptions of meaning – meaning as "signified," as "content," as "association," etc., all of which regard meaning as a significance without a context. Why "meaning" takes this form, when "one thing" would seem to be enough, is explained by our evolution model in the next chapter. In short, the way that language began imposes this kind of meaning.

Suppose a speaker intends to describe Sylvester ascending the pipe on the inside. This is not yet in itself a "meaning." She must also fashion a context or field of meaningful oppositions wherein this intended significance is newsworthy (he tries a stealth approach: inside the pipe then has this significance). Often context and point of differentiation emerge simultaneously. They differ in function, not in the sequence of arousal. The shaping of the context is not passive; it is an active process. Where fields of oppositions differ, even though the objective references are the same, different GPs – idea units – must form (as shown below in the "inside-only" and the "outside-inside" examples in Figures 2.4 and 2.5).

Control of the context by the speaking individual ensures that GPs establish meanings true to the speaker's intentions and memory, with revisions and rejections when self-monitoring finds meanings that don't fit these standards.

2.3.2 Psychological predicates – a natural experiment

The bowling ball episode is the second of Sylvester's attempts in the cartoon to reach Tweety by means of the drainpipe. In his first attempt, which appeared immediately before it, he clambers up the pipe on the outside, using it as a kind of ladder; as usual, his effort fails. He tries again, now the stealth approach on the inside that we have seen, leading to the bowling ball and its aftermath. This quirk in the cartoon lends itself to a natural experiment showing that GPs differentiate newsworthy information within immediate contexts.[9]

The natural experiment is the following: describing the first attempt, the field of meaningful oppositions would be something like *WAYS OF USING THE DRAINPIPE* (this is first mention of the pipe) and the psychological predicate something like *CLIMB IT*. With the second attempt, climbing itself is no longer newsworthy. It has become background and the field of meaningful oppositions would be updated to something like *WAYS OF CLIMBING THE DRAINPIPE*. In this field interiority is newsworthy: *ON THE INSIDE*.

If a speaker recalls both attempts, in the correct outside–inside order, the psychological predicate relating to the second attempt should thus focus on interiority. This follows from the psychological predicate concept; then in the updated field of meaningful oppositions, interiority becomes the newsworthy feature.

However, if a speaker recalls only the inside attempt and fails to recall the outside attempt, or recalls both attempts but reverses their order, interiority should *not* be newsworthy. This also follows from the psychological predicate, wherein "one meaning" is two things. Interiority, lacking a field of meaningful oppositions it differentiates, is not meaningful, even though the speaker has perceptually registered it and recalls that Sylvester did climb the pipe on the inside. Recalling and meaning are not the same. This is so because interiority does not contrast with exteriority in an inside-only or inside–outside context. The speaker does not mention many irrelevant details, and interiority is just one more without contrast to exteriority. The field of meaningful oppositions would be about climbing, and interiority, even if perceived and remembered, would not form the psychological predicate (no one in any experiment has ever recalled the outside attempt only).

2.3.2.1 Inside alone

The first two speakers (Figure 2.3) recalled only the inside attempt. For them, interiority had no newsworthy significance and their gestures did not contain it, even though they went on to describe the bowling ball and its aftermath, demonstrating that they had in fact recognized interiority as a feature of the story. It is just that it did not form a psychological predicate or GP.

Cel. he tries **climb**<u>ing up th</u>e rai]n barrel

No interiority. Hand simply rises. Cel. continued her description by explaining that "Tweety . . . drops a bowling bal][l down the rain b][arrel]," showing that she had registered the ascent as internal.

Den. and <um> / he tries crawling up the drainp[**ipe** /] to get Tweety.

Right thumb (entire gesture) lifts for ascent. No interiority. Den. continued with "Tweety drops a bowling ball down the drainpipe," again showing that the internal ascent had been registered.

Figure 2.3 Isolated "inside" gestures that do not highlight interiority. Used with permission of University of Chicago Press.

2.3.2.2 Inside after outside

Three other speakers recalled both attempts in the correct order. In each case, their second gestures highlighted interiority (Figure 2.4) but their preceding outside gestures showed path alone, without anticipation of the inside feature.

2.3.2.3 Exception that proves the rule

The final speaker, Lau. (Figure 2.5), remembered both attempts in the correct order, but picked out a different significant contrast, a twist conceivably triggered by her word-choice error when she described the first "outside" ascent as Sylvester's climbing "a ladder." Her gesture seemed to depict grasping the rungs of this imaginary ladder. By the second ascent she

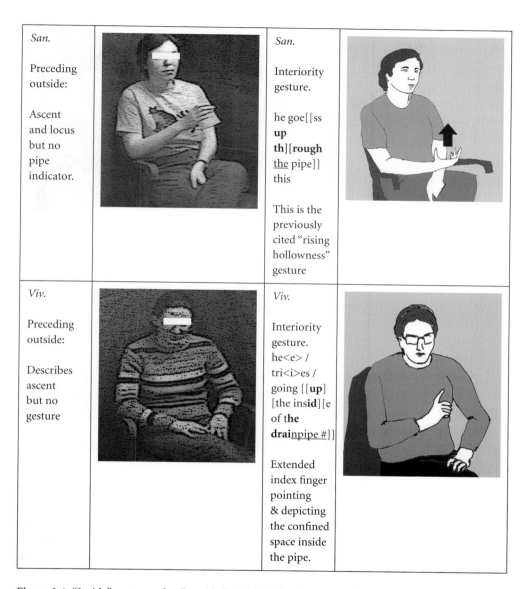

Figure 2.4 "Inside" gestures after "outside." All highlight the newsworthy interiority feature, by three speakers (San, Viv, and Jan). Drawings used with permission of University of Chicago Press.

did mention the pipe, which, for her, was its first mention. So the second ascent contrasted not in terms of paths (inside versus outside) but in terms of *landmark elements* (pipe versus "ladder"). Her handshapes and timing also suggest this interpretation (her hand cupped as if around the ladder, then curved more loosely and vertically in the shape of the pipe, synchronized

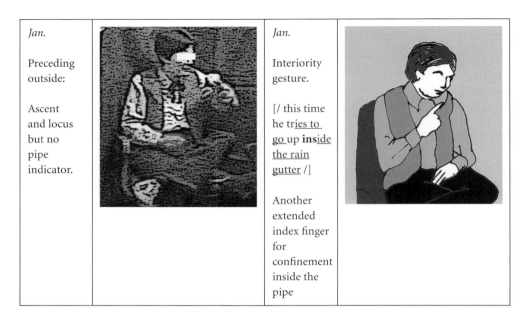

Jan.		Jan.	
Preceding outside: Ascent and locus but no pipe indicator.		Interiority gesture. [/ this time he tries to go up inside the rain gutter /] Another extended index finger for confinement inside the pipe	

Figure 2.4 (*cont.*)

with "climbing").[10] The extended index finger, while similar to Figure 2.4, was not angled upward and may instead have metanarratively segued to the next big event, "and the bird, the canary throws, puts a bowling ball into the drain spout."

Thus this natural experiment shows that a psychological predicate, as the essential point of the GP, captures exactly what is newsworthy in the immediate field of meaningful oppositions but ignores the same information even if perceived when, through narrative mischance, it is not newsworthy. Again, this severe selectivity follows from the psychological predicate concept of "one meaning" being two things, one the context, the other the differentiation of it.

2.3.3 Psychological predicates – a designed experiment

Fey Parrill (2008) devised a method for cueing discourse focus with flashing arrows, and was able in this way to change gesture and speech, so that they coalesced around the arrow-indicated ("newsworthy") content. In effect, she could create psychological predicates on demand. Participants saw the portion of the animated stimulus just after Sylvester exited the pipe with

Lau. (outside the pipe) and he trie[s / cl**imbing** up a la]dder #

Exception that proves the rule #1. Gesture with "climbing up a ladder."

Lau. (inside the pipe) he tries[s **cli**]m[[bing u<u>p the <nn> dra</u>**inspout** / <u>/</u>]

Exception that proves the rule #2. Gesture with "drainspout."

Figure 2.5 Exception that proves the rule – highlighting ground elements – "pipe" (not interiority) when the contrast is to the (misremembered) first ascent on a ladder. Drawings used with permission of University of Chicago Press.

the bowling ball inside him. The **ball prompt** was a flashing arrow pointing at Sylvester's rounded bottom (where the bowling ball had ended up) and resulted in more *ball-subject utterances*, compared to the **cat prompt** (arrow pointing at his head) – for example, "the ball rolls him down the street," rather than "he rolls down the street." The ball prompt also resulted in co-expressive manner in gesture – the manner of the ball's motion, the hand rotating rather than moving in the straight path that was common after the cat prompt. The induced point of focus thus became the newsworthy co-expressive speech–gesture psychological predicate, creating through deliberate manipulation the cohesion of this meaning bundle in context.

A Outside (upward gesture with "climbs up")	**B Inside** (similar upward gesture skips "climbs up" to go with "through")
	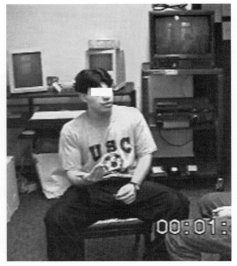
"and then the second part / [is he **climbs up** the drain]"	"<uuhh> let's see the next time / is he tries to* <uh> /tries to cliimb / [up / in / **through** / the] [drain* /"

Figure 2.6 Timing shift highlights interiority with similar gestures. **Panel A**. outside ascent. **Panel B**. inside. Right hand rises, palm up, in both cases but shifts from "climbs up" to "through." Used with permission of University of Chicago Press.

2.3.4 Gesture timing embodies context

Sometimes the form of a gesture does not embody the newsworthy content in the speaker's current field of meaningful oppositions but its timing does. Following the principle that a psychological predicate synchronizes co-expressive imagery and linguistic categorization, the timing of speech and gesture should always reflect the point of newsworthiness (allowing for variation due to mechanical factors, as mentioned in §2.2.4.1). To illustrate, one speaker used the same verb ("climbs up") and performed similar gestures for the outside and inside ascents, but with the "inside" occurrence, when climbing was no longer newsworthy but interiority was, the gesture skipped over the verb, where it had synchronized before, to time with the verbal expression of interiority ("tries to climb / [up / in / **through** the drain" (Figure 2.6).[11]

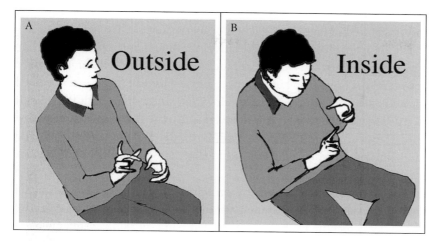

Figure 2.7 Gestures with the Taiwanese Sign Language sign for "animate being with more than two legs," deformed at the same discourse junctures where gestures occur by hearing speakers. **Panel A**. Outside the pipe ascent in a Canary Row narration: fingers "walking" up virtual pipe. Note that the thumb is also extended, which reinforces the conclusion that we see here a modified sign (extension of the thumb is part of the canonical sign form). It is not clear why the fourth finger also was extended, but perhaps it was to maintain something of the "extended-fingers" feel of the canonical sign while the first and second fingers "walked." **Panel B**. Inside ascent: single finger possibly for compression as well as deixis; cf. similar use by English speakers in Figure 2.4. Used with permission of University of Chicago Press. Data from Duncan 2005.

2.3.5 GPs in sign languages

One expects sign languages to be animated just as are spoken languages, via GPs and imagery–(sign)language dialectics. Figure 2.7, based on Duncan (2005), shows a canonical sign in Taiwanese Sign Language (TSL) "deformed" to incorporate newsworthy content. Duncan suggests that the deformation could be a gesture synchronized with the sign. It then could create an imagery–language dialectic and GP. Liddell (2003) also argued that signs (in ASL in this case) are accompanied by gestures but these gestures, pointing, are integrated into the grammatical form of the sign sentence, and belong to the "language-slotted" position on the Gesture Continuum. The TSL gesture, deforming a regular sign, seems closer to a true gesticulation and could pose the same kind of semiotic contrast of gesticulation and linguistic form that fuels spoken language but entirely within the visual-actional mode. As with the spoken examples, Sylvester was climbing first on the outside of the pipe, then on the inside. The dialectic predicts that iconic and/or metaphoric gesticulations should appear alongside canonical signs, and this is seen in Figure 2.7.

The signs involve a TSL classifier for Animate Beings With More Than Two Legs (cats, infants, etc.). The standard form of the classifier is the palm down and the thumb, the index finger and the middle finger extended and spread apart, the others curled in. However, when describing the outside ascent (Figure 2.7a) the signer adopted this sign but had the first and second fingers, instead of extending outward, "walk up" the space above the right hand (the left hand was also curved to show the pipe but did not provide the spatial locus for the "walking").[12]

Describing the second attempt, on the inside (Figure 2.7b), the signer highlighted interiority by reducing the canonical shape to just one extended first finger, which he pushed under his left hand, not unlike some hearing speaker's spontaneous gestures for this event.

These deformations occurred at just the discourse junctures where hearing speakers also perform their gestures, and are plausibly actual sign-accompanying gestures in TSL, co-occurring, as deformations, with conventional signs. They capture the same contrast of outside–inside paths that the psychological predicates of English speakers did, and suggest an imagery–language dialectic with signs, no different in its essentials from that with speech.[13]

2.4 HOW UTTERANCES OCCUR

While it is not possible to give a full analysis, including all the contextual sources, of how an utterance in its totality arises, we can cover some of what takes place even now. I divide this description into two parts for convenience. First, the GP itself; then how it was unpacked. However, in reality, they are inseparable – a fact of importance for our origin analysis in Chapter 3. The point will emerge there that the GP calls for its own unpacking. Unpacking does not require a third-party or agent; it is self-unpacking and is done by the GP itself. The GP evokes, on its own, a construction that does the job (usually). In so doing the GP is possibly related to other forms of self-organization (cf. Kelso 1995). A GP and its unpacking-construction can arise together (as in the example to follow and many other cases) or in sequence (and I do not rule out the possibility of the unpacking coming first and the speaker scratching up a GP that makes use of it). This current-day fact suggests that syntax could have been selected at the dawn by pressures to form unpackings with syntagmatic values, like those we see now emerging from GPs.

2.4.1 The catchment

The field of meaningful oppositions of which the GP is the point of newsworthy differentiation can frequently be discovered directly in the gestures themselves. *Catchments*[14] are when space, trajectory, handshape, etc. recur in two or more (not necessarily consecutive) gestures. We have already seen an example in Figure 2.2. There, the hands in the second panel occupied the same space as in the first, tying the two depictions visually. They are also tied thematically. The recurring gesture imagery, in that case space, is examined to see if it embodies a discourse theme, and it did – the theme of happenings at the entrance to the pipe. Catchments show the effective contextual background and provide an empirical route to the discovery of the context of GPs.

A convincing demonstration of the force of the catchment comes from an ingenious test by Furuyama and Sekine (2007). They noticed a systematic avoidance of gestures with a certain spatial content (involving a reversal of a predominant direction). The avoidance occurred precisely where this content, had it been included, would have disrupted an ongoing catchment. The catchment was the actual force and it blocked imagery that was referentially correct but inconsistent with it.[15]

So, to define the catchment:

- A catchment is recognized from recurrences of gesture form features over a stretch of discourse.
- A catchment is a kind of thread of consistent dynamic visuospatial imagery running through the discourse and provides a gesture-based window into discourse cohesion.
- The logic of the catchment is that discourse themes produce gestures with recurring features; these recurrences give rise to the catchment.
- Thus, reasoning in reverse, the catchment offers clues to the cohesive linkages in the text with which it co-occurs.

An illustration of several catchments from another of our early participants, Viv., is her description of Sylvester's inside ascent, his encounter with the bowling ball and its aftermath. The example shows how a GP may "drain" multiple catchments. Viv.'s full description is in Figure 2.8. The "it down" GP that we analyze is in panel 2.

(1) he tries going [[**up**] [the in**sid**] [e of **the drain**pipe #]] and *1 hand: RH rises up 3 times with the first finger extended*	C1	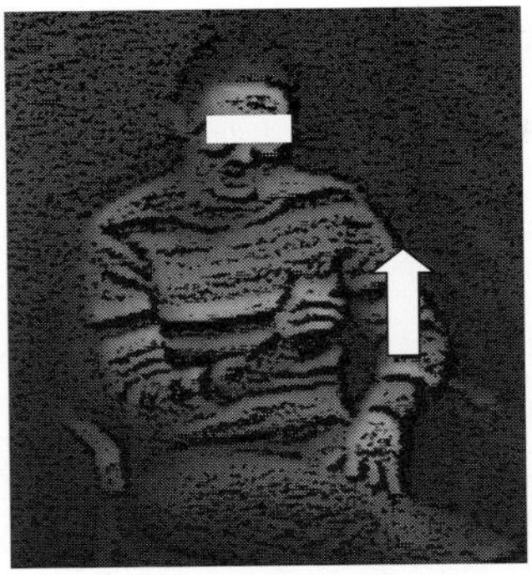
(2) Tweety Bird runs and gets a bowling ba[ll and drop<u>s</u> **it** **do**<u>wn</u> the drainpipe #] *Symmetrical: 2 similar hands move down* This gesture is selected below to illustrate a GP and how it relates to context.	C2	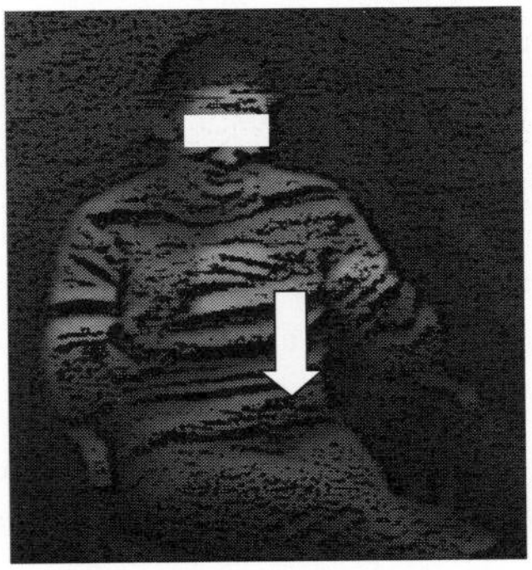
(3) [<u>and / </u>as **he's** co<u>ming</u> **up**] *Asymmetrical: 2 different hands, LH holds, RH up 2X*	C3	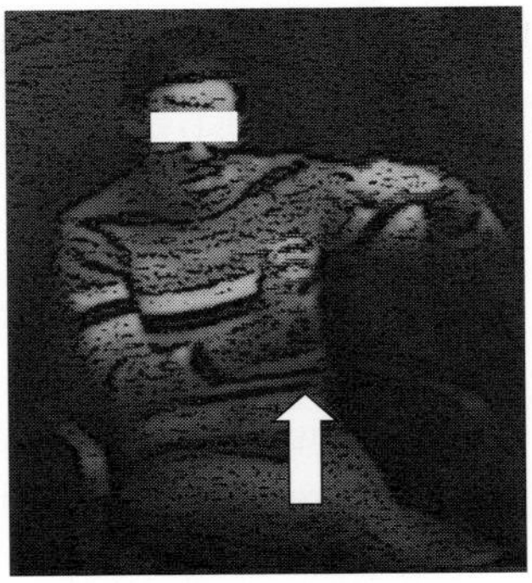

Figure 2.8 Catchments in Viv.'s bowling ball episode description.

First, to describe the GP itself. The gesture was made with two symmetrical hands – the palms loosely cupped and facing downward as if placed over a spherical object, and moving down and holding during the linguistic segments "**it do**<u>wn</u>." The inferred GP is this image of downward movement *plus* the linguistic content of the "it" (i.e., the bowling ball) and the path

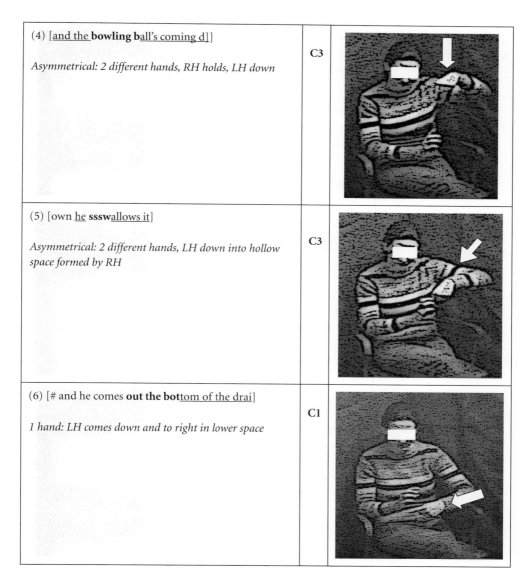

(4) [and the **bowling b**all's coming d]] *Asymmetrical: 2 different hands, RH holds, LH down*	C3	
(5) [own he **sssw**allows it] *Asymmetrical: 2 different hands, LH down into hollow space formed by RH*	C3	
(6) [# and he comes **out the bot**tom of the drai] *1 hand: LH comes down and to right in lower space*	C1	

Figure 2.8 (*cont.*)

particle "down." The poststroke hold continued the shape and position of the gesture until "down" was fully uttered; then the stroke dissolved.

The first point to notice is that the timing of the gesture (boldface) is somewhat off, if we think that gestures should line up with synchronically definable linguistic constituents (a "lexical affiliate," Schegloff 1984). The stroke *excluded* the verb "drops"; it coincided instead with "it down," and

(7) [npipe and he's **got this** big bowling ball inside h]im *Symmetrical: 2 similar hands move down*	C2	
(8) [and he **rolls on down**] [into **a bow**ling all] *Symmetrical: 2 similar hands rotate as move forward 2X*	C2	
(9) [ey and then **you hear a** sstri]ke # *Symmetrical: 2 similar hands move apart*	C2	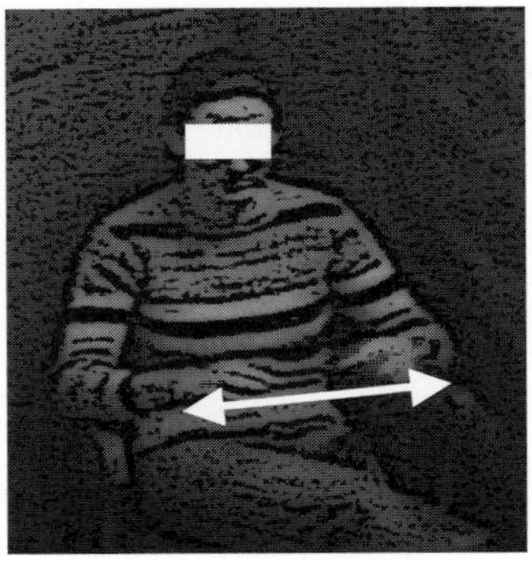

Figure 2.8 (*cont.*)

in this way combined two constituents, the Figure and Satellite (using Talmy's 2000 categories), but excluded another, the Activating Process, to which the Figure, "it," is actually more tightly coupled in the structure of the sentence. However, grammatical structure comes from the unpacking construction and is not necessarily part of the GP ("it" and "down" each have combinatoric potential but do not include the other).

This exclusion of "drops" was no accident. First, the preparation phase of the "it down" gesture has two features that skip over the verb. Preparation began at the first mention of the bowling ball, in the preceding clause (also indicated in panel 2), which suggests that the bowling ball was already part of the discourse focus at that moment. Second, preparation continued right *through* the verb, suggesting that the verb was not part of this focus. Further, a brief prestroke hold may have preceded "it down" (although coding varies), which, if present, suggests that the stroke waited for "it down." Finally, the unmistakable poststroke hold lasted exactly as long as it took to complete the spoken "down." This hold preserved the semantic synchrony of the gesture stroke with the complete articulation of "it down." So the stroke fully and exactly timed with just these two words, and actively excluded a third, "drops," which happens to be the closest lexical approximation to it. But why? To explain it we must examine the catchment structure into which the "it down" GP fits.

The important catchments for the description in (1) through (9) appear in hand use. The thematic values are apparent when we coordinate gestures with their accompanying verbal descriptions (Table 2.2).

Table 2.2 Catchment themes

Catchment themes	Utterances belonging to catchment
One-handed gestures – items (1) and (6) – tie together references to Sylvester as a solo force.	(1) he tries going up the inside of the drainpipe and (6) and he comes out the bottom of the drainpipe
Two-handed SYMMETRICAL gestures – items (2), (7), (8), and (9) – group descriptions where the bowling ball is the antagonist, the dominant force. The 2-handed symmetric gesture form highlights the shape of the bowling ball.	(2) Tweety Bird runs and gets a bowling ball and drops it down the drainpipe (7) and he's got this big bowling ball inside him (8) and he rolls on down into a bowling alley (9) and then you hear a strike
Two-handed ASYMMETRICAL gestures – items (3), (4), and (5) – group items in which the bowling ball (LH) and Sylvester (RH) are equals differing only in position and direction of motion.	(3) and as he's coming up (4) and the bowling ball's coming down (5) he swallows it

C1 – 1 handed = Sylvester as a solo force.
C2 – 2 similar handed = the bowling ball as an antagonistic force.
C3 – 2 different handed = the relative spatial positions and directions of the bowling ball and Sylvester inside the pipe.

The table reveals these three catchments, recognizable from hand use and handshape/hand position – right hand or left; one hand or two and, when two hands, whether same or different handshape and/or hand position. Each hand configuration embodies a certain thematic content, and this content is what motivates it: **C1** is about a single moving entity and its recurring gesture feature is a single moving hand; **C2** is about the bowling ball and what it does, and its recurring feature is a rounded shape ("2 similar hands"); **C3** is about the relative positions of Sylvester and the bowling ball in the drainpipe, and its recurring feature is the two hands in the appropriate spatial configuration ("2 different hands").

The second catchment (**C2**) involves the two-handed symmetrical gestures in (2), (7), (8), and (9). These gestures group descriptions where the bowling ball is the antagonist, and the dominant force. Sylvester becomes what he eats; a kind of living bowling ball and the symmetric gestures accompany the descriptions where the bowling ball asserts this power. In (2) the bowling ball is just beginning its career as antagonist. The rest of the catchment is where it has achieved its results (thus **C2** is about the bowling ball as a force, qua force). The two-handed symmetric gestures highlight the shape of the bowling ball or its motion, an iconicity appropriate for this antagonist role.

The occurrence of (2) in the symmetrical catchment shows that one of the factors comprising the field of meaningful oppositions at this point was the various guises in which the bowling ball appeared in its antagonist role. The catchment or field sets the bowling ball apart from its role in **C3**, where the bowling ball was on a par with Sylvester. This difference involving the bowling ball shows that the critical dimension here is the context, the field of meaningful oppositions, not the identity of the bowling ball itself. The *significant contrast* in (2) was the downward motion of the bowling ball. Because the field of meaningful oppositions was the bowling ball as an antagonistic force, this downward motion had significance not as simply a bowling ball going down the pipe but as a force against Sylvester. We can write the field of meaningful oppositions and GP as:

ANTAGONISTIC FORCE: BOWLING BALL DOWN

These were the context and differentiating contrast respectively: the GP at this instant, out of which speech and gesture arose. Thus, "it down," unlikely though it may seem as a unit from a grammatical point of view ("it" and "down" belonging to different grammatical constituents), was the cognitive core of the utterance in (2) – the "it" indexing the bowling ball, and the "down" indexing the significant contrast itself in the field of meaningful oppositions.

The verb "drops," therefore, was excluded from this GP. The verb came from the second process, unpacking, as we will see shortly. As noted before, exclusion is evidenced in the fact that the stroke did not synchronize with the verb; in fact, it was withheld from the verb by continued preparation and the possible brief prestroke hold. The verb describes what Tweety did, not what the bowling ball did (it countered Sylvester by going down), and thus was not a significant contrast in the field of meaningful oppositions involving the bowling ball as an antagonistic force. The core idea at (2) was the bowling ball and its action, not Tweety and his.

The timing is off only if we disregard gesture and speech as conveying the concept of an antagonistic force. From this vantage point, the synchronized gesture and linguistic segments could not coincide more precisely. The "it" indexes the bowling ball, the metaphoric force in question, and the "down" refers to the direction the force is taking. The verb, "drops," in contrast, refers to Tweety, the character who was the agent of the dropping or thrusting but was not the force in question.[16] In short, "drops" was outside the antagonistic force meaning and was excluded from the gesture that carried it.

2.4.2 Unpacking and further meanings

The essence of unpacking is to come up with communicable, socioculturally mandated constructions that (a) stabilize the imagery–language dialectics of GPs, without (b) disrupting how fields of oppositions are differentiated. Regardless of whether they occur together or in sequence, the GP and its unpacking are functionally on different levels. Unpacking results from a kind of self-organization; the GP *unpacks itself* by calling forth a construction (Goldberg 1995: a construction is a syntactic template, deployed as a whole, with slots for other elements – words or other constructions).

Something similar could have existed at the dawn. Early GPs seeking dialectic resolutions, constructions, produced pressures to develop ways of achieving them. Thus arose a force in the origin of syntax. Unpacking is a model, even now, of the natural selection pressures for syntax arising out of the GP itself.

The GP is the core idea at the moment of speaking, differentiating a field of oppositions; its unpacking cradles it, and intuitions of well-formedness comprise the dialectic stop-order. Some constructions unpack their GPs and nothing more. Others add further meanings, and this raises the potential of

Figure 2.9 Left panel: Sylvester's interior ascent gesture with "he tries going **up** the in**side** of **the drain**pipe" – the gesture (not shown, referred to as (a) in the text) goes with panel (1) in Figure 2.8.
Right Panel: (b.1) Start of the preparation phase of Tweety's downward thrust of the bowling ball gesture with "Tweety Bird runs and gets a bowling ba[ll." The gesture goes with panel (2) in Figure 2.8.
Then (b.2), the stroke phase of the gesture with "and drops **it do**wn the drainpipe #]."
Used with permission of University of Chicago Press.

mismatches (a case is shown in Chapter 3, §3.5.6.1). The aim of this section is to demonstrate the process of stabilization and how further meanings enter into it, again using the "it down" example.

Figure 2.9(b) illustrates the downward thrusting gesture for Tweety's launch of the bowling ball as the speaker said, "and drops (the possible *pre-stroke hold*) **it do**(the *gesture stroke*)wn (the *poststroke hold*) the drainpipe." This is the speaker's individualized concept. For her the bowling ball was more than an object; it was part of a contest of opposing forces, Tweety ("The Good")-down *versus* Sylvester ("The Bad")-up. In this contest the bowling ball became Tweety's surrogate, and part of the unpacking was to shift the Good-force from Tweety to the bowling ball, so that "it down" differentiated the *WAYS OF COUNTERING SYLVESTER* field of oppositions.

The complete text for Viv.'s bowling-ball episode, leading to and including "it down," is as follows:

(a) he tries going up the inside of the drainpipe (Figure 2.8, panel 1)
(b.1) and Tweety Bird runs and gets a bowling ba[ll (Figure 2.9, left panel)

(our GP started, seemingly in advance, in the clause with the "[" preparation onset – the hands would not have begun to move up other than to present the imagery of the bowling ball going down; however, we shall see that this was not an "anticipation" but an exact synchrony within the larger context).

(b.2) and Ø$_{tw}$ drops **it do<u>wn</u>** the drainpipe] (figure 2.9, right panel)

Line (c), the GP and its unpacking, is a caused-motion construction. The second clause in (b.1) may have been this type of construction as well. If so, (b.1) could have primed (b.2), but the priming would be irrelevant until the GP had sent out feelers for it, and this is what unpacking negotiated. The "it down" GP, its field of meaningful oppositions (the antagonistic force), and the cartoon story itself (to continue the story, the bowling ball had somehow to be mentioned) conspired to evoke the already primed caused-motion construction. The GP unpacked itself into caused-motion, in which the agent was Tweety and the entity caused to move was the bowling ball, thus achieving the transfer of Tweety's Good-force to the ball. Had the speaker begun differently in line (b.1), with "and Tweety sees him . . . ," for example, we predict there would have been a different GP/unpacking, something like "and stops him with a bowling ball." Such a beginning, however, would not have provided an opening for Viv.'s basic idea, the paradigm of opposed forces, suggesting the presence of this idea from at least the start of (b.1).

In this instance caused-motion and the GP became active at the same moment. It is not that the GP arose and the construction followed. Simultaneous activation is shown in that, as the speaker first mentioned the bowling ball, in (b.1), her hands arched and turned down, preparing to thrust the ball downward. Thus they already took on the agentive role they would play in (b.2). The shape was not an iconic depiction of the cartoon event – there, as we also see in Figure 2.10, Tweety supported the bowling ball with his hands facing *upward* and released it, letting gravity do the rest. But in the gesture version, she pushed the bowling ball into the pipe, her hands turned downward. The speaker had (presumably unconsciously) transformed the cartoon event to make Tweety the caused-motion agent. This illustrates the process of discourse formation shaping thought as much as the reverse, thought shaping discourse.

This situation with caused-motion is a good model of the selective forces that emanate from GPs to create constructions in the first place. We return to this selection pressure in Chapter 3, §3.5, the origin of syntax.

2.4.3 The "molecule analogy"

One might suppose that a GP could be something like a molecule.[17] The whole has properties that cannot be found in the parts. Just as combining a

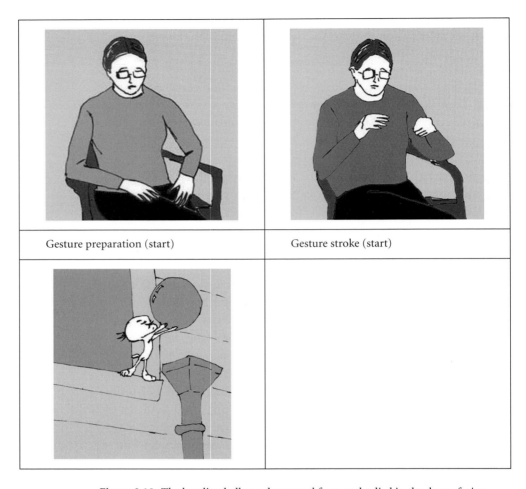

Gesture preparation (start)	Gesture stroke (start)

Figure 2.10 The bowling ball as a downward force embodied in the down-facing hands at the start of preparation; also, hands shaped over the bowling ball were those of an agent launching it. This imagery was altered from that of the cartoon, where there was no downward thrust but rather a release, gravity doing the rest. Used with permission of University of Chicago Press.

couple of Hs and an O gives rise to something new, water, so combining a gesture and a linguistic fragment also yields something new, a GP.

The molecule analogy however is misleading in one crucial respect, and to see why further elucidates the concept of the GP. If the O and/or H *changed its own atomic character* when combined to make water, the analogy would be closer. For that is what happens in the GP. The "it down" GP illustrates this point as well. H_2 and O do exist as elementary units in water, but in a

GP speech and gesture are not elementary units; the GP is the only unit and it produces them.

The "it down" GP was not formed "out of" a gesture for thrusting down plus the linguistic segments, "it" and "down." This inverts the dependencies. The gesture was thrusting and the linguistic categorization "it down" because the GP was the basic unit; it was differentiating a field of meaningful oppositions, *WAYS OF COUNTERING SYLVESTER*, with a psychological predicate, *BOWLING BALL DOWN*. The gesture and the speech segments did not exist outside this particular GP. They were shaped to do this job and descended from it. We can be sure the dependency ran in this direction for two reasons. First, the **gesture** was not an iconic depiction but was an image altered precisely to make Tweety into the agent of the bowling ball's motion. Second, the **speech** of the GP was not a grammatical combination, a V plus an object, as would be expected if speech were an independent "atom," but instead "drops" was cut off by the gesture stroke from its object, "it," creating the non-grammatical yet co-expressive segment, "it down." Both speech and gesture, in other words, were products of the GP and not the other way around.

2.4.4 Metapragmatic orchestrations

We have seen that GPs and their unpackings orchestrate speech through fields of meaningful oppositions, and that this dialectic process explains a number of utterance details; but there is more. Viv. not only conceived of and unpacked a paradigm of opposed forces, she also had the overall goal of recounting the story, a sense of textual flow, and the need to make the story clear so that her listener could reproduce it later. These goals require a larger thematic frame than the immediate field of oppositions. This section presents an approach based on the work of my Chicago colleague, Michael Silverstein (2003), which I dub "metapragmatic orchestration." Reviewing what we have covered so far pinpoints its role. The caused-motion constructions (both (b.1) and (b.2)) with Tweety as subject, contrast with the spontaneous-motion construction of (a), with Sylvester the subject. This provides a part of the (b.2) unpacking. (a) introduced the upward-moving force of the antagonistic forces paradigm, (b.1) the downward-moving force, and (b.2) shifted it to the bowling ball, Tweety's surrogate but with Tweety still in the subject slot in (b.2), still paradigmatically opposed to Sylvester, the subject of the upward force construction in (a).

The rest of the selection of the (b.2) caused-motion construction (and some details of the GP as well) brings us into the realm of metapragmatic orchestration. We have now to address the question of the framework that guides and oversees the discourse as a whole, such questions as the speaker's intentions and sense of direction. These areas have always been a gap in the growth point story – areas of obvious importance and self-evident activity but not captured (so far) in our way of discovering psychological predicates and GPs as they emerge. Metapragmatic orchestrations reveal aspects of this larger discourse framework. They identify the perlocutionary and other intended effects of one's uttered speech, as well as the sense of overall direction in the discourse as they exist at the moment of speaking. Like the field of meaningful oppositions, what is indicated penetrates the GP, as the thought unit funnels this large framework into each conceptual instant. In our example we see that they zeroed in onto the caused-motion construction in (b.2). Silverstein provides an elegant schema for conceptualizing this entire metapragmatics domain, which I reproduce in Figure 2.11 (his Figure 1).[18]

Silverstein writes of this diagram (p. 195):

[A]ny such socially conventional indexical (Legi)sign [=type] is dialectically balanced between indexical presupposition and indexical entailment. That is, its indexical meaning is composed of two aspects. One is its indexical "appropriateness-to" at-that-point autonomously known or constituted contextual parameters: what is already established between interacting sign-users, at least implicitly, as "context" to which the propriety of their usage at t_0 appeals. The other is its indexical "effectiveness-in" context: how contextual parameters seem to be brought into being – i.e., causally and hence existentially entailed – by the fact of usage of the indexical (Sin)sign [=token] itself. The presupposition/entailment relationship is not simply linear or one-dimensional, like a temporal "before" and "after" to an indexical event, even though Figure 1 [= Figure 2.11] visually might suggest the intuition of left-to-right, earlier-to-later cause-and-effect. The relationship is, rather, a complex and mediated one, as the various arrowed lines try to capture, and they end, i.e., result, in a conceptual object called a text-in-context that I have diagrammed as a line solid up to t_0 . . . "

He uses this approach to look outward – how, for example, innovations of speech-ways in one domain (professional wine talk in his example) spread to other domains (yuppies anxious to show special knowledge). However, we look inward – how contextual links shape online thinking for and while speaking. When we first examined Viv.'s "it down" GP the emphasis was on her catchment (the bowling ball as an antagonistic force) and the specific form of GP that differentiated it (its going down). But much more was taking place. Knowing that she and her listener (not to mention the experimenter) regard coherence and explicitness to be the *sine qua non* of a cooperative narration she was concerned to keep the story line in focus,

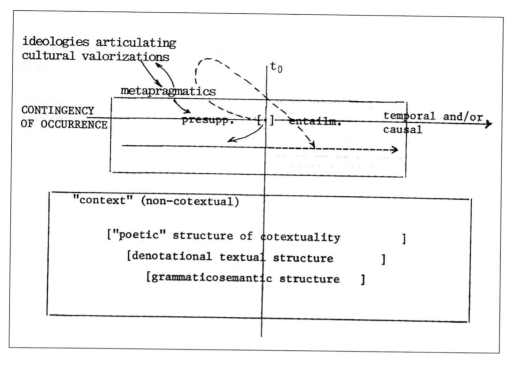

Figure 2.11 Micro-indexical context (Silverstein 2003). GP is at t_0. Co-text (or the non-contextual "context") consists of indexical links along the lines indicated to elsewhere in the "text" and thus adds co-expressivity on the linguistic side to go with the imagery in the GP. This range indeed exists, and the diagram suggests the mechanism of it. Diagram from Michael Silverstein. Used with permission of the author and Elsevier Press.

to have no inexplicable events and the like; but she also had to allow for the otherworldly cartoon logic of a small bird transporting and releasing a bowling ball many times its size and weight. These kinds of features are locatable in Figure 2.11 and are present in the GP in a number of places, in its imagery, its speech, and its field of oppositions. The multiple absorptions comprise the "delicacy" of thought and speech that Silverstein intends his diagram to explicate (the term "delicacy" is from Halliday and Hasan 1976 and refers to the fine modulations and contextual specificities of speech and thought).

Importantly, it was the metapragmatics of the situation that required incorporating the bowling ball into the narrative (it had to be mentioned); it also, given Viv.'s own characterization of the cartoon as a paradigm of opposed forces, spotted the necessity of shifting the downward force of The Good (Tweety) to an instrument, the bowling ball, in the battle against the upward force of The Bad (Sylvester). *This* was the selection pressure that summoned caused-motion. Moreover, metapragmatic selection accounts for the verb, "drop" over alternatives like "throw" or "thrust." This verb fits caused-motion but, more, attributes the motion of the bowling ball to the force of gravity, as was depicted in the original cartoon (Figure 2.10). It is the one verb choice among the possibilities that allows both caused-motion agency for its grammatical subject (Tweety), while remaining referentially correct with respect to the role of gravity.

The GP was shaped, as Silverstein makes clear in another context, not by lines of information flowing through Figure 2.11 but by the "complex and mediated" absorption of the indexically linked values and presuppositions that it displays. Instead of lines of information flow there is "all-at-onceness" in the realization of the elements of the diagram (a concept from Liesbet Quaeghebeur, see Chapter 4, §4.1.5.1). The gesture with hands arched down imaged Tweety as the bowling-ball launcher, and this embodied the above cartoon-logic; the pronoun "it" was anaphoric but it further reflected the presupposition that objects introduced at one point do not vanish a moment later. The GP, coming to life at the opening bracket in the middle of this noun ("Tweety Bird runs and gets a bowling ba[ll . . . "), was itself forming in the midst of the speaker's first mention of the bowling ball. The GP's linguistic side, in other words, was equally "ball" and "it" from the start. Noun and pronoun were *concurrent* in the speaker's experience, even though the pronoun did not surface until later. This would be because the "it" reflected not just anaphora in this case but the assumption that the bowling ball did not vanish and, crucially for this speaker's narrative metapragmatics, that the bowling ball was changing its role from an object to a force against Sylvester. So thinking of the bowling ball simultaneously as both noun and pronoun embodied the speaker's narrative intentions.

These details I attribute to the upward dotted loop of Figure 2.11, up into the metapragmatics context and back down to t_0 where the onflash of the GP was taking place. The metapragmatics of storytelling also came down over the same loop with the understanding that the bowling ball had somehow to appear in the narration, since it was part of the cartoon story, and had to become the force countering Sylvester, since this was Viv.'s construal. It thus had a direct impact on the GP. For this same reason, "drop" appeared in the unpacking – the lever ratcheting the force from Tweety to the bowling ball, fulfilling the metapragmatics supposition that the performance of the bowling ball had to be explained lest the suppositions of a coherent narration be violated. The construction unpacking the GP and wielding "drops" was caused-motion, also answering the call of Viv.'s construal. Silverstein calls the micro-contextual semiotic in Figure 2.11 a dialectic (understood as "competition" and "balance"), but it is a different dialectic from that in GPs (understood as "opposition" and "instability"). Competition and balance do not show thought and language fueled and changing but rather show the stability of the background. Such a viewpoint, far from conflicting with the imagery-language (GP) dialectic, shows the interplay of external factors as GPs take form and unpack themselves. To the GP a balanced dialectic takes various forms, as catchment (the bowling ball as a force), as imagery (hand-shape for Tweety's agency), as linguistic form (the pronoun "it" for object continuation and the bowling ball's new role), and as unpacking ("drops" and caused-motion). So imagery, the catchment, the linguistic component, and unpacking each absorbed parts of the micro-indexes of Figure 2.11.

Combining catchments and metapragmatics indexicals gives a plausible picture of how the utterance emerged. At the same time it also sets a problem that evolution solved. All of these factors, GPs, psychological predicates, unpacking, context, and metapragmatic orchestration were naturally selected. We shall see next how this could have come about, and why a popular hypothesis is eliminated by it from consideration.

3 | How it evolved (in part) – Mead's Loop

3.1 CHAPTER PLAN

Here begins our main topic. Now that we have an idea of what evolved, we can consider explanations of how it came about.

The sources of language dynamics sketched earlier are: (1) the imagery–language dialectic within each GP; (2) the incorporation of contexts into psychological predicates as GPs; (3) the further meanings and contexts generated in unpacking the GP; and (4) the larger-scale purposes and cultural beliefs and practices encompassed metapragmatically. The GP model applies at the intersection of the dynamic and static – and is itself the dynamic dimension's minimal Vygotskian unit.

The exposition in this chapter is straightforward. I start with a currently popular theory, "gesture-first," and explain what it is and what is wrong with it, that it does not predict (and could not have led to) this dynamic dimension. Then I introduce an alternative, called "Mead's Loop," and explain it in detail, including how it could have been naturally selected and the changes it would have caused in mind and brain. I take up next the origin of syntax as explicated by Mead's Loop and the brain model it suggests, including the forging in the evolving brain of a specific thought–language–hand link, and end with a proposed time-line for the beginning of language.

3.2 "GESTURE-FIRST"

The popularity of this theory was sparked by a discovery, that of the mirror neuron (Rizzolatti, *et al.* 1996, Rizzolatti and Arbib 1998), but interest in gesture-first far antedates this discovery, going back to the eighteenth century at least (Condillac, cf. Harris and Taylor 1989, Fitch 2010). Mirror neurons have been directly recorded in monkeys and presumably exist in all primate brains, including the human brain, and play a role in recognizing the intentions and actions of others. Concisely put in a Wikipedia article, "[a] mirror neuron is a neuron that fires both when an animal acts and when the animal observes the same action performed by another." Rizzolatti and Arbib (1998), in their exposition, explain similarly that mirror neurons are "neurons that discharge not only when the monkey grasped or manipulated the objects, but also when the monkey observed the experimenter making a similar gesture" (p. 188). Gesture-first had a modern advocate well before the mirror neuron discovery in Gordon Hewes (1973). The gesture-first theory says that the first steps of language phylogenetically were not speech, nor speech with gesture, but were gestures alone. Vocalizations in non-human primates, the presumed precursors of speech without gesture's assistance, are too restricted in their functions to offer a plausible platform for language (cf. papers in Call and Tomasello 2007), but gestures appear to offer the desired flexibility. Thus, the argument goes, gesture could have been the linguistic launching pad (speech evolving later). The gestures in this theory are regarded as the mimicry of real actions, a kind of pantomime, hence the appeal of mirror neurons as the mechanism. In some versions the gestures are also said to have been structured as a sign language (Armstrong *et al.* 1995). The gesture-first view has inspired a surprising range of enthusiasts, and has taken on something like the default assumption about the place of gesture in the origin of language – Hewes, as mentioned, Tomasello, Corballis, Armstrong *et al.*, Arbib, Rizzolatti, Volterra in some publications – and a smaller but increasing group of Doubting Thomases: we (the co-authors of McNeill, *et al.* 2008), along with Woll (2005/2006), Dessalles (2007), and Kendon (2010).

We (my co-authors and I) agree with gesture-first in asserting that language could not have come into existence without gesture. The error, as we see it, is in the explanation for why this was so; that gesture had to precede speech; that is, the very idea of "gesture first." We argue on the contrary that speech and gesture had to evolve together – speech and gesture were "equiprimordial."[1] If a gesture-only form of language did exist at some early stage of evolution (and we do not deny it) *it could not have led to human language.* Instead, this gesture-only language would have landed at a different point on the Gesture Continuum, at pantomime, and in this case gesture would have been separated from speech as an evolutionary by-product.

3.2.1 Problems with gesture-first

Even if mirror neurons were a factor in the origin of language, our basic claim is that a primitive phase in which communication was by gesture or sign alone, if it existed, could not have evolved into the kind of speech–gesture combinations that we observe in ourselves today. We see two problems. First, gesture-first must claim that speech, when it emerged, supplanted gesture; second, the gestures of gesture-first would be pantomimes, that is, gestures that simulate actions and events; such gestures do not combine with co-expressive speech as gesticulations but rather fall into other slots on the Gesture Continuum, the language-slotted and pantomimic.

3.2.1.1 Did gesture scaffold speech, then speech supplant it?

See Table 3.1 for a roster of gesture-first advocates, and note how all at some point say that speech supplants the original gesture language and then is marginalized. This is the first wrong assertion. Gesture-first commits one to the false prediction that speech replaced gesture rather than, as we see in ourselves, speech and gesture united as one "thing."[2] We say that gesture-first incorrectly predicts that speech would have supplanted gesture, and fails to predict that speech and gesture became a single system. It thus is falsified – twice in fact. The contradiction of gesture-first is that speech supplants gesture, it says, yet ends up integrated with it. The logic of gesture-first, at its very core, means that supplantation, overt or hidden, is inescapable. This is why every advocate naturally posits it.

Empirically, there is this perfect correlation of those advocating gesture-first and the supplantation step. Moreover, there is this conceptual point that explains it; namely, that supplantation is built into the gesture-first theory. It is important to see that gesture-first is a theory about the origin of *speech* (not gesture). Given that aim, it must logically consider that from gesture one gets to speech; and here supplantation enters: it is unavoidable. Even Sweet (Table 3.1), who envisions a transition from hand gestures to tongue gestures, and with them to speech, wants to leave hand gestures out at the end as "superfluous." He has no way to say from his several transitions that gestures in the end are other than left-overs.

When it emerged, why did speech not gradually integrate with gesture? This is possibly what "scaffolding" intends in part, and it is not an unlikely scenario. But even if scaffolding took place (it would be gesture that absorbs speech), it could only have been a temporary arrangement. Sooner or later gesture and speech must have separated. The reason lies again in the gesture-first tenet. The whole logic of gesture-first is to picture one code coming after another. The models of supplantation immediately below show the effects. The most that can happen is that the codes divide the labor of communication, as will be seen with the second of the supplantation models. Even if speech integrates with the gesture-language (as a kind of vocal gesture) it must sooner or later become an encoded system of its own,

Table 3.1 Gesture-first advocates and their statements

Source	Statement (regarding supplanted gestures in boldface)
Henry Sweet (and presumably Henry Higgins) in Henderson, E. (ed.) 1971:	"Gesture...helped to develop the power of forming sounds while at the same time helping to lay the foundation of language proper. When men first expressed the idea of 'teeth', 'eat', 'bite', it was by pointing to their teeth. If the interlocutor's back was turned, a cry for attention was necessary which would naturally assume the form of the clearest and most open vowel. A sympathetic lingual gesture would then accompany the hand gesture **which later would be dropped as superfluous** so that ADA or more emphatically ATA would mean 'teeth' or 'tooth' and 'bite' or 'eat', these different meanings being only gradually differentiated" (pp. 3–4). (Thanks to Bencie Woll for bringing this passage to my attention.)
Rizzolatti and Arbib 1998:	"Manual gestures progressively lost their importance, whereas, by contrast, vocalization acquired autonomy, until the relation between gestural and vocal communication inverted and **gesture became purely an accessory factor to sound communication**" (p. 193).
Stefanini *et al.* 2007 (referring to Gentilucci and others):	"the primitive mechanism that might have been used to **transfer a primitive arm gesture communicative system from the arm to the mouth**" (p. 218).
Tomasello (2008), thinking in terms of primates and very young (one-year and less) human infants but with the suggestion that something similar took place in phylogenesis:	"Infants' iconic gestures emerge on the heels of their first pointing... **they are quickly replaced by conventional language**...because both iconic gestures and linguistic conventions represent symbolic ways of indicating referents" (p. 323).

and the would-be integration is then lost, supplantation taking place, and gesture withering. The first of the models below shows this happening – encoded gesture and speech refusing to synchronize. Each is on a track of its own and they do not unify; instead they fly apart. It does not help to point to gestures in non-linguistic primates. There is nothing in them to show how they could lead to language without encountering the same roadblock of supplantation.

3.2.1.2 Models of supplanting and scaffolding

To see what may happen when two codes co-occur, as they would at the hypothetical gesture-first/speech supplantation crossover, we have two models: Aboriginal signs performed with speech, and bilingual ASL signs and speech. In neither case is there the formation of packages of semiotic opposites. When a pairing of semantically equivalent gesture and speech is examined in these two models, the two actively avoid speech–gesture combinations at co-expressive points. They repel each other in time or functionality or both, and do not coincide at points of co-expressivity.

3.2.1.2.1 Warlpiri sign language

Women use the Warlpiri sign language of Aboriginal Australia when they are under (apparently quite frequent) speech bans and also, casually, when speech is not prohibited. When this latter happens signs and speech co-occur and let us see what may have occurred at the hypothetical gesture or sign-speech crossover. Here is one example from Kendon (1988a):

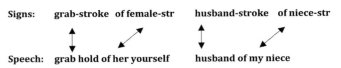

The spacing is meant to show relative durations, not that signs and speech were performed with temporal gaps (both were performed continuously). Speech and sign start out together at the beginning of each phrase but, since signing is slower, they immediately fall out of step. Speech does not slow down to keep pace with gesture, as would be expected if speech and gesture were unified. They then reset (there is one reset in the example) and immediately separate again. So, according to this model, co-expressive speech–gesture synchrony would be systematically interrupted at the crossover point of gesture and speech codes. Yet synchrony of co-expressive speech and gesture is what evolved.

3.2.1.2.2 English-ASL bilinguals

The second model is Emmorey *et al.*'s (2005) observation of the frequent pairings of signs and speech by hearing ASL/English bilinguals. While 94% of such pairings are signs and words translating each other, 6% are not mutual translations. In the latter, sign and speech collaborate to form sentences, half in speech, half in sign. For example, a bilingual says, "all of a sudden

[LOOKS-AT-ME]" (from a Sylvester and Tweety narration; capitals signify signs simultaneous with speech). This could be "scaffolding" but it does not create the combinations of unlike semiotic modes at co-expressive points that we are looking for. First, signs and words are of the same semiotic type – segmented, analytic, repeatable, listable, and so on. Second, there is no global-synthetic component, no built-in merging of analytic/combinatoric forms with global synthesis, and the spoken and gestured elements are not co-expressive but are the different constituents of a sentence. Of course, ASL/English bilinguals have the ability to form GP-style cognitive units. But if we imagine a transitional species evolving this ability, the bilingual ASL-spoken English model suggests that scaffolding did not lead to GP-style cognition; on the contrary, it implies two analytic/combinatoric codes dividing the work. If we surmise that an old pantomime/sign system did scaffold speech and then withered away, this leaves us unable to explain how gesticulation emerged and became engaged with speech. We conclude that scaffolding, even if it occurred, would not have led to current-day speech-gesticulation linkages.

Corballis (2002), in an argument for speech supplanting a gesture-first system of communication, points out the advantages of speech over gesture. There is the ability to communicate while manipulating objects and to communicate in the dark. Less obviously, speech reduces demands on attention since interlocutors do not have to look at one another (p. 191). While valid, these qualities do not single out gesture-first. There are also positive reasons for gestures not being language-like, and they would be so even if gesture and speech co-evolved as a single adaptation. All across the world, languages are spoken/auditory unless there is some interference to the channel (deafness, acoustic incompatibility, religious practice, etc.), and no culture has a visual/gestural primary language. Susan Goldin-Meadow, Jenny Singleton and I (1996) once proposed that gesture is the non-linguistic side of the speech–gesture dual semiotic because it is better than speech for imagery: gesture has multiple dimensions on which to vary, while speech has only the one dimension of time.[3] Given this asymmetry, even if speech and gesture were jointly selected, as proposed here, it would work out that speech is the medium of linguistic segmentation.

3.2.1.3 The pantomime problem

The second problem for gesture-first is that the gestures, given the mirror neuron phenomenon, would be pantomimes. Michael Arbib has advocated an origin role for pantomime (2005). In the pantomime version of gesture-first the initial communicative actions were symbolic replications of actions of self, others and entities, and these pantomimes later scaffolded speech. This process appeals because it so clearly taps the mirror neuron response. Merlin Donald likewise posited mimesis as an early stage in the evolution of human intelligence (1991). It is conceivable that pantomime is something that an apelike brain is capable of and was already in place in the last common chimp–human ancestor, some 8 million years back. Contemporary bonobos are capable of it (cf. Figure 3.2), supporting this idea.

The problem is not a lack of pantomime precursors but that *pantomime repels speech*. The distinguishing mark of pantomime compared to gesticulation is that the latter is integrated with speech; it is an aspect of speaking. In pantomime this does not occur. There is no co-construction with speech, no co-expressiveness; timing is different (if there is speech at all), and no dual semiotic modes. Pantomime, if it relates to speaking at all, does so, as Susan Duncan points out, as a "gap filler" – appearing where speech does not, in the language-slotted position for example. Movement by itself offers no clue to whether a gesture is "gesticulation" or "pantomime"; what matters is whether or not two modes of semiosis combine to co-express one idea unit simultaneously. Pantomime does not have dual semiosis. It and the ("straight") mirror neurons below producing it were thus unlikely to be the origin of language.

3.2.2 Last word on gesture-first

Whether you are persuaded by these arguments depends, ultimately, on taking seriously the idea, argued at length in Chapter 2, that *gesture and speech comprise a single multimodal system*, and that gesture is not an accompaniment, ornament, supplement or "add-on" to speech but is actually part of it. Gesture-first does not predict language–gesture integration. When we look at models of speech–gesture crossovers of the kind that, in theory, gesture-first would have encountered when speech supplanted the original gesture language, we do not find conditions for the GP dialectic, but instead non-co-expressiveness or mutual speech–gesture exclusion.

Joining the damage is Woll's (2005/2006) argument that not only does gesture-first leave gestures unable to integrate with speech but it also blocks, within speech itself, the arbitrary pairing of signifiers with signifieds that is characteristic of (or, Saussure says, *defining* of) a linguistic code.

The upshot is that gesture-first has little light to shed on the origin of language, as we know it; at best it explains the evolution of pantomime as a stage of phylogenesis that, if it once occurred, went extinct as a code and landed at a different point on the Gesture Continuum. We return to this possibility in the final section of the chapter.

3.3 MEAD'S LOOP

3.3.1 Overview

We now consider "Mead's Loop," an explanation of how an imagery-language dialectic and the GP could plausibly have been naturally selected at the origin. Mead's Loop refers to a posited new adaptation in the evolution of humans, wherein mirror neurons were "twisted" to respond to one's own gestures, as if they were from someone else. This did two crucial things. First, it gave to one's own gestures the sense of being social and public. This sense comes from straight ("untwisted") mirror neurons, which have social referencing by responding to the actions of others as if they were your own (whereas our posited "twisted" ones respond to one's own gestures as if they were from another), and this social-referencing property the newly evolved "twisted" mirror neurons inherited. And second, by mirroring one's own gestures and their significance, the new "twisted" mirror neurons made the gesture and its imagery available in Broca's area, the organ *par excellence* for complex action orchestrations; so vocal movements, originally for ingestion, could be orchestrated in new ways, by gesture imagery. These two achievements opened a door to the dynamic dimension. Of course one's gestures emerge from the same motor areas, but co-existing gestures and speech do not create gesture–speech unity. The gesture could well be pantomime and repel speech. But gestures over the "twisted" mirror neurons network, orchestrating speech, are meaningful in the dual semiosis sense that we seek on the dynamic dimension.

3.3.2 Straight mirror neurons

These are the already mentioned neural circuits in the motor areas that respond to the actions of someone else, as if the responder had performed the action herself (if a hand is seen picking up a raisin, certain mirror neurons fire; if the hand is just present or if the raisins are visible but no action, they do not fire; and these same neurons also fire when you pick them up yourself – they thus respond to the actions of another as if they were your own). While mirror neurons could underlie many social, empathic responses they do not carry the nervous system outside the significance of the actions to which they respond and have no way to enlarge the range of meanings beyond the significance of these actions. They naturally produce pantomime, as Arbib and others emphasize, but that is as far as they go. Accordingly, straight mirror neurons could not have produced the unified imagery–language dialectic that we ourselves embody.

3.3.3 The "twist" and its implications

The origin of language, we say, involved a novel adaptation of the mirror neuron circuits. This adaptation is named after G. H. Mead who wrote that a gesture is a meaningful symbol to the extent that it arouses in the one making it the same response it arouses in someone witnessing it. The Mead's Loop "twist" would be adaptive wherever sensing one's own actions as social and public is advantageous. Rizzolatti and Arbib (1998) linked straight mirror neurons to case grammar – a high-level grammar of semantic connections, such as action-on-object (Fillmore 1987), reflecting a straight mirror neuron semiotic. However, this linkage bypasses more immediate steps, which in our view were more likely in any case to have been the objects of natural selection, and which, in the adaptation described as Mead's Loop, could have lifted language out of the grip of a purely action-based semiosis.

Mead wrote:

Gestures become significant symbols when they implicitly arouse in an individual making them the same response which they explicitly arouse in other individuals. (Mead 1974, p. 47, but written earlier – probably in the 1920s)

Mirror neurons could be the mechanism of this response to oneself. Not the usual "straight" version, but the mirror neurons we posit with a "twist." This "twist" is what we hypothesize evolved – a new kind of response, a self-response to one's own gestures via mirror neurons.

The hypothesis is that part of human evolution was that mirror neurons participated in one's own gesture imagery. This hooks into Mead's loop – one's own gestures activating the part of the brain that responds to actions including gestures by someone else and thus treats one's own gesture as a social stimulus. Mirror neurons complete Mead's loop in the part of the brain where action sequences are organized – two kinds of sequential actions, speech and gesture, converging, and with meaningful imagery as the integrating force. This co-opting of sequential actions by socially referenced imagery made a new kind of action (and with it cognition) possible.

This hypothesis is meant to explain:

a. The synchronization of gesture with vocalization on the basis of shared meanings other than those of the actions themselves;
b. The co-opting of brain circuits that orchestrate sequential actions by meanings – those meanings carried by gestures.

Since Mead's Loop treats imagery as a social stimulus it explains why gestures occur preferentially in a social context of some kind (face-to-face, on the phone, but not to a tape recorder; Cohen 1977).

Mead's Loop had both semiotic and motor effects:

- Semiotically, it brought the gesture's meaning into the mirror neuron area. Mirror neurons no longer were confined to the semiosis of actions. One's own gestures (such as "rising hollowness") entered, as if it were liberating action from action and opening it to imagery in gesture. Extended by metaphoricity, the significance of imagery is unlimited. So from this one change, the meaning potential of language moved away from only action and expanded vastly.
- At the motor level, in Brodmann's areas 44 and 45 (i.e. Broca's Area), the areas of the brain where speech movements are orchestrated, Mead's Loop enabled significant imagery – gesture – to "chunk" vocal motor control, the foundation of the GP.

3.3.4 How Mead's Loop launched GP properties

I list here the chief properties of the dynamic dimension, and how Mead's Loop would have launched them. Mead's Loop would thus have opened the dynamic dimension. Without it, using only the general primate motor cortex, the ensemble of dynamic dimension properties would not have come together. It goes without saying that other factors also could have influenced the dual semiotic, social reference, psychological predicate and catchment properties, but all stemmed from the semiotic and motor effects of Mead's Loop.

3.3.4.1 The dual semiotic dialectic

The new form of mirror neuron response in Mead's Loop merged vocal movements and gesture, and synchronized them at points where they were co-expressive of the gesture image and its significance. Some languages, such as Japanese, have codified these imagery schemes in the form of "mimetics," or vocal imagery, codified onomatopoeia, which Kita (1997) found to correlate strongly with iconic gesticulation. Mead's Loop laid the ground for the imagery–language dialectic and the dynamic dimension of language. Once linguistic form evolved (and this was immediate, as suggested in §3.5 of this chapter), a dialectic would be the natural response. Without Mead's Loop, gesture and speech would have had only a loose connection, as seen with pantomime today, and language would not have escaped the single-semiosis box.

3.3.4.2 The social reference

The social orientation of mirror neurons with the Mead's Loop "twist" in general gave gestures and GPs a social reference character. Without Mead's Loop gestures could have social reference only if directed at an interlocutor. But gesticulations are not necessarily aimed at someone else (indeed, in contrast to emblems, points or pantomimes, they rarely are) yet gestures and their GPs, in themselves, are social ("public") entities. Also, crucially, a foundation in Mead's Loop opened a route over which the social conventions of speech and thought could form, GPs absorbing social-interactive content. An important effect of the inherent sociality of GPs due to Mead's Loop arose in the origin of syntax, namely, "sharaeability" (Freyd 1983), described later in the chapter (§3.5).

3.3.4.3 Origin of psychological predicates

The psychological predicate, the differentiation of the newsworthy in the immediate context, was inherent to Mead's Loop by virtue of how it brought gesture in as a speech-orchestrating force. From this, too, comes an explanation of why "one meaning" is "two things" – the thing differentiated, which is inseparable from the thing being differentiated, the field of meaningful oppositions. This inseparability from context of the psychological predicate resides in Mead's Loop's self-response-to gestures. A gesture of the gesticulation kind (in contrast to emblems or signs) is not portable from context to context. Over Mead's Loop it orchestrates vocal movements under the gesture's significance. The result is inherently context bound. Moreover, given the social reference of Mead's Loop, the contexts that gesture differentiates mesh with ongoing social interactions. So what is newsworthy is meaningful as a social framework. Eventually, the clever Mead's Loop creature was able to shape contexts to fit intended differentiations. This was an elaboration of the inherent psychological predicate functionality of Mead's Loop and may or may not have been part of it from the beginning (it seems possible that the ability to shape context to fit the intended meaning is linked to another ability, which also had to grow, to use metapragmatic indicators to orchestrate unpackings for goals and intentions – together, they promote utterances that will be true, respectively, to Silverstein's (2003) "indexical 'appropriateness-to'" (= goals) and "indexical 'effectiveness-in'" (= intentions) contexts; cf. Figure 2.11).

3.3.4.4 Origin of catchments

Threads of consistent imagery attached to themes – catchments – also arose with Mead's Loop as a matter of course. Mead's Loop binds imagery with speech and brings the meaning of the image into the "twisted" mirror neuron circuit. Each time the "it down" speaker regarded the bowling ball in a certain way (as an antagonistic force) its iconic imagery returned along with this theme. Theme and image were bound together. The theme is bound to the image because mirror neurons, echoing the gesture, also echo its significance as an antagonistic force plus whatever other referential iconicity it had. These details varied but the recurring theme was a constant. A similar analysis explains other instances – the single hand for Sylvester, the two different hands for the arrangement in the drainpipe.

3.3.4.5 The equiprimordiality of speech and gesture

Finally, to select Mead's Loop, speech and gesture had to evolve together. One could not have come first and the other later. There could not have been gesture-first *or* speech-first. To create the dual semiotic of Mead's Loop they had to be equiprimordial. This perhaps is the one step, if we try to single out one, that sets human evolution apart. Some avian species (crows, ravens) have evolved surprisingly elaborate vocal and gestural repertoires (Pika and Bugnyar 2011) but have not taken the step that led to language, evolving a unit that is both sound production and gesture integrally. The entire process involves one's own gesture impinging on the same area of the brain where vocal actions are being orchestrated, so both are necessary.

3.3.4.6 But not theory of mind

Mead's Loop however is not theory of mind (Wimmer and Perner 1983). In a sense, they are opposites. The Mead's Loop adaptation brings self-awareness of one's own behavior as social, not a theory of the cognitions and intentions of another (a theory of mind ability could evolve from straight mirror neurons in any case, which further limits its role in the origin of language).

3.3.4.7 And not imitation

Nor is Mead's Loop imitation. A report in *Science* summarizes a controversy among primatologists (*Science Magazine* 2008), whether chimps learn through imitation (the consensus being that they do), but Mead's Loop is not about this. In a learning situation, imitation and Mead's Loop can function collaboratively but each has a different role; the Loop fortifies the "instructor" with the sense that her own gestures are social entities. Imitation provides a response mechanism by the learner. Thus Loop and imitation can work together but are not the same.

3.4 NATURAL SELECTION OF MEAD'S LOOP

To summarize, G. H. Mead said that a gesture is meaningful when it evokes the same response in the one making it as it evokes in the one receiving it. For evolution, this suggests a kind of "twist," in which mirror neurons came to respond to one's own gestures as if from another. They thereby brought gesture imagery and its significance into the motor areas for orchestrating. They also built into speech an inherent social orientation. While "straight" mirror neurons reproduce the actions of another, with speech meanings that are those of the actions, the Mead's Loop "twist" responds to one's own gestures as social objects, and brings different meanings into the action-orchestration areas of the brain, those of the gestures. With metaphoricity, the expansion of meaning is unlimited. Everything from prosody to syntax, the inseparability of GPs from context, the differentiation of fields of meaningful oppositions with psychological predicates and the dynamic dimension in general, can be seen to stem from the Mead's Loop twist.

A hypothesis concerning the evolution of a new ability needs to describe the scenarios in which it plausibly would have been adaptive and thus naturally selected. For Mead's Loop, such a description begins with the gestures it used. Gestures did not begin with Mead's Loop; they were raw material and were co-opted by it. They did not have to be much like the gestures we produce now. Indeed they should not have been much like them. Gestures have developed along with speech. Current-day Great Apes may provide a better mirror of the gestures available to the Mead's Loop creature back then.

3.4.1 The gestures Mead's Loop could have co-opted

And we spot several candidates – chimp gestures with vocalization, bonobo iconic replicas of movement, chimp and orangutan movements with social interactive content, and old gestures adapted by chimps to new purposes (cf. Call and Tomasello 2007). In the creature evolving Mead's Loop gestures with these qualities would be the raw materials. They provide, one by one, the ingredients of Mead's Loop but circle around and do not close in upon it. They thus suggest "precursors" – social and meaningful actions that, given the right selection scenarios, could be co-opted for the new evolution, the "twist," but which has not (at least, not yet) occurred in chimps or bonobos.

One such precursor is suggested by the discovery that chimpanzees show a right-hand dominance for gestures only when the movements co-occur with vocalization (see Figure 3.1 and Hopkins and Cantero 2003). Barring independent evolution, such combinations could also have existed in the last common human–chimp ancestor[4] and provided raw material for co-opting the dominant left motor areas of the brain for speech. Such precursors combine vocalization and gesture but the significance of the gesture is redundant to that of the vocalization. Both are orchestrated by the same demand for goods and services (in Figure 3.1, the chimp is urgently requesting a banana).

A second precursor is seen in observations by Pollick (2006). She recorded bonobos performing pantomimic/iconic gestures to induce movements by other bonobos (not, so far as I know, ever directed at humans). The gestures in Figure 3.2 are distillations of the left-bonobo's action of shoving the right-bonobo but without making actual contact. It is unclear whether

Figure 3.1 Gesture and vocalization together promote right hand dominance in Chimpanzee. Drawn from video provided by William Hopkins. Used with permission of University of Chicago Press.

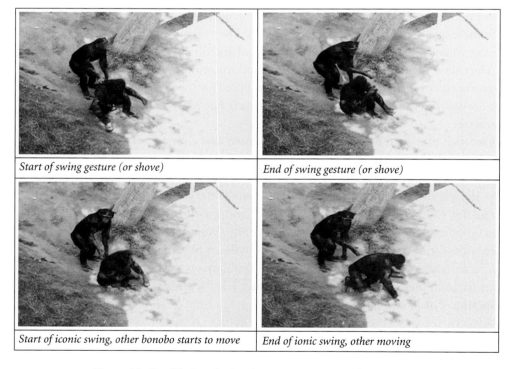

Start of swing gesture (or shove)	*End of swing gesture (or shove)*
Start of iconic swing, other bonobo starts to move	*End of ionic swing, other moving*

Figure 3.2 Possible Bonobo iconic gestures. Images with permission of Amy Pollick (bonobos at San Diego Zoo).

they should be called iconic or pantomimic.[5] The significance was clear to both producer and recipient, which was to get the second bonobo to move in the indicated direction. The gestures were totally independent of vocalization (there was no sound) and so, even though meaningful, were not in a position to orchestrate vocal actions. Nonetheless, if we imagine such gestures by the Mead's Loop creature, vocalization could also have been present and the left hemisphere (Broca's area or its precursor) awakened (as with the Hopkins chimp). This kind of gesture could then provide more raw material for the Mead's Loop "twist." That it has not happened (at least not yet) with the bonobo does not show it was unavailable as raw material to the creature in which we are presuming Mead's Loop to have evolved.

A potent third precursor is not a gesture in the classic sense but is the use of the hands to manipulate other animals for social interaction purposes. Such hand use is seen in the Great Apes but not in monkeys (Cartmill and Maestriepri 2012). This use merges the hand and social interaction, two ingredients of Mead's Loop, but does not (so far as I am aware) orchestrate vocal output or carry significances other than social interaction.

A fourth possibility, seen in us today, was perhaps also a precursor and this is the experience of mouth movements when one attempts some intricate hand manipulation. These non-functional movements show the close connection of the motor regions of hand and mouth in the human brain, plus an automatic activation of parts of the vocal tract by hand motion, a route that, if it existed in the evolving creature, would also have been a precursor.

Finally, chimps trained in a human-devised language (signs or keyboard symbols) produce rapid sequences of these imparted symbolic forms. This too could be a precursor (though symbolic forms do not spontaneously appear in current Great Apes). With Mead's Loop, they would have been orchestrated in a new way, by gesture imagery. In chimps, in contrast to signs produced by human users, sequences of signs are apparently not accompanied by gesture. They are structured by another principle altogether, desires and demands (see §3.7 below).

Thus a number of precursors can be found with contemporary Great Apes that plausibly would have been available to the Mead's Loop creature as well. Each is raw material for Mead's Loop but each is also limited as a form of speech–gesture unity. The missing link is a scenario selecting Mead's Loop itself. The one to be proposed arose in a form of family life that may not be accessible to apes, which is an answer to Kendon's questions in section §3.7: "What is missing? What holds them back?"

Figure 3.3 Tool use but not instruction. Youth on right watches and imitates; adult works. Lacking Mead's Loop the adult would not see her own actions as having the social resonance that "instruction" implies. Image from Haslam *et al.* (2009). Used with permission of Drs. Tetsuro Matsuzawa, Michael Haslam and William McGrew; also see Matsuzawa *et al.* (2011).

3.4.2 Adult–infant interaction: nurture into nature

The title of this section does not mean the inheritance of acquired characteristics but reverses the usual "nature into nurture."[6] Given the social references of Mead's Loop, natural selection for it would arise in situations where sensing one's own actions as social and public is advantageous – for example, as suggested here, imparting information to infants, where it gives the adult, typically a mother, the sense of being an instructor as opposed to being just a doer with an onlooker (the chimpanzee way, cf. Figure 3.3). Entire cultural practices of childrearing depend upon this sense (Tomasello 1999). The adult must be sensitive to her own gestures as social/public actions. Sensing actions as social would impact the next generation of children who, as a result of it, do better at coping, especially in an emerging cultural mode of life. Such children carry the genetic disposition to form Mead's Loop themselves, and pass it on more than their less inclined fellows, and then the Mead's Loop sensitivity increases over generations. The focus of this selection would be adults, and especially mothers – in this scenario *language began in female adults*. Their infants, both female and male, benefit from cultural inculcation and inherit any genetic dispositions. Sarah Hrdy (2009) has highlighted the group rearing of infants, including the infants of other adults, as an aspect of early human family life. The ability to engage in collective infant rearing clearly demands (and also naturally selects) seeing one's own actions as social. Such practices stand in sharp contrast to chimpanzee infant rearing, where infants, if left without their mothers, are neglected and vulnerable to attacks by adults in the same group.

Obviously, there would have been a range of instruction scenarios (passing on skills, planning courses of action, cultural inculcations of all sorts, including "Machiavellian" – or "Macachiavellian", as Maestripieri (2007) terms it – scheming but the adult (mother)–infant scenario stands out). Current-day mothers show the importance of self-awareness of their own agency. Iverson *et al.* (1999), observing the gestures of mothers directed to 16–20 month-old children, found that the gestures were mostly deictic points. A narrow focus on such gestures is (a) different from those to adults and older children and (b) an adjustment that reflects the mother's awareness of her gestures as social stimuli. Other hints come from Murray *et al.* (1996). The authors observed interactions (not necessarily involving gesture) with 18-month-old children by mothers suffering depression, versus mothers not so afflicted. The depressed mothers responded to children less sensitively, and the children were less developed cognitively. Both effects point to the importance, for children's cognitive and linguistic development, of the mother's awareness of the social context and of her own effectiveness within it.

These empirical indicators point to a factor of self-awareness in current-day mother–infant interactions that the Mead's Loop evolution would have introduced. It also links to MacNeilage and Davis' (2005) proposal that "the first words might have been parental terms formed in the Baby Talk context of parent-infant interaction" (p. 1830). Baby talk itself could be a product of Mead's Loop evolution in this envisioned adult–infant scenario. A role of self-aware agency also appears to be closely tied to the onset of the GP ontogenetically (Chapter 5).

Cartmill and Byrne (2007) point to what could have been a self-aware agency precursor in orangutans – mothers visually monitoring their infants when the infants are performing the same action; similarly (as Cartmill also points out, pers. comm.) Washoe shaping signs in the hands of her adopted son. But mothers in these species do not monitor the infant's response to *her* gestures as they impart information, and this is the innovation that Mead's Loop enabled.

3.4.3 The scenario

All of this suggests a scenario of organized family life by bipedal creatures inducing changes in brain configuration and function. An important selection pressure for Mead's Loop would be the family circle (thus not exclusively "man the hunter" or "man the tool maker"), this setting offering a role for Mead's Loop where one's own meaningful movements are treated as social objects, especially in childrearing and infant care.

The origin of Mead's Loop cannot be tied to a single step. It took place through many converging steps over a long period. Missing a crucial step, family life in particular, it is unlikely to have occurred.[7]

3.5 ORIGIN OF SYNTAX

3.5.1 Introduction

How, when, or even why syntax emerged is far from obvious, but here began the static dimension. Over eons it has led to vast crosslinguistic diversity. Proposals for the origin of syntax range from a "big bang" single mutation, through cultural practices such as ritual or grooming, to no special sources at all (syntax as the outcome of human intelligence in general, e.g., Sinclair-de Zwart 1967). This chapter affirms a biological proclivity to form syntactic patterns during communicative encounters. I follow Lenneberg (1967) and claim that syntax rests on a biological foundation, hence is a topic in the origin of language. But I also say, as will be explained, that a major selection factor is what has been called *shareability* (Freyd 1983). I seek the natural selection of syntax (the general ability, not specific constructions, although we will look at cases) in three places – the nature of the GP and its unpacking; the new paths this opened; and shareability. These in turn suggest three kinds of adaptive advantages. First, syntax is crucial for a GP dialectic. Without morphs and combinations of morphs there cannot be a semiotic opposition to gesture imagery. Second and linked, syntax stabilizes the dialectic. It is the resting point *par excellence*. Third, syntax helps make language shareable in sociocultural encounters. Any or all of these factors could have favored an ability to form syntactic patterns, defined generally as creating meaningful wholes out of segmented and patterned speech parts; meeting standards of form; providing cultural identity; and transmitting and maintaining this system over space and time. As often announced in these pages, we are focusing on the dynamic dimension of language. This dimension crosscuts the static and is not reducible to it (nor vice versa, the static is not reducible to the dynamic; they are two dimensions, not one dimension in two forms). In past decades, and continuing, any number of grammatical models has been proposed for the static dimension but none has been designed with this crosscutting in mind. In Chapter 6, §6.2.2, I point out the advantages of constraining a static description by how it combines with the dynamic. Cognitive grammar (Langacker 2000), although also limited to the static dimension, is more congenial for this purpose than other static approaches.

3.5.2 Shareability

An area of life where a syntactic ability could evolve is the cultural and social encounter. The term "encounter" is understood broadly. It includes migration and trade, as well as interpersonal interactions of all kinds and especially, *pace* the Mead's Loop selection scenario, infant care by parents (or groups of adults, cf. Hrdy 2009). Encounters create selection pressures, not for syntax directly, but for what Freyd (1983) in her innovative paper called "shareability" – constraints on information that arise because it must be shared; constraints because:

It is easier for an individual to agree with another individual about the meaning of a new "term" (or other shared concept) *if* that term can be described by: (a) some small set of the much larger set of dimensions upon which things vary; and (b) some small set of dimensional values (or binary values as on a specific feature dimension). Thus, terms are likely to be defined by the presence of certain features." (p. 197, emphasis in original).

From shareability then comes the language-like semiotic that fuels the imagery–language dialectic and the stabilization of it through analysis and combination. Gesture assumes the guise of a social other in Mead's Loop and naturally invites shareability, creating in this process a "discreteness filter" such that the semiotic properties of morphology (discreteness) and syntagmatic value (combinations) arise and with them the analytic/combinatoric semiotic opposition to imagery in GPs. In Mead's Loop the orchestration provided by gesture imagery could *from the start* be paired with static structure forms.

In her concluding footnote, Freyd speculates that shareability may be relevant to the intrapsychic workings of individual minds as well as the interpsychic relations between individuals (as shareability primarily asserts). The virtual otherness of gesture provides the link. Given Mead's Loop and the reconfiguration of Broca's Area it caused, shareability distilled a companion static system and from this arose the dual semiotic of the GP.

3.5.3 Emerging syntax

That the static and dynamic dimensions arose together, also "equiprimordial," is explained by Mead's Loop's built-in social referencing, combined with gesture imagery, as earlier pointed out. From this vantage point, we can claim that words and sentences continue the evolution of the GP. Contrary to traditions both philological and Biblical, language did not begin with a "first word." Words emerged from GPs. There was an emerging ability to differentiate newsworthy points in contexts; a first "psychological predicate" perhaps but not a first word.

The paradox of an emerging syntax (which for our purposes includes morphology) is that it is almost invisible in current humans. Infants today show a remarkable facility for acquiring language but, because there is an input language, this facility does not display the ability we seek. The original adaptation was an ability to create *sui generis* morphs and syntagmatic values to be part of GPs (recursion in the creation of syntagmatic value was the ability singled out by Hauser *et al.* 2002 as central; see Rossini 2012 for an illuminating discussion). Children now of course are presented with fully formed languages. If the ability to create a syntax is latent but still present in humans today perhaps we can coax it out in adult speakers when the usual avenues of speech are blocked. If adults form novel morphs and morph combinations, and especially if the responses are immediate, we may glimpse the ability we seek. Of course it is still not the ability in pure Edenic form since adults naturally draw upon the language(s) they use in daily life, but if we can find novel deployments that are not borrowings or analogies, we may be seeing the fundamental ability to form a novel syntax at work; all the more so if the new forms come forth immediately.

Participants in the experiments to follow were told to avoid speech and communicate information to a listener, using only gestures. They were telling a well-known story, Snow White (Bloom 1979), or describing brief video vignettes featuring motion (Gershkoff-Stowe and Goldin-Meadow 2002). What speechless gestures reveal could have arisen with speech and gesture jointly at the dawn, gestures without speech effecting the emergence of static dimension properties for reasons given in Goldin-Meadow, *et al.* (1996, p.34):

when communicators are forced to rely solely on gesture, that is, when gesture...must assume the full burden of communication, the manual modality is liberated from the constraints imposed on it by speech – only to be constrained to take on the grammatical properties essential to human language, most notably segmentation and hierarchical combination.

Adult speakers not allowed to speak do in fact show a robust emergence of novel static dimension properties, suggesting the response of a "bioprogram" (Bickerton 1990).

3.5.3.1 Experiment with speech-denial 1 – birth of paradigmatic values

Morphemes are the atoms of language, the indecomposable minimal units of form and meaning. In contrast to GPs, which are dynamic units of thinking-for/while-speaking, morphs are fixed, repeatable, listable, held to standards of form and meaning, bind form and meaning together by convention rather than by one's own inhabitance, and have combinatoric potential. They thus have the roster of semiotic properties that contrast with the global-synthetic semiotic of gesture imagery. Given our premise, an aspect of language origin was an ability to create these morph-like entities with which to make information shareable. Selection for discreteness, repeatability and portability (not just selection for specific morphemes) is what we consider.

A morph implies among other qualities that it meets, consciously or not, standards of form and is open to violations, such that changes of form can cancel the morph (e.g., making the "OK" sign with the second finger instead of the first touching the thumb). Spontaneous gestures do not have this potential (e.g., any finger touching the thumb embodies the idea of precision, possibly different aspects).

One question therefore becomes, when do standards emerge? Several things seem to take place all at once. First, the new gesture morph becomes analytic, as opposed to holophrastic; this results from shareability. Second, it becomes stable and repeatable and thus extractable from context. Third, it combines with other gesture morphs to create constructions with syntagmatic values. Fourth, it contrasts with other gesture morphs paradigmatically. Explicit mention of standards appears in the Snow White (SW) wordless narration, and novel syntagmatic values in the Gershkoff-Stowe and Goldin-Meadow vignettes. In SW the gestures for the Queen (Q) and King (K) contrast paradigmatically from their inception.[8]

Communicative encounters such as were present in both the SW and vignettes settings (the subject speaking to an interlocutor in both) could induce this critical attention to form. To spin the metaphor, a communicative encounter is midwife to the birth of a morph and syntagmatic value. The speed – the *immediacy* – with which the K and Q morph births took place is breathtaking and suggests an inbuilt capacity. In a post-experimental interview the SW narrator was able to provide the experimenter, Ralph Bloom, with descriptions of the gestures and their distinguishing features, so the contrasts had solidified into standards (moreover, he criticized the listener's variations of these forms as – he actually said – "violations").

What was novel was not the sign ensembles themselves but how they were constructed to contrast paradigmatically. The signs employed clichéd male/female, crowned-head features but the specific choices of what was similar (crowns on heads) and what different (breasts vs. muscles), while stereotypical, was novel: just those features that created (a) a paradigm (crowns) and (b) contrasted female to male within it. The paradigm is not from English or any other languages the speaker knew. That it seems "obvious" is the point: the "crowned-heads" paradigm reflects an ability that we share as a gift of the origin of language to create new systems of *langue.*

In the Queen sign especially, we find a number of morph hallmarks occurring from the first instance (the essential distinguishing features are maintained throughout, although there is streamlining – a directed process different from lack of stability): stable and repeatable, analytic rather than holophrastic, and extractable from context (the gesture appears in the same form and with the same value in multiple contexts). There was also dialogic use of "King" and "Queen" by the listener. He preserved the crucial male vs. female distinction, as well as the two morpheme structure of each gesture ("has-crown" + "has-muscles" or + "has-breasts") but embarked upon a "dialect" difference in how the "has-crown" feature of both the Q and K signs and the male feature of the K sign were formed – the first without revolution at the head, the second with a downward slice with the hands in front of the chest rather than the narrator's iconic braced arms. The meaning of Morph 2 may thus have shifted along with the form to something like "flat-chested" or "has-*no*-breasts" for "King," losing touch with the original "has-muscles" meaning, and possibly making the less frequent K sign also dependent on the Q sign. So linguistic drift, another *sui generis* feature, was taking place in the same encounter. Had the listener used this morph with fresh listeners, a kind of experimentally engineered migration, a new branch of the original language could have been set in motion. See Figures 3.4, 3.5, and 3.6 for illustrations of all these points (from McNeill and Sowa 2011; used with permission).

Canary Row gestures also show a tendency to stabilize on certain forms – for example, a single-finger (pointing) hand for Sylvester; a loose open flat "B-hand" for Granny; character viewpoint enactment and various hand-shapes for Tweety. These may be protomorphs but, in contrast to the stability of the K and Q signs, the forms are inconsistent. Non-single-finger hand-shapes were also used for Sylvester and the single-finger handshape appeared for other references. In short, there was gravitation to a certain form, often with an iconic start (the first of the Sylvester single-finger gestures was

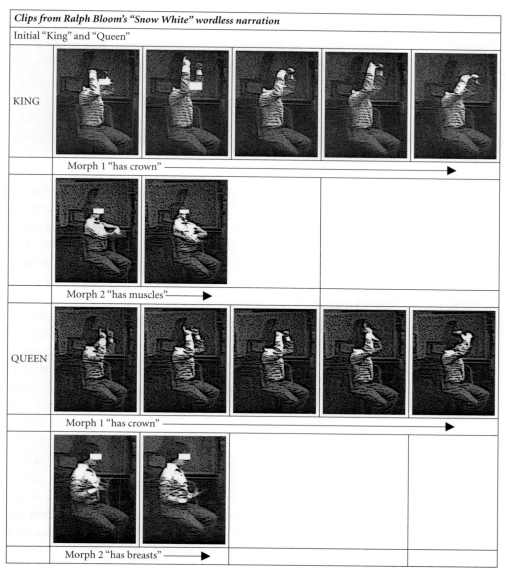

Figure 3.4 First occurrences of King and Queen morphs. Shows immediate paradigmatic contrast of the two morphs in first occurrence. The gestures are two-morph combinations. Note the contrast of Morph 2: "has-muscles" vs. "has-breasts." Morph 1, "has-crown," is the same. The two hands rotate around the head, forefingers pointing down, moving up and down as they rotate. The spatial head vs. torso distinction and pointing vs. cups for Morph 1 and Morph 2 are maintained despite later streamlining (see Figure 3.5). The duration of "King," the first gesture of the pair, was 4.3 seconds. "Queen," the second, was down to 2 seconds, and this acceleration continued. Used with permission from John Benjamins Publishing Company, Amsterdam/Philadelphia. www.benjamins.com. SW gestures from Ralph Bloom (1979).

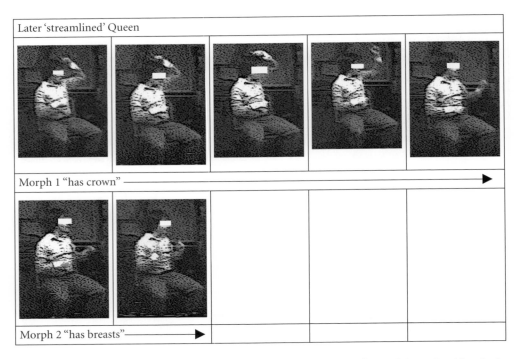

Figure 3.5 Later abbreviated "Queen." The "has-crown" morph is made with a single hand and only a partial revolution; the "has-breasts" morph is two still cupped hands but now rotates inward and is not held down with palms upward. The changes improve speed but also reduce iconicity, so already some alteration of form has begun that could end in arbitrariness. Duration is down to slightly more than 1 second for the entire two-morph "Queen" combination, about the span of a spoken word. The head–torso distinction is still present and indeed was never lost during the entire narration. Used with permission of John Benjamins Publishing Company, Amsterdam/Philadelphia. www.benjamins.com. SW gestures from Ralph Bloom (1979).

both deictic and iconic for squeezing into the pipe), but the form does not become fixed nor is it reserved for one meaning. If we call this polysemy, it is far beyond what one expects in a functioning linguistic system. However, a gesture quickly passes to actual morph status given minimal dedicated communicative use, as we see with the SW morphs. See Figure 3.7 for a collection across three speakers of single-extended-finger proto-morphs for Sylvester.

3.5.3.2 Experiment with speech-denial 2: birth of syntagmatic values

The second speech denial experiment brings out the combinatoric potential of the static dimension semiotic. Participants describing video vignettes in

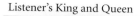

Listener's King and Queen

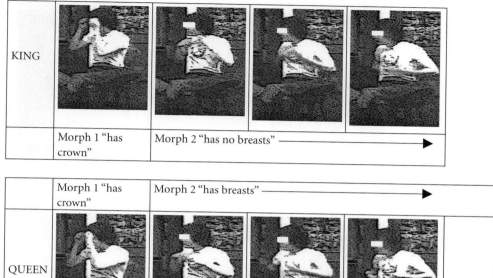

Figure 3.6 "Queen" and "King" signs by the listener, attempting to clarify which character, the King or the Queen, the narrator had just referred to. The Morph 1–Morph 2 distinction is preserved but a "dialect" difference has appeared in the "has-crown" and "has-muscles" features – the first without revolution, the second a downward slice with the hands in front of the chest. Morph 2 may be an instance of "language drift," shifting to something like "flat-chested" or "has-no-breasts," away from the original "has-muscles." The new meaning of "King" was "Not Queen," unlike the narrator's original. The narrator had just before used "flat-chested" in combination with his usual "has-muscles" and "crown," so it was modeled. The listener thus apparently did not arrive at these features by himself, and this seems to be the essence of a linguistic drift triggered by contact in microcosm. Used with permission of John Benjamins Publishing Company, Amsterdam/Philadelphia. www.benjamins.com. SW gestures from Ralph Bloom (1979).

gestures without speech showing a doll seeming to somersault through the air and land in an ashtray comparatively the size of a sandbox (a Supalla 1982 ASL verb of motion vignette) produce three gesture sequences with some frequency (Gershkoff-Stowe and Goldin-Meadow): S-M-A (S = "stationary object," the ashtray; M = "moving object," the doll; A = "action," the somersault arc), M-S-A, and S-A-M.

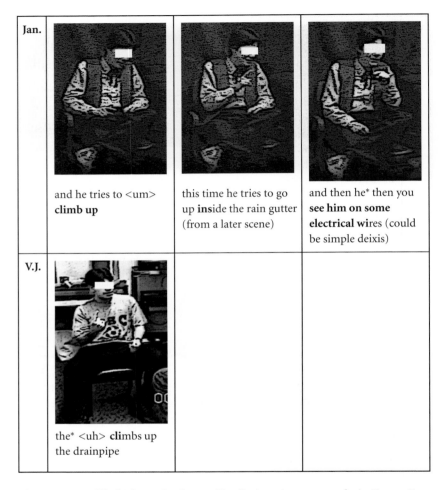

Figure 3.7 Possible "Sylvester" ephemeral/preliminary/ proto-morphs in Canary Row narrations by three speakers. There was no communicative contact among them. Thus, the spontaneous similarities across the three and the consistency within the two speakers from whom there are multiple examples are noteworthy: the beginning of form standardization. Lacking adoption, the proto-morphs would have disappeared, once out of the narrative situation. Used with permission of John Benjamins Publishing Company, Amsterdam/Philadelphia. Data compiled by Claudia Sowa.

These sequences correspond to different information packages that can be likened to "constructions" (see Table 3.2).

The hint of syntagmatic value in all this is that the same "M" (doll) gesture, for example, has different values in different combination (Table 3.2).[9]

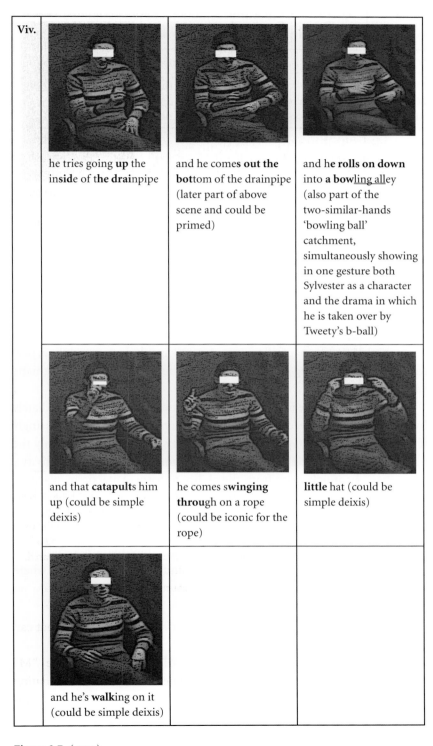

Viv.

he tries going **up** the in**side** of **the drain**pipe	and he come**s out the bot**tom of the drainpipe (later part of above scene and could be primed)	and he **rolls on down** into **a bow**ling alley (also part of the two-similar-hands 'bowling ball' catchment, simultaneously showing in one gesture both Sylvester as a character and the drama in which he is taken over by Tweety's b-ball)
and that **catapult**s him up (could be simple deixis)	he comes s**winging through** on a rope (could be iconic for the rope)	**little** hat (could be simple deixis)
and he's **walk**ing on it (could be simple deixis)		

Figure 3.7 (*cont.*)

Table 3.2 "Constructions" in wordless motion event descriptions
(Gerskoff-Stowe and Goldin-Meadow data)

"Construction'	Sequence	Example
MOTION (increasing activity)	(S-M-A)	ring-doll-somersault
LOCATION (where action occurred)	(M-S)-A	doll-ring-somersault
RESULT (end-state of action)	S-(A-M)	ring-somersault-doll

> *Doll* is "at-a-location" in the M-S-A "Location" package; the "phrase" is
> (M-S).
>
> *Doll* is "moving-object" in the S-M-A "Motion" package; the "phrase"
> is (M) alone.

and

> *Doll* reaches "end-state" in the S-A-M "Result" package; the "phrase"
> is (A-M).

To bring out these syntagmatic values, try mimicry (the effectiveness and
theoretical rationale of which are demonstrated in Chapter 4, §4.1.10.3):
while thinking of the particular semantic package shown on each line, perform the corresponding sequence of gestures, and look for the syntagmatic
value to emerge.

So, it may be possible to have new syntagmatic values created immediately
by gestures without speech. They come forth automatically, not surprisingly
if the experiment has tapped an inbuilt ability to create them.[10] Only the
S-M-A order is iconic (the sequence corresponds to increasing activity).
The others seemingly arise from the ability to form syntactic regularities.
Each syntagmatic value comes with a paired significance (Motion, Location, Result), and in this we find a basic property of a signifier-signified
combinatorics emerging.

A static dimension instantly emerges, as a bioprogram response is
expected to do, and generates novel forms and values in situations where
shareability constraints are invoked, communicating information to an
Other.

3.5.4 Rethinking syntax as action control

In the selection scenario where Mead's Loop had adaptability, adults incul-
cating cultural information in infants, actions, the overt behaviors of adults,

were put up to natural selection pressures. Gestures and speech are among other things actions and action is an obvious target of natural selection. Standards of form are not only about "good forms" but also about "good actions." Fluent bilinguals tell me that a different musculature engages when they shift languages. From an action perspective, morphs and constructions are templates for acting. Because they embody standards they ensure action that is recognizable and repeatable. Browman and Goldstein (1990) pioneered this approach on the phonetic level, and here we extend it to syntax. Syntax is a complex behavioral orchestration that achieves, within milliseconds, elaborate, hierarchical multimodal coordinated flows of movement under significances that have nothing directly to do with the movements themselves but can control them via imagery, and all of this is done effortlessly and at high speed. When we adopt this perspective the Saussurian synchronic method – analyzing language as a whole regarded panoramically – is redefined too. It is uncovering the standards of good behavioral forms. Linguistic intuitions are the individual's access to standards of action as well as of form, and play the role of signaling that speech (or manual sign) is "the way we do things around here." Rethinking syntax and language as action *in toto* appears again in Chapter 4, in a discussion of the "new actions" that Mead's Loop engendered in humankind.

3.5.5 Perception is special

Speech perception would have had its own evolution. It is reasonable to suppose that its trajectory and that of production were closely linked. Logically, perception would seem dependent on the Mead's Loop evolution of new actions.[11] Indeed, theories of perception such as the Haskins "motor theory" (Liberman 1996) make this linkage explicit, speech perception being, it says, in part "running" (as in a computer) the production of speech to oneself – a form of mimicry. At the same time, perception is the feedback channel for reaching the correct "forms" of vocal and manual actions, so the perception–production linkage runs in two directions.

3.5.6 Unpacking

To see how pressures emanating from GPs could have selected an ability to form morphs and constructions with internal syntagmatic values, it is useful to look at unpacking in its current-day form. "Unpacking" was introduced in Chapter 2, §2.5.2: it is the process of externalizing, with a construction, the GP's point of differentiation of a field of meaningful oppositions, and has the function both of bringing the meaning of the GP into the system of *langue*, and of providing a stabilizing "stop-order" to the GP dialectic. We took as our example one of the GPs for the bowling ball episode analyzed in McNeill (2005); the scene and the typical gestures that it evokes have already been described at several places. While this example is complex and is not at all plausible as a reflection of what the first speakers could have managed, everything in it shows how constructions answer the call of GPs. The example is a microcosm of what could have been selection pressures that ancient GPs also created. Shareability fulfilled the origin by analytically segmenting and combining the meanings that unpack/stabilize the GP. The unpacking construction in Chapter 2 was selected by the GP itself; it was a form of self-unpacking and a model of how at the dawn GPs could have created selection pressures for the syntactic abilities we have seen here. Shareability and its stabilization semiotic cemented these into the kinds of forms that we recognize as syntactic.

So from GPs and self-organization, structured by shareability, we see syntax as continuing the work of GPs, unpacking them from the start. There was no "holophrastic" or "single-word" phase in this picture. Did the Mead's Loop creature come up with discrete words that refer to objects, actions, locations, etc., and then, at some point, combine them; or on the contrary did he have words that globally indexed whole semantic complexes, and then come to divide them? And our answer is: neither; he (or more likely she) was forming imagery–language dialectic units, or growth points, and with these began thinking and acting in new ways, impossible without them, and required a syntactic ability from the very beginning.

3.5.6.1 Unpacking breakdowns

However, unpacking can be misaimed and cause breakdowns. It is not only a matter of finding the right words. A construction may not be found or the one found has semantic values that conflict with the GP and/or the field of oppositions. A case of the second kind was described in a paper with Nancy Dray (Dray and McNeill, 1990) – we dubbed it the "nurturing" example: a speaker in a conversation with a friend was attempting to convey a nuanced idea, that a third person she was describing was given to performing nurturing acts, but these good deeds were also intrusive, cloying, and unwelcome. Initial false starts were based on the use of "nurture" as a transitive verb (she would "nurture" someone) and were repeatedly rejected as inappropriate. Ultimately an oblique construction that circumvented transitivity was found in (2).

(1) The fact [that she's . . .] [she's nu- uh]
(2) [. . . she's somehow . . . she's] [done this nurtur] [ing] [thing and here you]

The problem was a mismatch at (1) of the transitive construction to the field of meaningful oppositions. Transitivity means, roughly, that the woman described has a direct transformative impact via nurturing on the recipient of her action. However, this meaning distorted the idea the speaker intended to convey – something that would differentiate a field of meaningful oppositions more like HER OTIOSE ACTS. The slight but successful updating in (2) separated effect from act and gave an unpacking that differentiated this context without clashing with it. Both successes and failures can be traced to a common source, the need to find constructions with semantic values that mesh with (or at least do not violate) the intended point of differentiation in a GP.

3.5.7 Summary

Important aspects of the static dimension – morphs, syntagmatic values out of combinations, constructions, and embeddings – are products of shareability, the form of information decomposition and standardization that arises when information must be shared. Part of the pressure to find shareable constructions arose from GPs themselves, to unpack and stabilize them. These static dimension aspects are candidate elements of the language "bioprogram."

3.6 SCENARIOS FOR SYNTAX

Much of the static dimension however, despite its roots in a bioprogram, is cultural and historical, shaped over time by intragroup and intergroup encounters, including during migrations. Shareability arises, we have said, in communicative encounters between individuals and groups. The encounter is basic. To have forms repeatable, standardized and non-context-bound makes them durable and portable from encounter to encounter. The encounter fosters linguistic identity and loyalty plus also the darker twins of shibboleths and xenophobia. Speakers recognize each other as orchestrating actions as they do, or not, and use these action signals to identify in- and out-groups. All of these factors create selection pressures. The following illustrate current-day aspects of such encounter scenarios.

3.6.1 Nicaraguan sign language, or encounters of cohorts

The first-ever school for the deaf in Nicaragua was established in the late 1970s. Deaf children who previously had lived in villages and rural areas with no contact with other deaf or with a sign language encountered each other on a sustained basis for the first time (such children typically would have already devised their own limited codes used with family in daily contacts, called "home signs"; see Goldin-Meadow 2003). The school was the setting for a new sign language whose emergence was documented on video – surely a first – by a dedicated group of linguists and psycholinguists, Judy Kegl, Ann Senghas, and Marie Coppola among others. As the language developed, its character changed and moved ever closer to patterns that also appear in other sign languages of the world (without any significant input from those sign languages). The process was punctuated: each new cohort, encountering former cohorts (an ever-growing number), made changes. Over cohorts, the new language emerged. At each encounter the language as a whole took a jump, a process modeling the role of encounters historically. To quote one of the researchers, Senghas (2003):

[N]ew form-function mappings arise among children who functionally differentiate previously equivalent forms. The new mappings are then acquired by their age peers (who are also children), and by subsequent generations of children who learn the language, but not by adult contemporaries. As a result, language emergence is characterized by a convergence on form within each age cohort, and a mismatch in form from one age cohort to the cohort that follows. In this way, each age cohort, in sequence, transforms the language environment for the next, enabling each new cohort of learners to develop further than its predecessors. (p. 511)

The importance of the cohort and the localization of each successive version of the sign language within an age-peer cohort shows the role of encounters, with one cohort and its phase of the language modifying the language's preceding version.

3.6.2 Language change/stability, or encounter frequency

An interesting paper by Pagel *et al.* (2007) documents how a tendency for words to change historically correlates inversely with the frequency of the words in daily speech – high-frequency words changing less. They say: "Greek speakers say 'ourá', Germans 'Schwanz' and the French 'queue' to describe what English speakers call a 'tail,' but all of these languages use a related form of 'two' to describe the number after one" (p. 717).

Pagel *et al.* list at the slow end words such as "two," "who," "tongue," "night," "one," and "to die." These compare to faster-evolving words such as "dirty," "to turn," "to stab," "guts," and "tail." What explains the distribution? Pagel *et al.* refer to social factors like status, the strength of ties, the size of the population, and the amount of outside contact; and no doubt there are others.

But how do collection-wide factors like these seep into individual speakers, so that, over time, as they speak, some words resist change, others are vulnerable and drift? No one speaker is responsible for change or persistence, since the changes (or lack thereof) stretch over many individuals and lifetimes but individuals must be involved as vectors at some level. Pagel *et al.* favor an account in which frequency affects how prone a population of speakers is to adopt a given change. This is still at the communal level and does not give a picture of individual speakers as vectors of change or its lack.

GP/Mead's Loop offers the following account of the inverse correlation. The important concept is how a GP embodies contextually newsworthy content at the moment of speaking. Let's consider this quality in relation to the diversification and the conservation of word forms.

First, diversity. Less frequent words appear in few GPs, but when they do they are likely to have high communicative value. This exposes them to a range of contextual and social influences in fields of meaningful oppositions, including the status of other speakers, who may model or impose diversity and induce mimicry, and in general induces the GP, in its capability of orchestrating vocal actions, to put pressure on signifier forms. The cumulative effect would be drift over time, forms branching out in separating groups and losing any discernible relationship.

Second, conservation. High-frequency words (at least many, like "two," "at," "and," "few," etc.) are less likely to be psychological predicates over many contexts, precisely because they are frequent. High frequency implies absence of newsworthiness. They are less likely to be the focal point of consciousness, less often parts of GPs, and less open for all these reasons to the momentary fluctuations of context, purpose, and thinking-for-speaking. Moreover, frequent words are more likely to appear in speech bundled in constructions as parts of GP unpacking, rather than as points of differentiation themselves, and be bundled there in the periphery of consciousness. This peripheral awareness could also protect them from wear and tear. All of this, at the level of individual speakers, seems to be a reflection of what Pagel *et al.* refer to, on the communal level, as the "purification" effect of high frequency (another not unrelated term might be the "cloistering" effect of it). Of course, frequent words also may appear in psychological predicates and not every occurrence of a rare word is in one, but there are these predictable tendencies.

3.6.3 Psycho-Babel, or encounters over space and time

Beyond words, there is also the preservation and diversification of syntax, and here again encounters play a crucial role. If we take the Tower of Babel story as a parable of migration it is not as far-fetched as one might suppose. The insight is that migration leads to encounters and breeds diversification; and the further the migration, the more the encounters, and the greater the diversification.

We can relate this diversification to Mead's Loop and the GP. What happens within individual speakers when languages spread? I mean at the level of the individual brain and mind; the spread of Indo-European, although a historical process in itself covering eons, would have necessarily also included this brain/mind process; it was the human brain/mind that responded to encounters and carried it.

Is there anything we can deduce of what might be a present-day relic of the first orchestrations that *H. sapiens* would have created as people migrated and encountered each other? Is such a hypothesis even conceivable? I no doubt incautiously put forth ideas for three pieces of the puzzle.

1. Mapping meanings onto temporal orders seems primitive – the orchestration of actions under some significance with shareability allots meaning fragments to segments of time. If this sounds like using English as a model of the original language, the reasons for the deduction are not English but considerations of possible brain mechanisms. A language in which meanings map onto time alone is one candidate for an early syntax. More derived are morphological complexes that dissociate meaning from temporal order. Other discourse and social forces then are free to orchestrate vocal and manual actions. It is perhaps no accident that languages spoken in the least accessible areas from the presumed southwest African starting point of world migration, thus taking the longest to reach and the forebears of current speakers having encountered more indigenous others on the way, such as the Arctic, are elaborate and the most altered from a mapping of meanings onto time.

2. Embedding plus syntagmatic values (the ability to embed one construction within another, accruing value as it goes, which Hauser *et al.* 2002 nominated as a linguistic universal) would likewise be coordinated in the most primitive action-orchestrations at temporally fixed loci – the embedded parts temporally isolated from the embedding parts, which in turn are continuous in time except for other embeddings. This creates levels of embedding but always holds the temporal sequences together. Thus a language in which embedding is handled by holding pieces in memory until an embedded piece is complete is another candidate for an early form. Notice that both the embedding and the basic mapping mechanisms assume that the creatures employing them have some way to know when some form is "complete" or "incomplete" – that is, have standards of form. Elaborations of this basic plan also would be correlated with migration and encounters.

3. A simple hypothesis would be that the IE type is one of the least elaborated language forms. Modern opinion ties migration to the invention and spread of agriculture starting about 11,400 years ago, but creatures with presumably a fully modern microanatomy (if not anything like modern cultures) were already dispersing over the range eventually inhabited by modern-day IE speakers and beyond. From geography, it would have been the initial area to be entered, hence would have the greatest likelihood of retaining time-based orchestrations. Probably no current language descends from the original inhabitants of where it is spoken; it descends instead from migrants who encountered earlier languages, and the farther the current-day language forbears migrated, the more encounters the language absorbed, both of earlier languages and of late-comers. Not unlike the elaboration of Nicaraguan Sign Language over successive cohorts, each encounter creates pressure to add embellishments as a reaction, either of assimilation or resistance. The indigenous languages it encountered on the way are probably long gone but their impacts remain, and long-travelled languages will have absorbed the greatest number of them. More outlying areas – the Arctic, the southern ocean, the New World – are thus expected to have developed more adorned languages (cf. Hale 1983, "non-configurational" languages, such a Warlpiri, an Aboriginal language of Australia, characterized by radical departures from time-based unpacking: Hale enumerates "(i) free word order, (ii) the use of syntactically discontinuous expressions, and (iii) extensive use of null anaphora" – this last a kind of invisible pronoun, the ultimate disconnection from a temporal-segments of speech syntax). This makes sense from the dispersion viewpoint, since these remote regions would have been the last to be reached through migrations and the forebears of current-day speakers, encountering more languages on

the way, the most likely to have elaborated their languages. Perhaps there is some such correlation – more remote, more departure from temporal sequencing. Are the languages with the greatest time depth in the original eastward migration route also the ones with the most temporally sequenced relations?

The Sapiran division of languages according to how they combine meanings into single words – analytic or isolating (e.g., Chinese), synthetic (e.g., Latin), polysynthetic (e.g., Inuit) (Sapir 1921, p. 128), may reflect degrees of adornment of the basic brain orchestration plans. There are of course all kinds of possible complications of this simple pattern. Multiple waves of migration and changes from other sources can induce changes on top of existing layers. Indo-European itself presumably was altered to become inflecting after the first migrations. DNA analyses (*Science* news item, issue of 4 Sept. 2009, p. 1189, vol. 325) suggest that the first farmers in Europe were migrants, replacing indigenous hunter-gathers, and modern European populations descend from these migrants. Per hypothesis, this further alters the language plan. There must be other forces also changing languages that move them in other directions of their own, further camouflaging ancestral forms. But the main point is that many forces concerning the dispersal of language – the Tower of Babel story – can be traced to the effects of migration encounters on the mechanisms of orchestration produced by Mead's Loop.

However, this entire theory appears to conflict with a view among some who reconstruct the history of languages, that when languages come into contact they simplify (e.g., Trudgill 2011). While I cannot present myself at all as expert on these topics, the conflict may be more apparent than real. The cases Trudgill cites as simplifications seem to be pidginizations or creolizations, where a new, partial and not surprisingly simple code arises out of contact, and speakers do not change their source languages. The cases where contact increases complexity involve speakers of fully established natural languages with at least one of the languages gaining complexity, and there is no pidginization or creolization. "Babel" encounters would be of this second type. Sarah Thomason, in a talk given at the University of Chicago, May 12, 2011, presented numerous examples of this occurrence in contemporary encounter situations: complexity increasing after contact. One impressive instance was how the Russian language that Finnish immigrants learned increased in complexity over its native form, adding a new opposition between the genetive and partitive, that traced back to the Finnish original (Russian had not possessed this distinction; example originally in Thomason 1997). Mead's Loop and shareability, active in the Finns's encounter with Russian, offer an explanation. A speaker attempts to create (to him) a new form of Russian vocal action orchestration with an existing Finnish schema. Blends or even new forms of orchestration then occur that permit the process to proceed smoothly. Importing an existing template (which the genitive/partitive opposition from Finnish provided) resolved a specific orchestration difficulty. The import occurred where, in Russian, an "opaque," obsolete, not-useful-for-differentiation-or-unpacking distinction existed; so it was replaced by the speaker's new version just where GPs could use it in appropriate contexts (and this then was taken up by others). It would be of interest to see if other instances of L1 importation can be explained similarly, as meeting the need for smooth orchestration.

Two papers appearing almost simultaneously, one in *Science* (Atkinson 2011) and one in *Nature* (Dunn *et al.* 2011), shed further light on the migration theory. Straight mirror neurons seem to favor SVO (subject-verb-object) word orders (cf. Armstrong *et al.* 1995), but the Mead's Loop "twist" does not favor particular word-orders. According to Mead's Loop the "instinct" is more general, an urge to analyze global meanings into morphs; to combine morphs in GPs with gestures having co-expressive meanings; to create new syntagmatic values; to share it all; to carry it around to different contexts; and to learn it; but Mead's Loop is indifferent whether the order is SVO or SOV or some other sequence. Specifications of a particular word-order preference come from history and what forebear speakers have encountered. So failing to find any overarching grammatical plan, as in Dunn *et al.*, is a kind of confirmation of Mead's Loop. I completely echo their conclusion that "cultural evolution is the primary factor that determines linguistic structure, with the current state of a linguistic system shaping and constraining future states" (from the abstract).

In his paper, Atkinson deduces where language began, on the principle that small groups, as they migrate further, lose features of their original linguistic pool, a version of the "founder effect" in genetics (according to which populations, as they move from the origin, progressively carry fewer of the original pool of traits). The total phonemic diversity of languages decreases linearly from the southwest corner of Africa with distance up to 30,000 kilometers – whence the origin of language. Possibly Mead's Loop emerged there too and from this corner tendrils of migration branched out. If so, it predicts that the languages spoken in the southwest now should be of the isolating type. A hint they tend in this direction appears in Greenberg (1970), who reports that some 70% of noun, verb, and adjective roots in the Khoikhoi (Hottentot) language begin with clicks – an exceptionally rigorous time-based schematization. And the

Wikipedia article on the Khoisan languages of the region in general summarizes that they: "are generally fairly isolating, with word order being more widely used to indicate grammatical relations than is inflection." This is the prediction of the brain-mechanism role in Mead's Loop when there has been few encounter events. So the Mead's Loop creature may have lived in this remote area and from there her descendants have reached everywhere else. Atkinson's discovery applies to the phoneme inventories of languages. But what of syntax? How does our scenario – more elaborate, non-time based syntax building up over space – co-exist with less phonemic diversity at greater distances? We avoid conflict if we posit some kind of trade-off, whereby syntax takes over from sound. That trade-offs take place in general is a frequent assumption. As phonemic diversity reduces, syntax elaborates. The encounter and its impact on syntax becomes the driving force of a compensation for reduced phonetic diversity.[12] Even a two-phoneme language could in imagination evolve if it had a sufficiently elaborate non-temporal syntax.

3.6.4 Loyalty

One last aspect of the encounter is that it tends to highlight language likenesses and differences. Encounters of groups have the potential both to close off, to protect, and to open, to find ways to communicate. To emphasize either similarities or differences would in turn have developed selection pressures for morphology and syntax. As a scenario in which a syntactic ability was adaptive and could have been naturally selected, the encounter connected syntax and psychological identity with language. Language loyalty answers encountered differences by raising a sense of one's own language as unique, shared by fellow speakers, distinguishing them from others not inhabiting the same mode, whose very "inhabitance" is different, and leads finally to xenophobia and shibboleths. An interesting and unexpected instance of language identity is in the attitudes of children at the start of language-thought unity in ontogenesis. White American children of 5–6 yrs. consider it more likely that an English-speaking white child they are introduced to will grow up to be an African-American adult but still speaking English, than an adult of the original race but speaking French (Kinzler and Dautel, 2012), suggesting a charmingly low priority for race as a criterion of what is essential for one's being and/or greater weight to inhabitance in language as the basis of identity. Older children (9–10 year-olds), as do adults, choose race. The "unchanging" dimension for African-American 5–6 year-olds, on the other hand, is already race. Kinzler and Dautel point out reasonably that racial identity is likely to be more salient to African-American children.

On the other hand, multiple inhabitances seem to coexist in native bilinguals (those who grow up with two languages simultaneously). Informants tell me (Pamela Perniss, native in English and German) that, to themselves, they exist either "in" one language or the other and whichever language it is the language appears to them self-contained, a whole. Inhabitance is in two modes, each experienced singly (paradoxically, then, translation from one language to the other is difficult since it requires shifting entire modes of being).[13] The same principle applied to successive bilingualism (the more typical kind, the "second" language being acquired second) can result in the new language supplanting the first as a mode of being. Not only full linguistic systems but people who master a prestige dialect can experience an altered mode of being (the Eliza Doolittle effect), not for show or because they are rejected in their former milieu but because their mode of being has shifted.[14]

These effects, according to Mead's Loop, are products of how language itself came to be with its connection to action and modes of being, all geared to encounters as a setting for the evolution of syntax and the new forms of action it structures.

3.7 LANGUAGES WITHOUT MEAD'S LOOP – THE APE-LANGUAGE EXPERIMENTS

Taking our perspective from Mead's Loop and the GP we can consider the many attempts to teach a human language to non-humans and see what remains of the language after it has been filtered through the workings of a brain capacious but lacking Mead's Loop. The question is not whether chimps and other non-human primates can learn what we can plausibly call a "language" (the word itself has often been the battleground) but what this "language" without Mead's Loop actually comprises.

We see some language-like features but other features are strikingly absent. What remains is a candidate precursor; conversely, what is absent may reflect the requirement of having something like Mead's Loop. In the animals signs and sequences of signs occur in abundance but they are structured in ways quite unlike those of a human language. Sequences appear to be organized by desires and demands and follow an iconicity that is basically a diagram of the demand for, and the receipt of, a donation from the "addressee" (although "mark" in the sense of someone panhandled may be a better word). If these features signal precursors of human language, they also show that Mead's Loop was a major breakout from the kind of ape mental world that Kendon described in 1991:

Evidently, then, chimpanzees in wild and semi-wild conditions refer each other to features of the environment by means of a sort of eye and body pointing, they do sometimes give evidence of partially acting out possible, rather than actual courses of action, they are able to grasp the nature of the information their own behaviour provides to others and to modify it accordingly if it suits their purposes, and in respect to some kinds of gestural usage, as we have seen, they are able to employ them in new contexts with new meanings [referring here to attested cases by infants lifting their arms overhead as a signal of non-aggression, based on a natural postural adjustment to being groomed]. They are on the edge of developing a use of gesture that is representational. The studies in which chimpanzees have been taught symbolic usage, whether of gestures or of keyboard designs, not only confirm the cognitive capacities that these observational studies imply but also show that chimpanzees *can* use behaviour representationally if shown how.

Chimpanzees, then, seem on the verge of developing a language, yet they have not done so. What is missing? What holds them back? (p. 212)

Kendon proposes an answer to his question, that chimpanzee social life is full of "parallel actions" but has little in the way of collaboration (cf. the ape group in Figure 3.3). Parallel action is a form not evoking pressures to select anything like Mead's Loop. On the contrary, parallel action is emblematic of interaction styles that find no advantage in sensing one's own gestures as social and yet leave ample room for making demands; so if anything it actively blocks the emergence of Mead's Loop. This is the current hypothesis for "what holds them back."

What then passes through the language filter and what does not? Whatever makes it through we can place with the potential gesture precursors identified earlier (right hand dominance when vocalizing, deictic/iconic gesture production, the hands manipulating others for social purposes, and others). I think it is likely that language-trained chimps grasp something of the notion of signs as signifier–signified units, reacting to them as more than just signals evoking responses. The chimps combine signs productively and often into strikingly novel usages, such as "drink" + "fruit" for a watermelon, inventions that evoke admiration and quotations from their handlers. However, the chimps also very often combine signs to make what seem to a human a structureless jumble; for example (in succession, each English word a separate sign), *open gimme key in open help help key in open key help hurry*

(Washoe attempting to get a human handler to open a food box – "Washoe" being a chimpanzee subject of the Gardners's original sign-language study). There is nothing in this sequence of meanings being mapped onto temporal orders (see "... *in open help help key in open key help*..."). While to us structureless, such strings follow an accumulative iconic principle of **more urgency** ⇒ **more signs** (or, more generally, **more urgency** ⇒ **more effort**). This long string, regardless of its appearance as a jumble, accurately reflects Washoe's urgent desire to get the prize. And it could be a precursor – Mead's Loop, when it arose, could build on this kind of rapid-fire expressive outburst, the raw material for what became, with Mead's Loop, orchestrations in a new way, by imagery. Kanzi, the bonobo described below, shows a similar ability to rapidly produce discrete expressive actions.

Some years back (McNeill 1974), long before I perceived anything of the existence of Mead's Loop, I collected all the examples of Washoe's sign sequences that I could glean from various lists and examples the Gardners (1969, 1971) had cited, and concluded that, as well as having numerous signs, Washoe did indeed produce sequences of signs in certain regular ways. I found three orders (two of which the Gardners had identified as well). After eliminating various redundancies and mechanical constraints, the sequences boiled down to one pattern that Washoe truly followed; this was Addressee-Action-Non-Addressee. I wrote of this sequence:

The chimpanzee may therefore have imposed her own formula on the sentence structures she observed her handlers using. Washoe's formula does not capture what the handlers themselves encoded (agent, action, recipient), but instead emphasizes a novel relationship as far as grammatical form is concerned, that of an interpersonal or social interaction (addressee-non-addressee). (1974, p. 83)

The Addressee (or "Donor")-Action-Non-Addressee (or "Recipient") sequence is an iconic model – besides the quantity principle above, it is a *diagram* of the desired event. It is a social-manipulative "syntax," if we can call it that. The "sentence" diagrams the desired result and is not unlike reaching out to grab something from someone: the addressee (the donor) offers the non-addressee (always Washoe) the desired prize or action – iconically, the path Washoe wanted the food or other desirable to follow. So, for Washoe, the meanings orchestrating her actions are specifically demands to meet wants, with her as beneficiary. And as noted in the quote, Washoe and her handlers could look at the same sequences of signs and relate them to different meanings, addressee/donor for Washoe, agent for researcher, etc.

Moreover, this is a single mode of semiosis. Washoe's "sentence" is iconic for a direct action, which it maps in its own form, and in making it there is no opening wedge for the dual semiosis of human language and thought.

Pointing to this same conclusion, another important clue is that Washoe and other signing apes never perform, so far as I know, gestures with their signs, as human signers do (see Figure 2.7 for examples from Duncan 2005, and other examples in Liddell 2003 and Bechter 2009). Thus they don't form semiotically opposed imagery–sign units, and there would seem to be no possibility of a dialectic of imagery and "language."

Kanzi, the famed bonobo subject of Sue Savage-Rumbaugh's language learning experiments (Savage-Rumbaugh *et al.* 1998), was highly successful at utilizing a keyboard with buttons corresponding to lexical words (each button with a distinctive visual sign). From the published reports that I have seen (involving common chimpanzees, Sherman and Austin, using the same or a similar keyboard system; Savage-Rumbaugh 1986), the button sequences appear to follow the same **more urgent ⇒ more presses** principle (it is unclear from descriptions how repeatable if at all such sequences are). From the videos of Kanzi that I have studied ("Bonobo People," NHK), there is no indication that Kanzi uses gesture as the orchestration medium, and it does not appear that anything like Mead's Loop is part of his repertoire. Kanzi shows an impressive ability to understand spoken English commands. However, comprehension is so multifaceted it offers little clue to where he stands regarding Mead's Loop.[15]

The realization that non-human primates are unable to orchestrate speech sounds (as has been known for many decades and was indeed one of the original reasons for using sign language and a keyboard) also suggests the same limit of the chimp brain for language: it's not only that ape vocal-anatomy differs (a higher larynx, for one thing), it is that apes do not have Mead's Loop and a thought–language–hand brain link to orchestrate these mouth-part movements around imagery.

So, the animal-language experiments yield a fairly clear picture. Part of what evolved in our lineage was the ability to use our own gestures to orchestrate movements of the vocal tract under significances other than those of the actions themselves. Rather than communicative dynamism, which is the human mode of increasing materialization where quantity reflects newsworthiness or unpredictability, chimps show a kind of "demand" dynamism, where quantity reflects the animal's urgency, and the resulting "syntax" is an icon of the process of receiving donations. The animals are indifferent to shareability because of parallel-action, and so experience no pressure to decompose complex wholes into repeatable parts. Precursors are that they are able to learn signifier–signified signs, and are thus not limited to a fixed repertoire, and are able to output signs sequentially, and thus can structure meanings (in their own way).

3.8 THE THOUGHT–LANGUAGE–HAND LINK

What changed in the evolving human brain to make Mead's Loop and the GP superstructures resting on it possible? I describe next the already-mentioned thought–language–hand link, a possible new brain structure that emerged with Mead's Loop and resides in all humans but is observable most directly in cases of deafferentation, in which there is a dissociation of practical-actions and gestures, action-actions being lost while gesture-actions are kept.

3.8.1 The IW case

The unique features of gesture and its differences from practical action at the level of brain orchestration is brought home with clarity in the remarkable case of Mr. Ian Waterman, sometimes referred to as "IW."[16] His condition exposes what otherwise would remain hidden, a specific *thought–language–hand link* in the human brain that Mead's Loop would have created.

IW suffered at age 19 a sudden and total deafferentation of his body from the neck down – a near total loss of all the touch, proprioception, and limb spatial position senses that tell you, without looking, where your body is and what it is doing. The loss followed a never-diagnosed fever that is believed by Jonathan Cole (pers. comm.) to have set off an autoimmune reaction. The immediate behavioral effect was immobility, even though IW's motor system was unaffected and there was no paralysis. The problem was not lack of movement per se but lack of control. Upon awakening after three days, IW nightmarishly found that he had no control over what his body did – he was unable to sit up, walk, feed himself or manipulate objects; none of the ordinary actions of everyday life, let alone the skilled actions required in his vocation.

To imagine what deafferentation is like, try this experiment suggested by Shaun Gallagher (pers. comm.): sit down at a table and place your hands below the surface; open and close one hand, close the other and extend a finger; put the open hand over the closed hand, and so forth. You know at all times what your hands are doing and where they are but IW would not know any of this – he would know only that he had willed his hands to move but, without vision, would have no idea of what they were doing or where they were located.

After more than 30 years of constant effort, IW has developed an entirely new way of initiating and controlling movements. His movements depend on having constant visual contact with the environment, including the surrounding space, objects to be manipulated and other objects in the immediate vicinity, as well as his own body, arms, hands, legs. Every movement is planned in advance, the force and direction calculated intuitively, and the movement monitored as it is taking place. Given all these requirements, it is impressive to see IW move without visible flaw at normal speeds. However, if vision is denied, IW can no longer control his hands and arms accurately.

3.8.2 Significance of the IW case for language origins

IW also cultivated gesture performance. Gestures for him are equally planned in advance, controlled during performance, and timed. He refers to them as "constructed" gestures and distinguishes them from "throw-away" gestures that are unplanned, untimed, unwitting and "just happen." For us, it is just these "throw-aways" that are of principal interest. Considering only them the IW case shows that, without vision and in the absence of all proprioception and spatial position sense, gestures continue to occur with co-expressive speech, attaining complete accuracy at the level of what the motion signifies ("morphokinetic" control), although not at the level of fine motor adjustments ("topokinetic" control). The gestures possess the same tight binding with speech at points of co-expressiveness that marks the performance of unaffected individuals. Moreover – a crucial point – IW is able to perform these "throw-away" gestures with full exactitude *without vision*, without therefore feedback of any kind: there is simply *no decrement*. Yet he cannot control practical actions under the same conditions. This juxtaposition, that "throw-aways" are accurate without vision but practical actions are not, reveals something hidden in the human brain, a dedicated *thought–language–hand* brain link, in part dissociated from the brain circuits involved in world-related actions, underlying semiotically unlike and co-expressive speech and gesture meaning combinations; that is, underlying GPs. Part of the origin of language was the emergence of this thought–language–hand brain link.

Figure 3.8 IW's iconic gesture with vision. Used with permission of University of Chicago Press.

3.8.3 IW's gestures with and without vision (1997)

With vision, IW's gestures are like those produced by normal speakers except that they are fewer in number and tend to be isolated and performed one by one, in keeping with a constructed-gestures strategy. Figure 3.8 shows a narrative gesture accompanying speech made with vision. IW was describing Sylvester after he had swallowed the bowling ball. Both morphokinesis and topokinesis are indistinguishable from normal. His hand appears to bracket a small figure in the central gesture space and move it downward, wobbling right and left slightly as it goes down. The motion is co-expressive with the synchronous speech: "he wiggles his way down." The only clue that control is other than normal is that IW continually looks at his hand during the gesture.

Figure 3.9 illustrates a coordinated two-handed tableau without vision.[17] The left hand is Sylvester and the right hand is a trolley pursuing him in another Canary Row scene. IW was saying, "[and the $_a$tram $_b$**caught** <u>him up</u>]" (a, b referring to the first and second panels). His right hand moved to the left in exact synchrony with the co-expressive "caught." Moreover, a poststroke hold (underlining) extended the stroke image through "him" and "up" and thus maintained full synchrony of the meaningful config-uration of the stroke and the still unfolding co-expressive speech. It is important to recall that this synchrony and co-expressivity were achieved without proprioceptive or visuospatial feedback. We thus see, without any

Figure 3.9 IW's morphokinetically coordinated two-handed iconic gesture without vision (blind conceals his hands). The hands enact pursuit and contact in a coordinated image. Note however the topokinetic misalignment along with the morphokinetic precision. Used with permission of University of Chicago Press.

feedback, the double semiosis of synchronous gesture and speech of a GP. The use of space is especially informative. Although IW has no exact sense of where his hands are topokinetically (as seen in the slight misalignment), he synchronized them morphokinetically with the co-expressive speech to create an image of "catching up to," a feat that seems impossible without a thought–language–hand-linked GP controlling both speech and gesture.

3.8.4 IW's instrumental actions without vision (2002)

In contrast, instrumental actions are essentially impossible for IW lacking vision. Figure 3.10 shows his attempt, under the blind, to remove the cap of a thermos bottle. The left panel is immediately after Jonathan Cole has placed the thermos into IW's right hand and placed his left hand on the cap (IW is strongly left handed, the dominance surviving deafferentation); the right panel is a second later when IW has begun to twist the cap off. As can be seen, his left hand has slipped off and is turning in midair. Similar disconnects occurred with other simple actions – threading a cloth through a ring, hitting a toy xylophone, etc. – this last of interest since IW could have used acoustic feedback or its absence to monitor when his hand had drifted off target, but still he could not perform the action.

Figure 3.10 IW attempts to perform an instrumental action without vision (removing cap from a thermos). Used with permission of University of Chicago Press.

3.8.5 IW slows speech and gesture in tandem (1997)

Another striking demonstration of the thought–language–hand link is that without vision IW can, *in tandem*, modulate the speed at which he presents meanings in speech and gesture. Without feedback he maintains speech–gesture synchrony through a change of speaking speed. While still under the blind and conversing with Jonathan Cole, we adventitiously observed IW reducing his speech rate at one point for prosodic emphasis by about one-half. As his speech slowed, *his gesture also slowed, and to precisely the same extent.* See Figure 3.11. This joint modulation could stem from his sense of how long his GPs remained active and took to unpack, a time sense that would circumvent the lack of feedback. The example is especially convincing since IW happened to use nearly identical words (and the same number of syllables) at the two speeds (bracketed in Figure 3.11) and we can directly compare the fast and slow rates.[18]

Normal Speed (bracketed material = 0.56 sec., 5 syllables) **"and [I'm startin' t'] use m' hands"**

Slow Speed (bracketed material = 0.76 sec., 5 syllables) **"-cuz[I'm startin' t'] get into"**

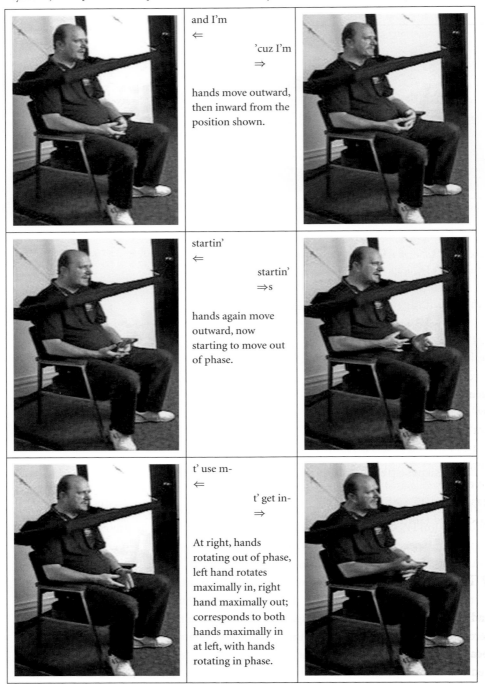

and I'm
⇐

'cuz I'm
⇒

hands move outward, then inward from the position shown.

startin'
⇐

startin'
⇒s

hands again move outward, now starting to move out of phase.

t' use m-
⇐

t' get in-
⇒

At right, hands rotating out of phase, left hand rotates maximally in, right hand maximally out; corresponds to both hands maximally in at left, with hands rotating in phase.

Figure 3.11 IW changes rate of speech and gesture in tandem without vision, maintaining perfect gesture–speech synchrony. Implies that the GP and its unpacking were the pacesetter as both slowed. Note that motion of hands outward and inward occurs at same speech points at the two speeds. IW rotated his hands together at the normal rate and in opposite phase at the slow rate; despite this difference, the maximal and minimal extensions of the hands occur at the same speech points.

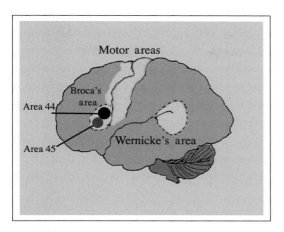

Figure 3.12 Annotated brain. Used with permission of University of Chicago Press.

3.8.6 Implications for the thought–language–hand link

The IW case suggests that control of the hands and the relevant motorneurons is possible directly from the thought–linguistic system. Without vision, IW reveals a dissociation of gesture, which for him remains intact, and instrumental action, which is impaired. His case implies that the "know-how" of gesture is not the same as the "know-how" of instrumental movement (using Gallagher's 2005 terms). In terms of brain function, it implies that producing a gesture cannot be accounted for entirely with the instrumental action circuits; at some point gesture diverges into a circuit of its own and there is tied to speech. The likely locus of this link is Brodmann's Areas 44 and 45, or Broca's area, where mirror neurons in Mead's Loop are also situated (see Figure 3.12).[19]

3.9 THE BRAIN, AND HOW IT CHANGED

Mead's Loop thus accounts for a thought–language–hand link in brain areas where actions are orchestrated. In this way it offers an explanation for why Broca's area *is* a speech area. In this section, I sketch a general brain model based on current understanding of gesture–speech semiosis and where this brain link fits into it.

We are hampered in our quest because so little is known about how the brain organizes gesture. Nonetheless, by invoking the principle that speaking is dynamically organized in a dialectic of imagery and language, we can predict some features of a "neurogestural" system. This system should engage the same brain circuits as language, in part. And conversely, if we discover something about brain action from gesture, we should be able to add this discovery to our picture of what the brain is doing when it handles language. I do not present myself as a neuroscientist, but I hope to bring basic information about the brain into contact with what has not been considered in this area previously – the insight that gesture is actually part of language and must be considered along with it. I believe the perspective of an imagery–language dialectic can lead to new understandings of some familiar facts.

The first of these is that Broca's area is more than a "speech center." It is *the area of the brain for orchestrating actions under some significance* – that is, it is the area of the brain that assembles sequences of movements and/or complexes of moving parts into performance packages unified by goals, meanings, and adaptability. We have seen that performance units in the case of human language are unified by imagery – a primary organizational factor – and Broca's area may be where actions (articulatory, manual) are organized around gesture images (visuospatial-actional), as Mead's Loop explains. A general orchestration function is suggested by brain imaging results. For example, Nishitani and Hari (2000) observed that activation of this region preceded activity in the motor area by some 250 ms and seemed to have the function of organizing the mirror neuron system, located in areas 44 and 45, including, per hypothesis, "twisted" mirror neurons. In a later paper, Nishitani and collaborators write: "Far beyond its classical language functions, Broca's region contributes to action planning, action observation, action understanding, and imitation. Speech production and comprehension can be considered a highly developed form of action execution/observation matching" (Nishitani *et al.* 2005, p. 66). Broca's area also mediates higher-order control of forelimb movement[20] and, in this, resembles the neuronal mechanisms subserving speech (Binkofski *et al.* 2000). Bonda *et al.* (1994) also found that Broca's area became active during arm and hand movements. Even more germane, Decety *et al.* (1994) found Broca's activity during *mental imagery* of grasping. Horowitz *et al.* (2003) report that a region in Broca's area (area 44) is activated by "generation of complex articulatory movements of oral/laryngeal or limb musculature" (from the abstract). Ferrari *et al.* (2003) observe activation in a region of the monkey brain known as F5, which is the presumed homolog of Broca's area, by communicative face gestures. And, Xu *et al.* (2009) conclude from an fMRI imaging study that the orchestrating areas of the brain are modality-independent, a semiotic system that encompasses the whole semiotic domain, language, gesture, imagery and environmental objects.[21]

All of these factors could have been co-opted by Mead's Loop evolution. It in turn would change how vocal movements are orchestrated – by imagery. It would also change how manual movements are orchestrated – also by imagery. The dual semiotic system of speech and gesture imagery developed here.

3.10 OVERALL MODEL

In the brain model the neurogesture system includes both the right and left sides of the brain in a choreographed operation with the following parts: The left posterior temporal speech region or Wernicke's area supplies categorial content, not only for comprehension (as classically supposed) but for the creative production of verbal thought; this content becomes available to the right hemisphere, which seems particularly adept at creating metaphor and imagery, and at capturing discourse content (McNeill and Pedelty 1995). The right hemisphere could thus play a central role in the creation of growth points. This is plausible since GPs depend on the differentiation of newsworthy content from context, require the simultaneous presence of linguistic categorial content and imagery (both of which seem to be available in the right hemisphere), and incorporate metaphoricity as a property from Mead's Loop. Metaphoric gestures, like the "conduit" (cf. Figure 4.3) could be formed there as well.

The prefrontal cortex may play a role in constructing fields of oppositions and psychological predicates, and supplying these contrasts to the right hemisphere, there to be differentiated by GPs. Such a role suggests that language depends on processes that are also crucial for discrimination and choice, for resisting impulsive action, and by extension on moral and social cognition. The prefrontal cortex develops in children slowly (Huttenlocher and Dabholkar 1997), and in fact does not reach a level of synaptic density matching the visual and auditory cortex until about the same age that self-aware agency appears and with it, per hypothesis, GPs differentiated from fields of opposition (Chapter 5).[22]

Underlying the rhythmicity of speech "pulses" (cf. Duncan 2006) and interactional entrainment (cf. Gill 2007), to which we add GP's on-switching, following the strong urgings of Lieberman (2002) that subcortical areas were important to the origin of language, we assume a continuous circulation of cerebellum inputs and feedback.

The results of all this processing (right hemisphere, left posterior hemisphere, frontal cortex, cerebellum) converge on the left anterior hemisphere, specifically Broca's area, and the Mead's Loop thought–language–hand circuits there specialized for action orchestration under meanings other than those of the action itself.

Broca's area may also be the convergence point of two other aspects of the imagery–language dialectic – the generation of further meanings (like "caused-motion," "expanded noun phrase," etc. – obviously not thought of in these words) connected to constructions for unpacking GPs, and intuitions of formal completeness that provide the "stop orders" to this dialectic.

All of these – left (front, rear), right, prefrontal – can be called the "language areas" of the brain. The particular anterior left-hemisphere (Broca's area) specialty, according to Mead's Loop, is not "language" per se (it draws on many areas) but the ability to use thought, language, and imagery to orchestrate actions under significances.

The language centers of the brain have classically been regarded as just two, Wernicke's and Broca's areas, but if we are on the right track in our brain model, metapragmatic and contextual background information must be present to activate the broader spectrum of brain regions that the model describes. Typical item-recognition, memory and production tests would not tap these other brain regions but discourse, conversation, play, work, and the exigencies of language in daily life, where language originated, would.

3.11 TIME-LINE OF ORIGIN, INCLUDING EXTINCTION OF GESTURE-FIRST (IF IT EXISTED AT ALL)

The phrase, "the dawn of language," suggests that language burst forth at some definite point, say 150~200 kya (thousand years ago), when the prefrontal expansion of the human brain was complete (Deacon 1997). But the origin of language has elements that began long before – 5 mya (million years ago) for bipedalism, on which things gestural depend (although I am told, again by Erica Cartmill, that gorillas, the least bipedal of the Great Apes, use manual gestures, even bimanual ones; so bipedalism perhaps is not as crucial for gesture as one would suppose; nonetheless, it seems necessary for prolonged gesturing). I think 2 mya, based on Wrangham (2001) and Deacon (1997), who separately date humanlike family life to then, for starting the expansion of forebrain and the selection of self-responsiveness of mirror neurons and the resulting reconfiguration of Areas 44/45. I imagine this form of living was itself the product of changes in reproduction patterns, female fertility cycles, child rearing, neotony, all of which must have been emerging over long periods before. So this says that language as we know it emerged over 1.8 million years and that not much has changed since the 150K~200K landmark of reconfiguring Broca's area with the mirror neurons/Mead's Loop circuit (although this date could overlook continuing evolution: there are hints that the brain has changed since the dawn of agriculture and urban living; Lahn group genetic investigations: see Evans, *et al.* 2005).

The Mead's Loop model doesn't say what might have been a proto-language before 2 mya – Lucy and all. It would have been something an apelike brain is capable of. There are many proposals about this – Kendon (1991), for example, proposed that signs emerged out of ritualized incipient actions (or incomplete actions). Natural gesture signals in modern apes have an incipient quality as well, the characteristic of which is that an action is cut short and the resulting action-stub becomes a signifier (as seen in Figure 3.2). The slow-to-emerge precursor from 5 mya to 2 mya may have built up a gesture language that derived from instrumental actions, as gesture-first envisions. It would have been an evolution track leading to pantomime. But the human brain evolved further to create a system in which gesture fuses with vocalization. Mead's Loop also does not say where language evolved (as described earlier, it may have been the southwestern corner of Africa according to Atkinson 2011), but "predicts" that wherever that was the languages spoken there now, apart from subsequent migrations, would tend to be of the isolating type, with grammatical structuring controlling temporal order without morpho/syntactic elaborations, as in the discussion in §3.6.3. In any case the origin point would have been an area where human family life also was emerging.

A proposed time line for the origin of Mead's Loop is as follows:

a. To pick a date, the evolution of a thought–language–hand link started 5 mya with the emergence of habitual bipedalism in *Australopithicus*. This freed the hands for manipulative work and gesture, but it would have been only the beginning. Even earlier there were presumably preadaptations such as an ability to combine vocal and manual gestures, to perform rapid sequences of meaningful hand movements, and the sorts of iconic/pantomimic gestures we see in bonobos, but not yet an ability to orchestrate movements of the vocal articulators by gestures.

b. The period from 5 to 3~2 mya – Lucy *et al.* and the long reign of *Australopithicus* – would have seen the emergence of various precursors of language, such as the protolanguage Bickerton (1990) attributes to apes, very young children and aphasics; also, ritualized incipient actions becoming signs as described by Kendon (1991).

c. At some point after the 3~2 mya advent of *H. habilis* and later *H. erectus*, there commenced the crucial selection of self-responsive mirror neurons and the reconfiguring of areas 44 and 45, with a growing co-opting of actions by language to form gesticulation type gestures, this emergence being grounded in the appearance of a humanlike family life with a host of other factors shaping the change (including cultural innovations like the domestication of fire and cooking). The timing of this stage is not clear but recent archeological findings strongly suggest that hominids had control of fire, had hearths, and cooked 800 kya (Goren-Inbar *et al.* 2004).[23] Thus, the family as the scenario for evolving the thought–language–hand link seems plausible, commencing no more recently than 800 kya.[24] Along with this sociocultural revolution was the expansion of the forebrain from 2 mya, described by Deacon (1997), and a complete reconfiguring of areas 44 and 45, including Mead's loop, into what we now call Broca's area. This development was an exclusively human phenomenon and was completed with *H. sapiens* about 200–100 kya (if it is not continuing; cf. Donald 1991). At least two other human species have existed, Neanderthals and the recently discovered *Denisova hominin*; each may have had a gesture-only form of communication but our species also developed Mead's Loop and GPs. These other humans went extinct, one factor in which could have been a confinement to pantomime and consequent inability to reach a new form of language, inhabitance with thought and action, just as, in our case having evolved this ability, we were spared the same fate (but it is also possible that Mead's Loop emerged earlier and Neanderthals also had speech–gesture units and extinguished for other reasons; see Figure 3.13 for two versions of when gesture-first extinguished and Mead's Loop evolved).

Considering the time-line, protolanguage and then language itself seems to have emerged over five million years (low hum more than big bang). Meaning-controlled manual and vocal gestures synthesized under meanings emerged over the last two million years. The entire process may have been completed not more than 100 kya, a mere 5,000 human generations, if it is not continuing.

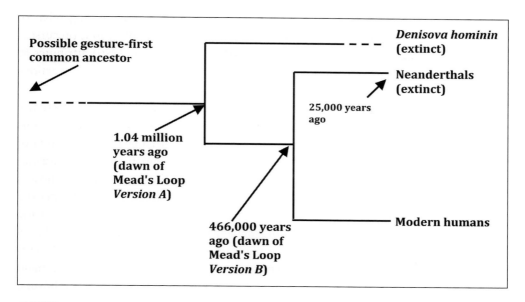

Figure 3.13 Two versions of gesture-first extinction.

Version A: The branch leading to modern humans and Neanderthals and away from the newly discovered *hominin Denisova* was the emergence of Mead's Loop. *Denisova* was the continuation of the gesture-first creature, and went extinct some 30,000 to 40,000 years ago – the date of the fossil finger bone from which its mtDNA was recovered by Krause *et al.* 2010. In this version, Neanderthals and modern humans share Mead's Loop but differ in other brain aspects (the temporal lobes and possibly the prefrontal area) and ontogenesis (Neanderthals, according to Rozzi and de Castro 2004, developing markedly faster, leaving less time for GPs to emerge before any critical period shutdown).

Version B: Mead's Loop arose instead at the 466 kya split between modern humans and Neanderthals, and in part defines this separation of lines. In this version, neither extinct *hominin* species evolved Mead's Loop, which may have been a factor in their extinctions. In an alternate version, the split at the 1 mya point separated the common ancestor of the Neanderthal and the *Denisova hominin* from modern humans. They left Africa while modern humans remained (possibly in the Southwest coruer, Atkinson 2011), eventually evolving Mead's Loop and migrating out of Africa themselves.

Diagram based on Brown (2010); Mead's Loop annotations added.

4 | Effects of Mead's Loop

Language, the *fact* of it, that it evolved, changed everything; how we communicate of course, but also how we act, think, become conscious, and live in social and cultural groups – whole spans of human life. I do not mean simply that since we speak, language is part of life but that these domains could not exist at all in the forms they take if mind and the mode of being that language shapes had not also evolved. My standpoint has been the mental and how the origin of language shaped it but the scale of change is much broader. This chapter is made up of 14 essays stemming mostly from Chapter 3, describing modern-day Mead's Loop effects – mental, actional, artistic, and social. The chapter is a kind of "gumbo," a pot of leftovers, tasty, boiling, and not to be missed. I have endeavored to order the essays so that earlier ones fulfill presuppositions that later ones make, but otherwise the essays are self-contained.

While Mead's Loop is not causally involved in each of the following, it created conditions whereby they emerged, as is fitting for a founding event.[1] The chapter as a whole demonstrates that small changes – mirror neurons becoming responsive to one's own gestures as if from another – can, over time, set in motion a wide range of consequences. Also, as a matter of scientific interest, since none of these consequences was foreseen, they count as "discoveries" by the Mead's Loop hypothesis and so as a kind of confirmation of it. I have divided them into "direct" and "indirect" effects. Mead's Loop can be said to have been a cause of the direct group effects. They of course have been vastly elaborated culturally and historically, but still Mead's Loop can be seen to have played a causal role. The second group is no less indebted to Mead's Loop but other factors have had greater weight, and so are deemed "indirect."

4.1 DIRECT EFFECTS

4.1.1 Origin of new actions

Given Mead's Loop, a prominent result of the origin of language was the emergence of a new kind of action. Actions are the logical target of the

Mead's Loop adaptive selection in any case, and seeing language itself as a means of controlling the actions of speech depends on the origin of this new-action effect.[2] The result of natural selection was that gesture imagery became a schema for vocal action orchestration, in Broca's area. This control is "new" in two respects: it is orchestrated by significances brought in from gesture instead of from practical goal-directedness; and the context of the action is under the creative control of the speaker instead of given by the environment. These qualities set Mead's Loop actions apart. Evidence from aproprioception indicates a dedicated thought–language–hand link in the brain to carry them (Chapter 3).

4.1.1.1 Two action theories, bracketing a third

We can localize the effects of the "new actions" by exclusion, comparing two action theories – one in which speech emerged from ingestion movements, the other where gestures emerged from object manipulations – and noting what they have left out. The missing ingredients, the new actions, Mead's Loop provides.

Peter MacNeilage and Adam Kendon both have seen a connection of language origin to action (as did the Enlightenment figure, Condillac; cf. Harris and Taylor 1989). The actions they consider however are not the new actions that emerged from Mead's Loop. MacNeilage's theory brackets them from below, Kendon's from above.

4.1.1.1.1 *Vegetative movements into speech*

MacNeilage in his 2008 book traces speech evolution to jaw movements during the ingestion of food. With phonation the basic mandible closing-opening maneuver creates CV (consonant-vowel) syllables. The structures thus formed are called "frames" (manifestations of which occur in infant babbling). Subsequent variations lead to full syllable repertoires – specific tunings of how, to what extent and for how long, etc. the closing/opening movements occur, and at this point are called "frames with content" (the theory also assumes that ontogenesis – infant babbling – recapitulates this aspect of phylogenesis).[3] However, we need to add to this explanation a bridge of some kind from mandible movements, significant at first as ingestion, to actions *symbolically* orchestrated. Mead's Loop provides this orchestration via gesture and its imagery.

4.1.1.1.2 Actions into ritualized actions

Kendon has described gestures as ritualized actions:

I argue that the manual actions that are coordinated with speech that we see in modern humans, are derived from forms of practical action. That is, they are "ritualized" versions of grasping, reaching, holding, manipulating, and so forth. Given their intimate connection with speaking, I make a speculative leap, and argue that speaking itself is derived from practical actions. Acts of utterance are to be understood, ultimately, as derived versions of action system ensembles mobilized to achieve practical consequences. The origin of language, that is to say, derives by a process of "*symbolic transformation*" of forms of action that were not communicatively specialized to begin with. Speech and associated gesturing does not descend from communicative vocalizations and visible displays but from manipulatory activities of a practical sort. (Kendon 2009b, p. 19; quoted with author's permission; italics added)

This action hypothesis also leaves an explanatory gap that the evolution of Mead's Loop fills. Mead's Loop explains the "symbolic transformation" mentioned in Kendon's quote.

4.1.1.2 New actions

What evolved is a unity of speech and gesture. To Mead's Loop language, among other things (a social interactive foray), *is* a means of orchestrating the actions of mouth and hand (and whole body) by significances of other kinds, and it naturally involves both structuring the actions themselves and their significances. These were the new actions, using their own thought–language–hand link in the brain, reconfiguring the motor orchestration area with gesture imagery and providing a gesture–speech unity that an imagery–language dialectic requires.

4.1.1.3 Gestures – do they stem from practical actions?

What remains of "old actions" in this new world? Many of my fellow scholars of gesture and action consider them to be the source of gesture. They adopt an action-based semiotic. The quote above from Kendon regards gestures as ritualized practical actions. Streeck (2010), LeBaron and Streeck (2000) and Müller (1998) have also proposed that gestures stem from practical, world-directed actions. Kendon in his plenary talk at the Frankfurt/Oder International Society for Gesture Studies conference (2010) likens a gesture of something being flat to "*making* something flat" (p. 14, emphasis in original) and more generally, alluding to Streeck, that "many of the actions [i.e., gestures] understood as meaningful can be understood as being derived from actions of the hands acting in relation to objects in the environment" (parenthetical insert added).

The idea that gestures derive from actions is plausible at first glance but there is more (or perhaps less) than meets the eye. A gesture may look like a pragmatic action but the action has changed at its core. To describe a gesture as "outlining" or "shaping" is useful as a description but to also say that such a practical action is still within the gesture is to disregard what makes the gesture a human sign. An example I have often cited, the "rising hollowness" gesture (Figure 2.1), looks like the action of lifting something in the hand, but this gesture is not lifting at all. It is an image of the character rising, of the interior of the pipe through which he rose, and of the direction of his motion upward – all compacted into one symbolic form to differentiate a field of meaningful oppositions having to do with *HOW TO CLIMB A PIPE: ON THE INSIDE.* This complex idea, as a unity, orchestrated the handshape and movement; it is the same motor response but it is not the action of lifting up an object.

While a gesture may engage some of the same movements and tap in part the same motor schemas as an "action-action" it has its own thought–language–hand link in the brain. In keeping with the unity of speech and gesture, the manual movements of gestures as well as the actions of speech are co-opted by Mead's Loop and orchestrated in new ways by significances other than those of the original vocal tract and manual actions. We observed the separation of "action-actions" and "gesture-actions" directly in the IW case where, without vision, action-actions were impossible but gesture-actions were normal.

To show the difference that "new actions" make for explaining gesture and speech, I will cite an example from a talk by Cornelia Müller (at the University of Chicago, 05/07/11). She described a conversation in which a speaker (of Spanish) first outlined an oval shape with a two-handed open-palm gesture (for the shape of a wall-plaque), then outlined it again with extended forefingers. Was he tracing an outline of the plaque with his fingers? In speech, he said "lo tenía **con un a marco redondo**" [lit. it he-was holding **with a frame round**].[4] From Mead's Loop's viewpoint, the speaker highlighted exactly the roundness of the plaque; this was the psychological predicate and GP in his immediate context of speaking. His forefingers embodied the differentiation specifically of "*ROUND*" in this field of meaningful oppositions (rather than, as well, the size, as in the first two-handed open-palm gesture) – something like *THE PLAQUE'S CIRCUMFERENCE:*

ROUND. The stroke was co-expressive with the synchronous speech and together they formed a plausible GP making this differentiation. Single forefingers contrasted with the previous full-palm gesture, and the tracing-fingers shape may therefore not have been tracing but the circumference of the plaque, *qua* a circumference, in contrast to the plaque's planar surface.

Some gestures do depict actions; they ritualize the actions they depict. They are more than actions – a kind of performance, a replication of the action, and may also include posture, spatial location, etc. as well as the manual action. These gestures are of two kinds. Some are pantomimes at their own locus on the Gesture Continuum. Others are "character viewpoint" (C-VPT) gestures, gesticulations with the viewpoint of the character that is being recounted. And here again the difference of pantomimes from gesticulations applies; I think the C-VPTs must pass through the thought–language–hand link. The C-VPTs are co-expressive with speech and their viewpoint is part of the semiotic with which they oppose it in a dialectic – a C-VPT is, among other things, *not* an "observer viewpoint," or O-VPT, a contrast that it has but that is not part of a pantomime. Pantomime is simulated action and has no such contrastive value. The "it down" example we have cited before: the speaker's hands were Tweety's hands, the space his space, her body his, and so forth – the speaker stepped into Tweety's shoes and added this to the utterance itself. It was part of the caused-motion unpacking, making Tweety the agent and the C-VPT perspective was shaped by this significance. The most telling difference from a replicated action is that the hands thrust the ball down, in contrast to the release of it in the stimulus. All of this could happen because the gesture was a "new" action, formed over the thought–language–hand link.

What looks to be an "action-action" gesture source is really often a metaphor in gesture form that uses the action-action as the vehicle. The gesture embodies this metaphor but is not itself the action. It is an iconic image of the metaphor that in is fact two steps removed from the action. The metaphor itself is one step. Müller's (2008) awakening process, in Mead's Loop terms, adds another.[5] If there is an action source of the *metaphor* then that action also can also be jolted to the surface. The "old" action circuit is activated along with the "new" thought–language–hand circuit as a kind of meta-gesture comment. The question is whether this old-action is necessarily active whenever the metaphoric gesture arises, and the answer is no. To see why, notice what happens to the gesture when you do awaken the action. In the case of a rejection metaphor (the hand slicing to the side, palm forward, in typical form) it becomes a simulated removal of the imagined offending object (as if flicking a fly with a finger, etc.); it has turned into a pantomime (speech may even cease). This is not to say that awakenings do not occur. They do, but to remain part of speaking, rather than detaching from it, the meaning also changes; the pantomime becomes a meta-gestural layer, as if saying that the gesticulation is *decorated* with the pantomime ("I am totally against your argument," plus flicking: the meta-comment of the awakened action is something like saying (if you dared), "your argument is puny, repellent and can be flicked away"). None of this shows that gestures derive from action-actions. Quite the contrary: the gesture *recruits* the action as an ornament.

Liebal *et al.* (2010), following Kendon 2004, describe what they identify as "gesture families," which in their study are families of chimp gestures based on shared action sources – slapping, pushing, offering, etc. If these gestures are what they seem, miniaturized and ritualized editions of the source actions and not chimp metaphors, they do what human gestures do not, preserve in the gesture the original significance of the action, and would count therefore as yet another morsel of what, on comparison, arose from Mead's Loop – new kinds of actions with their own significances that do not occur with the apes. Indeed, the key difference between ape-emblems (if this is what they can be called) and human-emblems is that those of apes are action-stubs, while those of humans are conventionalized metaphors – a precision metaphor within "OK," the image of removal metaphor within "negation," and so forth. It all points to the mode of human cognitive being that Mead's Loop engendered.

Part of the scope, creativity and distinctiveness of human thought lies precisely in its freedom from pragmatic action constraints. When the hands make a gesture, it is thought that controls them and not a hidden action with purposes in relation to the physical world.

4.1.2 Metaphoricity

The "new actions" of gesture and speech are thus intimately tied to metaphoricity. Mead's Loop made metaphoricity obligatory, the "experience" of one thing (or the "being" of one thing) in the form of something else.[6] This was, according to Mead's Loop, intrinsic to the very origin of language ("metaphors" = specific packages of meanings, "metaphoricity" = the semiotic they are based on). Metaphoricity came about when the orchestration of actions of the vocal tract and hands was undertaken in Mead's Loop by something other than those actions, meaningful gesture imagery. In this way the vocal tract movements took meaning from gesture. This is the semiotic of metaphoricity, one thing (voice) gaining significance in terms of something else that it is not (echoing in part Herder, who said that language gave to man "the art of changing into sound what is not sound." Herder 1986; reference thanks to Robin Allott).

"Phonetic symbolism" effects can be explained this way, as vocal maneuvers orchestrated by gesture imagery. Which is the better name for a large table – "mal" or "mil"? Sapir (1929) found that nearly 90% of respondents chose "mal." The imagery of something large gives meaning to the vocal tract maneuvers, so that a large vocal space (that of the open [a]) seems a better fit. We are saying that "mal" has meaning in the form of something else, the imagery of something large. This appears to reverse Sapir's explanation. Rather than saying that in the phonetic symbolism of "mal" vs. "mil" mouth shape (open) determines meaning ("large"), we are saying that the meaning (imagery) determines (orchestrates) the mouth shape (directing it to open). Phonetic symbolism is unique in that the orchestration is of the simplest kind, iconic replication of the imagery ("large" → large vocal space, "small" → small vocal space).[7]

Iconicity and metaphoricity are mutually dependent. It is not that iconicity has no place; far from it, metaphoricity *recruits* iconicity – a metaphor of a discursive "object" recruits an iconic gesture that depicts a container for it. Iconicity in turn provides the imagery with which to orchestrate the speech that the metaphor uses. Therefore, metaphoricity also depends on iconicity, but only as recruited. Without metaphoricity the significances with which iconicity orchestrates speech would be those of the vocal articulatory movements themselves (which may be what infants babbling in the first year are doing; see Chapter 5). This analysis applies to *sui generis* gestures as well as to established metaphors like the conduit hand "holding" a "discursive object," and explains why they occur at all. In such gestures, the speaker thinks one thing and finds her own image that can present it as something else. The reason again is to have the gesture imagery with which to orchestrate speech. The gesture iconically depicts something concrete, space, movement or form, and this is a metaphor of some other idea. The "it down" gesture (Chapter 2) iconically depicts a bowling ball, its downward path, and Tweety's agency in thrusting it (this last the speaker's addition, to make the GP fit the field of oppositions she was differentiating – ways to thwart Sylvester); all this a metaphor for Tweety's force against Sylvester's force, which orchestrated her description, "a bowling ba[ll and drops **it do**<u>wn</u> the drainpipe," with the cognitive core the gesture and the beyond-grammar "it down."[8]

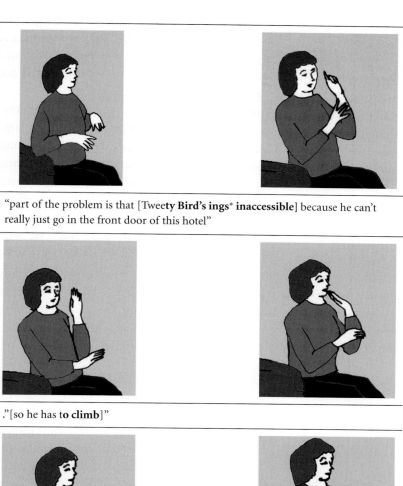

"part of the problem is that [Twee**ty Bird's ings*** **inaccessible**] because he can't really just go in the front door of this hotel"

."[so he has **to climb**]"

"<um> / tryi[ng to s<u>wing</u> **across** <u>by</u> a rope #]"

Figure 4.1 Impromptu metaphor for the idea of "inaccessibility." Used with permission of University of Chicago Press.

In a GP, accordingly, metaphoricity is more than a figure of speech. It is built into the very essence of language.[9] Metaphor, rooted in this Mead's Loop ability, carries the dialectic to meanings that lack imagery. It gives the imagery with which to organize speech and gesture to the unimageable – the abstract, the unspatial, the formless. Not surprisingly, *sui generis* metaphors are constantly invented as one speaks (McNeill 2008). Alan Cienki (2008) gives some interesting examples: "life is a banana." What do we make of that? It is an instance of what Cienki terms a metaphor of low conventionality. Given our Mead's Loop explanation, we should expect this metaphor, notwithstanding the low conventionality, to participate in a GP. And Cienki provides a field of oppositions that it could differentiate ("life is a banana – you should peel it carefully and enjoy every bite"). The metaphor of a peeled and bitten banana can orchestrate speech for the idea of life itself and how it should be led. Figure 4.1 shows another example, this time a metaphor for the concept of inaccessibility. It uses separation of the hands, iconically depicting the separation of the bird from the cat, as a metaphor of the idea of one character being inaccessible to the other, a meaning beyond the concrete referent itself. The speaker explicitly announces this metaphoric meaning with the gesture's first occurrence.

4.1.3 Emblems encoding metaphors

Emblems also depend on metaphoricity. The very possibility of an emblem can be considered another effect of Mead's Loop. Experiencing shareability as a force, cultures imbue gestures, mainly metaphorics,[10] with standards of form that carry them from gesticulation to other locations on the Gesture Continuum, above all to the emblem spot. Chapter 1 mentioned "OK" and the metaphor of precision, and "thumbs-up" and that of good-is-up. To illustrate an emblem and the metaphor it incorporates from Neapolitan culture we take the "finger-bunch" (named the *grappolo* by Kendon 2004). We see that underlying it is a widespread metaphor, the "conduit," originally identified by Reddy (1979) and Lakoff and Johnson (1980) with linguistic examples and, following a suggestion by Lakoff (pers. comm.), extended to gesture in my 1985 paper, "So you think gestures are nonverbal?" (McNeill 1985). Figure 4.2, from Kendon, shows a *grappolo* in use as a speaker introduces a discourse topic with the fingers in a bunch (shaped by standards of form), then followed by the hand opening to present the comment (also shaped by standards of form – both shapings attested by Kendon, pers. comm.); one of a family of *grappolo* usages that Kendon describes.

Figure 4.2 Neapolitan gestures appear to be standardized encodings of metaphoric images, in this case the discursive object (so-called "conduit") metaphor. Drawings and caption from Kendon with permission. Gesture notation converted to the format used in this book. Kendon writes of this example,

"A parsing or discourse structure marker gesture (*grappolo* – open hand) directionally inflected toward the location of the object the speaker is commenting on."

e allorë [/ s'adda ricërë ca **ë tipë vandaliscëmë**]

[1]   [2]

and well one must say that it is a type of vandalism

Grappolo hand lifted, directed left, as speaker states "topic." Note speaker looks in same direction as gesture, which is an additional clue to the deictic component this gesture has.

Hand opens as speaker gives his "comment" [1].

Opened hand lowered and speaker turns to look at interlocutor as he completes his phrase [2]." (Kendon 2004, p. 204). Figure from the author. Used with his permission and that of Cambridge University Press.

The *grappolo* hand, like the conduit, appears to hold a discursive object; the hand then opens and continues to support it. Both steps embody the imagery of a surface (first curled, then opened) and a substance in or on it.[11] Gesturally the conduit depicts "content" "in" or "on" the hand, which may be open or closed, partly or totally, as in the *grappolo*. In its raw (non-emblemized) form it appears all over the world; Asia, Northern Europe and North America at least (Africa, I cannot say). But in all these places it lacks the Neapolitan stabilization of how it should be formed and the discourse effects it should have. Nonetheless, like the *grappolo*, the conduit metaphor defines a container or surface that supports a discursive object. We have an early (possibly emblematic, perhaps even the *grappolo* itself) use of the conduit in a quote from Montaigne (sixteenth century), who attributes a series of conduits for degrees of epistemological certainty to Zeno of Elea (sixth century BC). The *grappolo*, in its topic-comment use, appears as part of this series (boldface):

> Zeno pictured in a gesture his conception of this division of the faculties of the soul: **the hand spread and open was appearance**; the hand half shut and the fingers a little hooked, consent; **the closed fist, comprehension**; when with his left hand he closed his fist still tighter, knowledge. (Montaigne 1958, p. 372)[12]

As with Zeno, the *grappolo*'s closed version is a bounded container that conveys a sense of certainty; in its second, open version, the certainty is less, corresponding to the Neapolitan codification of a comment.

Traces of metaphor can be discerned in many of Kendon's examples. It is noteworthy that in no case has the culture reversed or undone a root metaphor; it has stabilized, specified, and constrained them. To take another example, a gesture for warding off (the hand held upright, palm forward) metaphorizes something unwanted as an approaching force or emanation, and the hand as a barrier or wall, again a widespread metaphor the Neapolitan code has standardized.

The open hand, in addition to being the less certain end of the Zeno conduit sequence, conveys its own metaphor of openness – the idea of a discursive object that is "open" to discussion, dispute, etc., as is appropriate for the second half of topic-comment. Again, Neapolitan culture has codified form and use, so that the open hand zeros in from conveying something "open" to something where "the object being indicated is not the primary focus or topic of the discourse but is something that is linked to the topic" (Kendon 2004, p. 208).

Finally, in Figure 4.2, panel C, the open hand part of the gesture also included deixis, pointing. Multiple dimensions converged. Although in this example the deixis was to a concrete locus, deixis can readily take on metaphoric value, pointing to a space whose meaning is non-spatial and is established or recaptured by the deixis.

Figure 4.3 shows an English speaker's open-hand conduit gesture also holding a discursive object ("the final scene," the "object" in question). The gesture is not unlike the open-hand version of the *grappolo* but is also different from it. His gesture is *not* held to standards of form. The metaphor of a discursive object recruited an icon of a container to hold it. There is no

Figure 4.3 English speaker's non-culturally defined discursive object gesture with "the final scene was ... " His palm "holds" the object – the idea of the "final scene" of the cartoon. Used with permission of University of Chicago Press.

history or culture of gesture form behind it and the gesture has no standards other than to iconically depict the conduit's container. It arises exclusively out of the conduit image, and this is the only constraint on form.

4.1.3.1 Emblematicity

Finally, it is useful to consider how the "emblem," the category, is really the end-point of a dimension that Susan Duncan and Kamala Russell and others have started calling "emblematicity" – a dimension that, at its end, approaches the full conventionality that we call an emblem like the *grappolo*, "OK," or thumbs-up, but at earlier points includes, in limited combinations or separately, metaphoricity (hence virtually all gesticulations), recurrence (such as the forefinger for "Sylvester," Figure 3.7), awareness of one's own gesture as a communicative effort, shareability, intragroup solidarity, intergroup differences, and no doubt others. These intermediate points are affected by different forces (for example, thinking with a metaphor like the conduit, as in the palm up, open hand, produces recurrence without encoding) which, when present, offer raw material on which social groups can work in reaching the final state, a conventional emblem.[13] Communicative exchange is again the midwife and creates the emblem. What makes a society seize the available emblematicity and convert it into a codified emblem is not at all known. Nor is it known how long and irregular or smooth the emblematicity dimension must be before the magic moment, but to think of each emblem in this way, as the end of a "pre-encoded" line, is an important insight. Most importantly, *every gesture*, no matter how ephemeral, lies somewhere on this dimension and, along with its other dimensional loadings, has emblematicity and the potential to become an emblem itself; again, the "Sylvester" extended finger proto-morph is an illustration: it had recurrence of form with meaning, along with its iconic and/or metaphoric loadings, but it was not shared and fell into oblivion at the end of each narration in which it had appeared.

4.1.4 Material carriers

Another consequence of Mead's Loop is the creation of what has been termed the *material carrier* – a phrase used by Vygotsky (1987) to refer to the embodiment of meaning in enactments or material experiences.[14] The material carrier deepens insight into gesture and also into many other forms of motor execution, writing something down for example, the *very act of it, whatever it is* enhancing the symbolization's experiential potency. The source of the material carrier effect is ultimately Mead's Loop with its new modes of action orchestrated under significances other than the action itself: materialization follows ineluctably. In the case of gesture materialization implies that the gesture, this natural material image, *the actual motion of the gesture itself,* is a dimension of meaning. Experiential enhancement of language is possible if the gesture *is* the image in an imagery–language dialectic, not an "expression" or "representation" of it, but *is* it. From this viewpoint, a gesture, a global-synthetic whole, is an image in its most developed – that is, in its most materially, naturally embodied – form. The absence of a gesture is the converse, an image in its least material form. The material carrier concept thus explains how an imagery–language dialectic still is possible in the absence of visible gestural movement. When there is no gesture there is still imagery and a dialectic with linguistic categorization, still the simultaneous rendering of meaning in opposite semiotic modes – the dialectic in its essentials – but it is bleached, experience at the lowest level of materialization. This leads us to expect that gestures are more elaborate, more materialized and more frequent – more *present* – when the psychological predicate has greater newsworthiness.

In Figure 4.4 we see a range of materializations, from zero to full, on two continua – speech and gesture. "Communicative dynamism" (CD) is the extent to which a given spoken or gestured form "pushes the communication forward" (Firbas 1971). The continua correlate positively with CD in terms of the elaboration of the quantity of "substance" involved.

Communicative Dynamism (CD)

Most Continuous/Predictable　　　　　　　　**Least Continuous/Predictable**

Less Materialization ━━━━━━━━━━━▶ More Materialization				
Linguistic Form Continuum				
Ø	**Unstressed Pronoun**	**Noun Phrase**	**Modified Noun Phrase**	**Clause or Verb Phrase**
Gesture Form Continuum				
Referring term included in ongoing iconic	**Referring term excluded from adjacent iconics**	**Iconics that cover clause or Verb Phrase**	**O-VPT iconic with Noun Phrase**	**Deictics with Clause or VP** **O-VPT iconics (one hand)** **O-VPT iconics (two different hands)** **C-VPT iconics**

Figure 4.4 Communicative dynamism. Gesture continuum based on McNeill 2005, p. 55. Linguistic continuum based on Givón 1985. Used with permission of University of Chicago Press.

Thus the widespread economic/psychological assumption that "least effort" = "best result" is backwards. It is not that gesture expands as speech shrinks – speech and gesture respond in the same direction. The most elaborate NPs are accompanied by the most developed gestures, the least with the least. So the more discontinuous an utterance is with the previous context, the greater the CD, the more probable a gesture, the more internally complex it will be, and the more complex the synchronous speech as well.

A striking illustration of materialization is Cornelia Müller's (2008) "waking of sleeping metaphors," the breath of new life given to an inactive or "sleeping" metaphor by a gesture, the effect of the gesture as a material carrier. Müller gives an example of a German metaphor ("gefunkt," "sparked," the equivalent to English "clicked," for suddenly falling in love). The metaphor is usually hackneyed and inactive, not apprehended through the metaphor source but seen as a literal term. A speaker, describing her first love, said, "between us somehow it sparked ['clicked']" (Müller's translation). As she said "between us" her hand rose upward next to her face in a ring shape but with an unusual orientation – the fingers pointing at her own face; then, as she uttered the metaphor itself, "gefunkt," her hand abruptly turned outward – her gesture materializing the "dead" metaphor as a sudden event, an electrical spark emanating from the head.

Another striking illustration is the phenomenon Severance and Washburn (1907) more than a century ago called "semantic satiation." Staring at the printed word TREE, say, eventually disrupts the word. It ceases to be a meaningful symbol and suddenly turns into lines and spaces. Perceptually the transformation is quite striking. We seem to perceive words as material carriers before we see them as lines and spaces. A similar disruption takes place with speech: hearing the same word, "tree" over and over, changes it into a pure acoustic experience, the equivalent of the printed word's lines and spaces. It would be interesting to look for a similar "satiation effect" with gestures. Trying the experiment on myself, by deliberately repeating a gesture of my own that seems to be typical – according to Parrill (2007) it is my gesture for a growth point, and since reading her description and seeing a photo of it, I have caught myself making it many times – the gesture almost immediately shifts from significant symbol to mere hand rotation.

Finally, the sociality of Mead's Loop provides a basis for the dialogicity emphasized by Bahktin (1981). Dialogicity materializes Mead's Loop itself. Bakhtin commented concerning a literary source: "Thus the speech of another is introduced into the author's discourse (the story) in *concealed form*, that is, without any of the normal markers usually accompanying such speech, whether direct or indirect. But this is not just another's speech in the same 'language' – it is another's utterance that is itself 'other' to the author as well" (p. 303, italics and quote marks in original). This experienced-language of the other echoes the Mead's Loop "twist." Just as one's own gestures are mirrored in the orchestrating parts of the brain so is one's speech, as part of the same GPs. An ultra-self-aware author (Bahktin was referring to Dickens) would be almost expected to build this echo into his constructed prose, hence the "dialog" that is the "other" (cf. section §4.2.2 later in this chapter, on gestures hidden in written prose).

4.1.5 Inhabitance of symbols

The concept of a material carrier is raised to a whole new level when we turn to Merleau-Ponty (1962) for insight into the unity of gesture and language and what we expect of gesture in a dual semiotic process. Gesture, the instantaneous, global, nonconventional component, is "not an external accompaniment" of speech, which is the sequential, analytic, combinatoric component; it is not a "representation" of meaning, but instead meaning "inhabits" it:

The link between the word and its living meaning is not an external accompaniment to intellectual processes, the meaning inhabits the word, and language "is not an external accompaniment to intellectual processes."[15] We are therefore led to recognize a gestural or existential significance to speech . . . Language certainly has inner content, but this is not self-subsistent and self-conscious thought. What then does language express, if it does not express thoughts? It presents or rather it *is* the subject's taking up of a position in the world of his meanings. (p. 193; emphasis in the original)[16]

The GP is a mechanism geared to this "existential content" of speech – this "taking up a position in the world." Gesture, as part of the GP, is inhabited by the same "living meaning" that inhabits the word (and beyond, the discourse). The correlation of speech and gesture complexity in Figure 4.4 thus involves greater "inhabitance" (if this concept can be gradual, half in, half out); it involves more of the body, in movements more coordinated by the significance being differentiated from context. It is the thought–language–hand link that Mead's Loop created simultaneously affecting both motor domains.

4.1.5.1 Cognitive being

A deeper answer to the query, therefore – when we see a gesture, what are we seeing? – is that we see part of the speaker's current cognitive being, her very mental existence, at the moment it occurs. By performing the gesture, a core idea is brought into concrete existence and becomes part of the speaker's own existence at that moment (the opening motto of this book – "it's like seeing someone's thought" – registered this same insight). The Heideggerian echo in this statement is not accidental. Following Heidegger's emphasis on being, a gesture is not a representation, or is not only such: it is a form of being. From a first-person perspective, the gesture is part of the immediate existence of the speaker. Gestures (and words, etc., as well) are themselves thinking in one of its many forms – not only expressions of thought, *but thought, i.e., cognitive being, itself.* To the speaker, gesture and speech are not only "messages" or communications, but are a way of cognitively existing, of cognitively being, at the moment of speaking.[17]

The speaker who creates a gesture of Sylvester rising up fused with the pipe's hollowness is, according to this interpretation, embodying thought in gesture, and this action – thought in gesture-action over the thought–language–hand link – was part of the person's being cognitively at that moment.

To make a gesture, from this perspective, is to bring thought into existence on a concrete plane, just as writing out a word can have a similar effect. There is not a causal sequence: thought → speech/gesture; speech and gesture *are* the thought coming into being at that instant. The greater the felt departure of the thought from the immediate context, the more likely its materialization in a gesture. Thus, gestures are more or less elaborated depending on the importance of material realization to the existence of the thought (see Figure 4.4 again).[18] This philosophical position in turn discloses a property that Quaeghebeur (2010) has called "all-at-onceness":

> multi-modal face-to-face interaction is characterized by an "all-at-onceness" in the intrapersonal as well as in the interpersonal realm. Because thought coincides with expression . . . the multimodal display is produced and understood immediately and as a whole." (p. 97)

All-at-onceness in the GP creates room for the components simultaneously existing in a given GP to affect the other components in full or in part. We saw this elaboration of the material carrier in the infiltration of metapragmatic indicators into the "it down" GP discussed at the end of Chapter 2 (§2.5.4).

4.1.6 Notes on consciousness

With gesture and speech, thought is a materialized part of one's cognitive being. Consciousness itself, understood as the experience of this being, also is materialized, and this too is an effect of Mead's Loop. The topic of consciousness was once a major theme of scientific psychology but was swept aside in the behaviorist revolution of the early twentieth century. Interest has reemerged (e.g., Baars 1988, Chafe 1994, Chalmers 1996), fueled in part by the neurocognitive revolution (e.g., O'Regan and Noë 2001). The GP offers a perspective of its own. Wundt a century ago described the "sentence" as a dynamic psychological phenomenon in terms of consciousness:

> From a psychological point of view, the sentence is both a simultaneous and a sequential structure. It is simultaneous because at each moment it is present in consciousness as a totality even though the individual subordinate elements may occasionally disappear from it. It is sequential because the configuration changes from moment to moment in its cognitive condition as individual constituents move into the focus of attention and out again one after another. (Translation by Blumenthal 1970, p. 21)[19]

Wundt's insight is that two simultaneous consciousnesses occur in the "psychological structure" of the sentence, something that we are aware of all at once (like a GP) and something else, the same meaning but in another form, that we encounter in succession (like its unpacking).

No doubt all ambulatory creatures are conscious in some way; this is not questioned – mobility alone requires it, but this consciousness would not be the same across animal species. As Wundt described, ours is shaped by language. One form this takes is to yoke it to the emergence, growth and dissipation of GPs.

4.1.6.1 "L-centers"

The GP and its unpacking align and laminate consciousness in the two ways that Wundt described. GPs surface in speech as dynamic pulses that orchestrate the whole and are Wundt's "simultaneous" consciousness. The unpacking is the sequential version, encountered step by step as the GP is unfolded and further meanings generated. The impact of language was not just a matter of content being carried linguistically but also of ways of focusing consciousness, crystallizing it around GPs. By shaping fields of meaningful oppositions and GPs we are able to control our own consciousness, a GP coming to surface in an "L-center" (inspired by the "P-center," Morton *et al.* 1976), the temporal locus of consciousness concentrated in a particular linguistic–imagistic unit. This plane of focal consciousness includes the GP's imagery–language dialectic and its instability. Thus at the L-center an open and unfinished quality of consciousness exists. Unpacking is a second layer, peripheral but equally part of "the psychological structure of the sentence." While it is sequential, it is also unmalleable, partaking of the static structure of language engaged in unpacking the GP. Moreover, awareness has both a definite start and end point, respectively the moments the GP flashes on and its unpacking ends. There is accordingly a new focus of consciousness with each GP and a new periphery with each unpacking (GP and unpacking may arise simultaneously). These levels of consciousness then switch off at gesture's end, either the end of the stroke or retraction.

4.1.6.2 Double (or triple) consciousness

How can consciousness be extended?[20] L-centers have the ability to double (or triple) consciousness.

One means is to make other gestures simultaneously with a given gesture (indicated in transcriptions with multiple brackets). So doing adds a

[[₂ is **und**er Sylvester]	[₃ or in**si**de of him]]

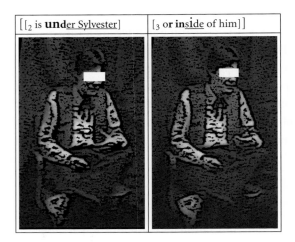

Figure 4.5 Hierarchies of consciousness. "you c[₁an't tell if the **bow**ling ball] [[₂is **und**er Sylvester] [₃or in**si**de of him]]"

linked but separate focus of consciousness. The gestures still have the global property. In Figure 4.5 a speaker is outlining an ambiguity she believed the cartoon had left concerning where the bowling ball ended up – in the cat or under him. The outer brackets mark the gesture phrase that coincided with her mentioning the ambiguity. There were two more gestures, one for each alternative. While the "under" gesture could be regarded as iconic, the "inside" gesture clearly is not, since it moves outward. The point of the illustration is that the three GPs materialize two layers of awareness – the top layer (1) "you can't tell . . . etc." plus the image of the two hands separated in space as a metaphor for the ambiguity; the second layer the alternatives themselves with a metaphor of opposition: (2) "is under Sylvester," plus the image of the hand moving inward; and (3) "or inside of him," plus the hand moving outward.

Still other multiple gestures focus within a focus, a kind of microscope effect. The same speaker, depicting Sylvester's outside ascent with a rising hand, then repeated the upward movement in enhanced form specifically with the path particle, "up" (Figure 4.6). Unlike hierarchical consciousness, there is not an overarching gesture that the other(s) then split open. The second GP is not a further differentiation of the first; both cover the same idea but the second enhances it as a materialization. Microscopic refocusing is a recurring style with this speaker (seemingly a metacommunicative strategy, bringing into sharper focus the point of highest communicative dynamism: "up" in this instance).

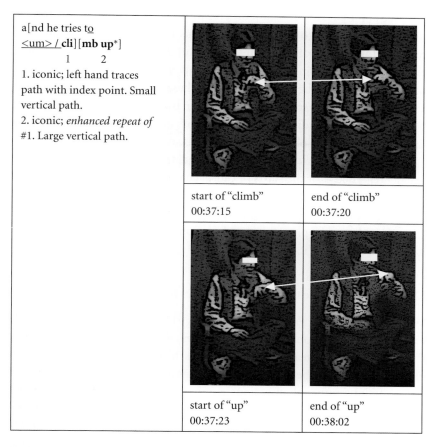

a[nd he tries to
<u><um></u> / **cli**] [**mb up***]
      1   2
1. iconic; left hand traces
path with index point. Small
vertical path.
2. iconic; *enhanced repeat of*
#1. Large vertical path.

start of "climb" 00:37:15	end of "climb" 00:37:20
start of "up" 00:37:23	end of "up" 00:38:02

Figure 4.6 "Microcsopic" consciousnss. Arrows indicate extent of upward movement.

4.1.7 Time and will

This concerns the distribution of GPs in time and the necessity, or not, of intending to speak when you are producing speech.

First, time. One notices new rhythmical speech pulses roughly every second or so. Gestures too bounce along at the same rate. Is there something in an imagery–language dialectic that determines this "speed of thought"? Any number of aspects of the dialectic could occupy this amount of time. One second may be how long it takes to create a gesture (a gesture is "instantaneous" in the sense that its meaning is not built up over time, but it may take a second or so to conceive of the image with the intended significance and to orchestrate its material form). One second might also be the natural pace of successive prosodic peaks and/or the time it takes to produce an unpacking and stop order. More deeply, it might be the time to make a contrast and/or shift to a new focus in it. It may also be the time required to conceive of a field of meaningful oppositions. Finally, it might be the time of carrying out an action unit and using it to update one's momentary state of being. Any or all of these could be the source of the 1~2 s. pulse. It is apparent that an evolution that made the dual semiotic of GPs possible would adjust to all these factors of attention, action, and idea unit formulation/dissolution.

Next, the will (to use the old-fashioned term). Will and purpose are usually regarded as at the starts of causal chains but they can be at the ends as well. For example, a new purpose – highlighting interiority in (2) with "inside the drain pipe" and "to go up through it" – was generated by the GP in (1), "through" plus an upward motion gesture; (2) reinforces (1) and has reinforcement as its only purpose:

(1) tries to climb [up- in **through**]
(2) the [drain- **inside the drai**npipe]- [tries **to go up th**rough it]

William James in his *Principles of Psychology* (1890) pondered why the will to carry out an action was not accompanied by a gap, first the willing, then the action. Instead the action seems to occur without a gap. This experience also may be an effect of language as it creates its own purposes out of actions rather than actions coming out of purposes. An amusing study published in *Science* shows illusory purposes. Johansson *et al.* (2005) devised an experimental setting in which they got university students (both men and women) to choose which of two presented photos of women's faces "was more attractive." Then the chosen photo was slid across the table before the student, who was asked to explain his or her choice. On a fraction of the trials, unbeknownst to the participant, the (light-fingered) experimenter switched the photos. Very few noticed; rather, they invented reasons to explain their "choice." The authors call this "choice blindness," and it seems to be another case of purpose flowing from action rather than action from purpose.

4.1.8 Affective-volitional tendencies and "the last why"

These terms and "the last why?" are from Vygotsky, and set the stage for linking goals (both causal and speech-created) to affect and the GP. Obviously, we expect different growth points and utterances depending on the propositional content of speech. However, we also should expect different growth points depending on the speaker's affect and purposes (including the purposes that the GPs themselves are creating). This too is part of what originated with language. Vygotsky, at the conclusion of *Thought and Language*, writes:

Thought is not begotten by thought; it is engendered by motivation, i.e., by our desires and needs, our interests and emotions. Behind every thought there is an affective-volitional tendency, which holds the answer to the last 'why' in the analysis of thinking. (Vygotsky 1987:252)

Classically, there are these two major systems of experience each with its own characteristic material carriers. Affect is materialized in the face and prosody, as well as in large-effector body motions. Propositional and discourse content are in linguistic form and gesture (as well as prosody, which embodies both systems). The two streams however merge in the generation of growth points. I have so far emphasized the context in which, say, going up the inside of a pipe (as opposed to the previous outside attempt) is the highlighted factor. Affect also can have an effect "on" (not "through") context via the same kind of highlighting process.

The analysis is as follows. A speaker who sees irony sees different oppositions and points of departure than a speaker who sees honest effort. Anger, fear, amusement, interest – are fields with different oppositions in them. "The next thing" in a story is defined by the actual events of the story, but the context in which these events are opposed is self-created. This is where the affective-volitional tendencies of the speaker enter in, since the utterance and growth point that come out of this context are shaped by the set of oppositions. We should therefore expect different growth points and utterances depending on affect. Here is one illustration. Tweety's dropping of the bowling ball can be recast in an ironic mood. This actually appears in some narratives. Although the propositional content is the same, the significant oppositions are not the interiority of the path but the convenient fact that the top of the pipe is right next to Tweety's window. The growth point then might be, not "down" + an image of interiority, but "contrived by the film maker" and an image of the pipe topping out at Tweety's perch. The sentence that emerges would be, not "drops it down the pipe," but something like "of course there's a drainpipe right next to Tweety," all this arising from the same objective content of the cartoon but interacting with an ironic mood that induces a different set of oppositions. *All* utterances would be formed in this way, not just ironic ones, so the affective-volitional tendency *is* the ultimate "why" of language and thought.

Moreover, affect varies not only in quality or coloration, which changes the field of meaningful oppositions, but also in strength. Here we predict a kind of upside-down "U" curve. The middle range of affect should energize thinking and meaning through the mechanisms of fields of oppositions formation outlined above. But at extreme levels – intense or minimal affect – there may be interference with thinking and the generation of new meanings. At very high levels, there seems to be a kind of paralysis; the body freezing in some attitude and this temporarily stopping any material carriers from emerging or changing. At the opposite end, there is again stasis but of a different sort, lassitude rather than paralysis. It is hard to separate cause and effect since the absence of thought may dampen affect, or the absence of affect may dampen thought.

Our method of eliciting narratives does not yield much variation of affect strength. The best we can do is look at the energy drain that occurs when a narrator temporarily loses track of the story line, and the reciprocal energy surge when she finds her way back. Losing your way may in itself be affectively negative and regaining it positive. The process does in any event show what energy loss and restoration look like. Figure 4.7 is Cel. losing steam and then regaining it. The detail to observe is that the size and complexity of her gestures correspond to her energy level – a decline then a restoration. This appears to be in accord with Vygotsky's affective–volitional tendencies as the ultimate "why" of thought and speech. From an evolutionary point of view this "U"-shaped energy curve again suggests that the origin of language was linked to the organization of action.

4.1.9 Memory

How did language and its role in shaping consciousness affect memory, and vice versa? Consciousness and memory are closely linked (cf. Baars 1988), and memory, like consciousness, would have been affected by Mead's Loop. A GP with an L-center imposes a kind of rhythmical pulse on memory. There is focal awareness followed by a change of state every one or two seconds or so. The state change is a change from immediate "working" memory to some other kind of information state. Without this quick-to-change system, thinking in terms of language could not itself have evolved with Mead's Loop; the action orchestration it provides would have clogged into unusability and never been naturally selected. The state change at the end of the cycle is an active step, part of the continuation of the discourse. The GP then loses

and then uh climbs up the build- the side of the building (full energy)	*large iconic*	
and jumps in the window (possible energy decrement – the culturally specified form of pointing demands less effort)	*deictic*	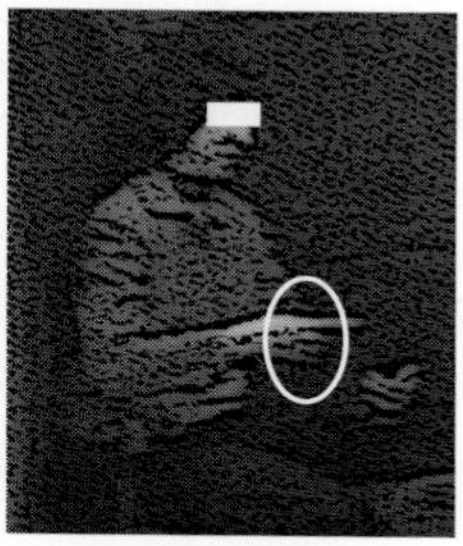
this way he can fool Granny (possible energy decrement – the culturally specified form of the metaphoric demands less effort)	*metaphoric*	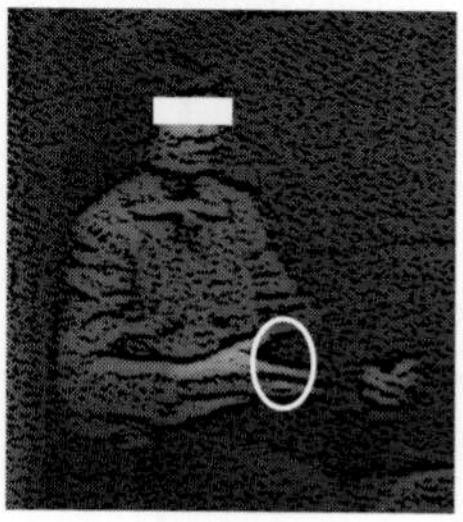

Figure 4.7 Decline and return of energy in gesture size and complexity as a speaker momentarily loses the narrative thread and then recovers.

cohesion and identity. The pieces do not disappear and may be swept up into the next GP, e.g., as part of the next field of oppositions. Metapragmatic indicators guide the process, such as the sense of direction the storyline provides. Such GP → field of meaningful oppositions continuity was shown in the outside–inside the pipe examples in Chapter 2. The outside GP was fragmented (or fragmented itself) and the pipe-climbing feature from the "outside" event became part of the next field of oppositions (i.e. outside: *WAYS TO USE A PIPE: CLIMB IT*; then inside: *WAYS TO CLIMB IT: ON THE INSIDE*).

let's see what happens (zero energy at this point)	*no gesture*	
he tries to find out where Tweety Bird is hiding in the house (gradual return of energy – beats are minimal in effort)	*beats*	
and the Grandmother sort of catches on to him (return to level of metaphoric just before zero – again, pre-specified form demands less effort)	*metaphoric*	

Figure 4.7 (*cont.*)

The question is not whether a short-term memory exists without language (for which the evidence is clear – it does exist in much the same form in monkeys, e.g., Paule *et al.* 1998) but whether the 1∼2 s rhythmic pulse interval followed by a change of memory state has adapted to memory, and possibly altered it.

A provocative approach in this domain that helps to understand these questions was launched by Cowan (2001) and continued by Oberauer (2005). The essence of their approach is that there is but one memory, a long-term storehouse, which is functionally differentiated into working memory and within working memory into a focus of awareness. It is a view that contrasts to the modular separations proposed by Baddeley and Hitch

and she says here's a nice new penny for you little monkey or something and she (full energy from here on)	*large iconic*	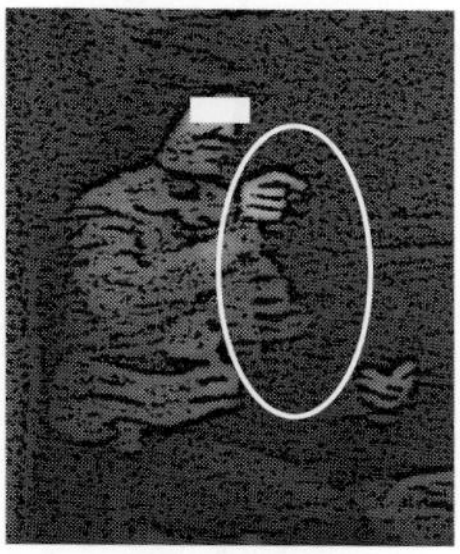
he holds out the can and she drops the penny in the in the little cup	*large 2-handed iconics with dual C-VPTs*	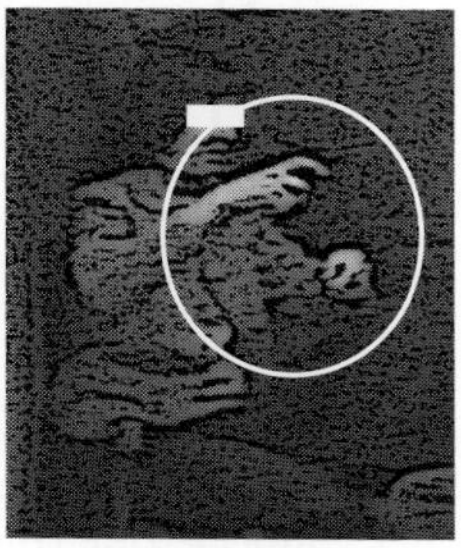
and he takes off his hat to her	*large full-body iconic in C-VPT*	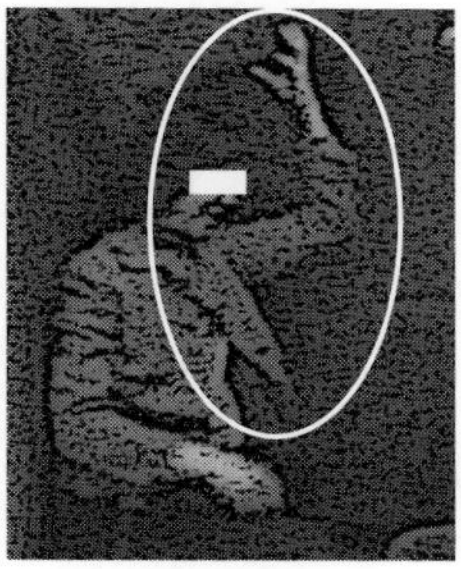
and then it's obvious that he's really a cat and she says ahhh! and whaps him with her umbrella	(further large gestures, not illustrated)	

Figure 4.7 (*cont.*)

(1974), for whom working memory is a product of separate processors, an executive, a phonological loop, and so forth. I see no natural mapping of memory so described onto the dual semiotic of language conceived dynamically. Cowan's non-modular, function-based approach, on the other hand, especially as particularized by Oberauer, adapts well to the GP and L-center. The GP adds functionality to memory and the L-center provides the focus of awareness within it.

Oberauer diagrams his "embedded-component model of working memory" as a net (illustration thanks to Klaus Oberauer):

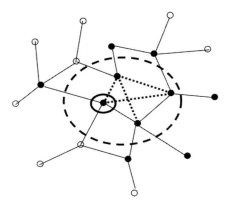

And explains that:

Nodes connected by continuous lines represent the associative network of LTM; the subset of black nodes stands for the activated part of LTM. The large oval in broken line delineates the direct-access region, which has a limited capacity that permits holding a small number of activated representational elements at any time. The small circle in continuous line represents the focus of attention that selects one element at a time as the object of the next cognitive operation. (Oberauer 2005, Figure 1 and caption, p. 716)

This can be aligned with GP equivalents:

Large dotted oval = *gesture imagery* (an inhabited action unit).

Small solid oval = *L-center focus* (the GP surfacing).

Black nodes = *field of meaningful oppositions.*

Black node links = field of meaningful oppositions *structured to make the GP possible.*

White nodes = *potential next field of oppositions or GP* (depending on macro-factors of intention and metanarrative/pragmatic considerations).

Memory researchers are interested chiefly in capacity issues whereas here our interest is in the evolution of the dual semiotic of language, and how it affected memory in turn; how, in terms of Oberauer's diagram, the emergence of linguistic dynamism influenced what is "white" and "black," where the large and small ovals form and the linking of black nodes by meta-factors to structure the field of meaningful oppositions.

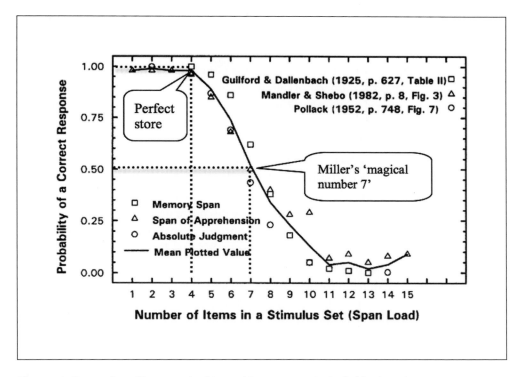

Figure 4.8 Proportion of items retained in working memory. As Bachelder (2001) points out, the 50% point is the "magical number 7 ± 2" (Miller 1956) and the largest number without loss is 4 (Cowan 2001). Graph from Bachelder (2001), whom to see for citations in the chart. Used with permission of Cambridge University Press.

4.1.9.1 The GP has adapted to working memory capacity, and vice versa

Figure 4.8, from Bachelder (2001), shows the fall-off of working memory as the number of chunks of information increases (working memory is information immediately available, without search, for cognitive work; a "chunk" is one or more bits of information structured as a unit and handled as one item in this memory). Bachelder points out that the 50% mark is exactly the "magical number 7 (± 2)" that G. A. Miller famously identified in 1957, but 4 is the capacity of working memory without loss that Cowan (2001) has claimed. This latter number is quite interesting for our discussion. First of all, it is an upper bound. Linguistic awareness would have adapted to this limit and would not have exceeded it. A 4-chunk span accommodates, without loss: a gesture, its co-expressive linguistic segments (chunked), a field of meaningful oppositions (also chunked), and the point of differentiation within it; together they are one GP. In Oberauer's net, it is the dotted oval. In this way, *a GP and errorless human attention and working memory seem mutually adjusted.*

Given Mead's Loop, however, the GP-cycle has equally shaped memory. A GP has the property of "all-at-onceness" and this takes up just one chunk of memory. A separate short-term memory built around the GP seems to exist. It has adapted "chunking" so that GPs have internal complexity without coming close to the 4-item memory limit, and the creation of speech, including unpacking (Wundt's second tier of consciousness), stays well within the perfect-score limit. Four becomes one in this adapted memory, and this one includes the context, its differentiation plus metapragmatic indicators that may index the entire discourse up to the moment of speaking and foretell the future. This enormous expansion of memory capacity is due to the orchestration by gesture that Mead's Loop provides. It is thus conceivable that language has evolved a dedicated short-term memory in this functional sense along Cowan's and Oberauer's lines. Such a memory would be tied to GPs, contextualization and differentiation, as well as inhabitance. The usual short-term memory tests in clinical practice and in many classic psychological experiments are deliberately de-contextualized and do not activate this dedicated memory. But if it exists it would explain how speakers with impaired memory continue to produce, without disturbance to themselves or others, socially and cognitively integrated speech.

4.1.9.2 How gestures protect incidental memory

We can apply this reasoning to a discovery by Goldin-Meadow *et al.* (2001) that memory for something improves if you talk about something else and perform gestures as you do. The experiment was as follows. The subject, a child or an adult, solved math problems (an equivalence problem for children, finding factors for adults), and then explained the solution to the experimenter. While giving this explanation, he or she was also told to retain in memory a set of letters or names the experimenter provided; the items had no connection with the problem or the explanation. When no gestures were made, subjects recalled fewer letters or names. This was true if the subjects were told not to gesture and also if a subject, on her own, although allowed to gesture, did not. Clearly, therefore, any extra effort to obey the instruction not to gesture cannot explain the decrement. In both the no-gesture cases, memory was poorer for the incidental information and by the same amount. Thus, one infers that making gestures increases the capacity of incidental memory, and/or not making them decreases it.

Gesture may provide some positive benefit to memory. It enhances the materialization of GPs and fosters the enlarged memory functionality described above. This may extend to incidental information floating by. But there is a second, more direct benefit of gestures to incidental information in particular. Gesture both possibly enhances the GP but also, by commandeering forgetting, protects incidental information.[21] If the focal information in working memory changes state not during the 1~2 s span of memory but discretely, at the end of a GP-cycle, then this is when focal information can be lost and incidental information benefit from the reduced competition. When there is no gesture, focal memory undergoes less state change and incidental information receives less benefit. Since incidental information is not in a GP-cycle it does not take part in a state change. So, paradoxically, it is not lost, and as a gesture clears memory of focal information, more incidental information is retained when there is a gesture than when there is not, and this is the Goldin-Meadow *et al.* finding.

4.1.9.3 A way to test

Looking at the flipside of the Goldin-Meadow *et al.* effect, if the materialization of GP imagery in gesture encourages a memory state-change, then no gesture should make this change less likely and/or less robust. The contents of the focal task should then be still "in memory." So, somewhat counter-intuitively, no-gesture trials should show better memory for the focal task (and poorer memory for the incidental task, as shown).

4.1.10 The social fabric

Language and thought in Mead's Loop are social from the beginning. In this section we look at elaborations of this intrinsic property. We see first how the GP can be a joint social product. Also we see that mimicry of GPs is possible; that, when applied to gesture and speech, it recreates, in the mimic, the GP and field of meaningful oppositions of a social other. Current-day speakers show absorptions of the social context of speaking into their own GPs and fields of oppositions. Özyürek (2000) showed this kind of absorption experimentally. A narrator recounting the Canary Row bowling ball episode has gesture imagery that differs depending on the number and the spatial locations of the listeners. With a single listener, in front, the imagery for Sylvester's exit from the drainpipe is "out" of the shared space between speaker and listener, which is typically to one side or the other. With two listeners, however, one to the left, one the right, "out" is away from all and over the speaker's shoulder is the typical path – "out" of the shared space without favoring one listener over the other. Both spaces incorporate aspects of social context – the number and the loci of the listeners.

So far in this discussion we have emphasized the family circle (possibly expanded with surrogates) as the milieu of Mead's Loop evolution, but other social forces could have had an impact as well. The earliest communities of humans are thought to have been bands of one to two hundred individuals, including children (Dunbar 1996), a milieu where self-awareness as a social force would be a daily presence and Mead's Loop would be under pressure to evolve in this kind of communal living. The sensitivity included in gesture to the number of listeners documented by Özyürek is perhaps an illustration. Dunbar argues that language was triggered when a threshold community size was crossed – in his colorful terms, then grooming changed to gossip. The imagery–language dialectic of GPs was formed during this transition as well. Quaeghebeur (2010) connects the phenomenon to the experience of social interaction:

This [conversational participants as an 'interactional unit'] exemplifies well Merleau-Ponty's (2007) concept of "intercorporeity": in social or linguistic inter-action our bodies become aspects of a shared dynamic system; we "share a body" because it has been formed the same way (we speak the same verbal and non-verbal language) and because we find ourselves in this concrete situation together, i.e. a shared framework for making reference to.... A full multimodal analysis shows that when engaged in conversation, we are at all times immediately attuned to each other's meaningful behavior, so that it is better to say that we think, speak and listen "along." (2010, p. 119)

We see in GPs this inclusion of others' meaningful bodily movements through mimicry and the joint construction of gestures. This inclusion and mimicry could reflect the small-group (but larger than the family) form of life that Dunbar identifies. The links are seen in the role and ultimately the power of gesture mimicry and gesture absorption to form GPs and make them joint products of two or more individuals.

4.1.10.1 "Mind-merging" – the "Mr. A–Mr. B" conversation

We begin with "mind-merging," in which speakers in conversations con-verge on shared GPs at turn-shifting points.

A conversation is an approximation of the presumed natural selection scenario of the social fabric that had shaping effects on GPs. The "Mr. A. and Mr. B conversation" compellingly illustrates the incorporation of social interaction factors into GPs. The conversation was recorded in the early 1970s by the late Starkey Duncan as part of a larger investigation of face-to-face interaction (see Duncan and Fiske 1977 for the full study). It was named "the Mr. A–Mr. B conversation" by Silverstein (1997). The participants were previously unacquainted male graduate students at the University of Chicago. A and B were introduced, placed in front of a video camera, and told simply to "have a conversation." As would be expected in such a situation, the participants started out exchanging academic biographies. Each already knew that the other was a graduate student and the specific school within the university the other attended, but nothing more. Mr. A, a budding lawyer, made a determined effort to uncover Mr. B's academic past, about which Mr. B was strangely unforthcoming. After several false starts, Mr. A. finally pinned Mr. B down with Q$_{A}$8 "an' [you went to undergraduate here or . . .]," which elicited R$_{B}$8 "[in Chicágo] át, uh, Loyola," the reluctant Mr. B divulging his academic homeland (see Table 4.1).[22]

The analysis of Mr. B's state of mind at this critical point shows the incorporation of the social fabric into his R$_{B}$8 GP. The gesture space between A and B had acquired meaning as a discourse topic. It initially had meant Mr. B's academic past in Iowa, before he had arrived in Chicago, "Iowa-then." The meaning of the deictic field changed to "Chicago-now" at R$_{B}$7.6, when B said "so I [came back]" and pointed to the shared space that previously had meant "Iowa-then" (the status of the shared space at R$_{B}$7.4–5 is unclear). This meaning shift could have hinged on temporal updating. Mr. B wanted to move the topic away from his Iowa past and into the present and thus contrasted "now" to the "then" that had been the left space at R$_{B}$7.2–3. However, if this was his goal, he was hoisted on his own petard, for along with "now" at R$_{B}$7.6 came "Chicago," and it too became part of the shared space. But which "Chicago" – the City or the University?

Examining the way B divided the gesture space, we see that at this moment, if not sooner (for we can't be sure about R$_{B}$7.4–5), the shared space meant for Mr. B the *City*. The crucial indication is that Mr. B pointed to the *right* at R$_{B}$7.7 and hedged the reference to coming back with "[kind of /]." He was evidently saying that he had come back to Chicago, but hadn't come back to *Chicago*, and placed this Chicago-1 versus Chicago-2 opposition on a new shared versus *right* space axis (the only use of the right space in the snippet).

Table 4.1 "Mr. A–Mr. B" conversation snippet. Used with permission of University of Chicago Press

Mr. A	Mr. B
Qᴀ6 how do you like Chicago compared to	
Qᴀ7 did you [go to school thére] or uh *points to shared space*	
	Rʙ7.1 I did go to school [there] *points to shared space*
	Rʙ7.2 [I went to school hére] *points to left*
	Rʙ7.3 [álso] *circles to left*
uh-huh	
	Rʙ7.4 [I] *points to shared space*
	Rʙ7.5 [/ um] *points to left*
	Rʙ7.6 so I [came back] *points to shared space*
oh, uh-huh	
	Rʙ7.7 [kind of /] *points to right*
Qᴀ8 an' [you wént to undergraduate hére or ____ (A's gesture held)_____] *points to shared space*	
	Rʙ8 [in Chicágo] át, uh, Loyola *points to shared space*
óh óh óh óh óh I'm an óld Jésuit Boy mysélf / / unfórtunately	

The shared and right spaces cannot have had the same meanings: one was the City and the other was the University (or at least *not*-the-City), although we cannot say yet which was which. Subsequent pointing however makes clear Mr. B's thinking.

Mr. A now asks his fatal question (Qᴀ8): "an' [you wént to undergraduate hére or]" and points again to the shared space with an extended hold that is maintained during Mr. B's answer. Mr. A's use is unambiguous: The space means for him the University. Mr. B's answer at Rʙ8 also points to this space while saying, crucially, "[in Chicágo] át, uh, Loyola" – the capitulation after his efforts at evasion.

The preposition "in" shows that the shared space for Mr. B at this point meant the City, not the University. This in turn suggests that the *right* space at RB7.7 meant the University and not the City.

This meaning allocation would explain the hedge "kind of." What Mr. B meant when he said "so I came back kind of," was that he had returned to one kind of Chicago (the City), but it was not the Chicago that might have been metacommunicatively supposed – the University, where Mr. B and Mr. A were students and where the conversation was taking place.

That Mr. B hedged and introduced a new spatial contrast also suggests that he was aware of the "$^{c/u}$Chicago" ambiguity. Had he been thinking only of his own meaning of "^{c}Chicago," there would have been no motivation for introducing the hedge and a new space for "^{u}Chicago" (or "*not* ^{c}Chicago"). In other words, Mr. B, without realizing it, tipped his hand that the "$^{c/u}$Chicago" ambiguity had been intentional.

That Mr. A and Mr. B had conflicting meanings for the shared topic space and that Mr. B was aware of this also explains why Mr. B gave up his resistance at this very moment. Mr. B could have continued dodging Mr. A and perpetuated the City–University ambiguity, had he wished, merely by answering QA8 with a "yes."

However, the shared space and "here" then would have meant the City for Mr. B whereas they meant the University for Mr. A. This contradiction confronted Mr. B with an interactional problem on a new level: the need to cease being evasive and to start lying; he balked at this step.

It may seem that Mr. B could have avoided his dilemma by not pointing but this was not an option for him. Mr. A had already pointed into the shared space with the unambiguous meaning of "^{u}Chicago" and Mr. B had previously pointed to it with the opposite meaning of "^{c}Chicago;" moreover, Mr. A was *continuing* to point at the shared space with the contradictory meaning; the shared GP with Mr. A could mean only the University, and Mr. B's confrontation with possible immorality was inescapable.

That Mr. A maintained his pointing gesture during the entirety of Mr. B's response suggests that for Mr. A, also, there was a sense that the central gesture space had become a field of divergence.

Thus, the role of pointing into the gesture space was an active one in this stretch of conversation. Pointing contributed to the dynamics of the conversation and included such interpersonal factors as evasion, probing, and confession.

Mr. B's field of opposition, as he construed it, was something like *TO LIE ABOUT LOYOLA VS. TO TELL THE TRUTH ABOUT LOYOLA.*

Mr. B's chosen contrast was the *TO-TELL-THE-TRUTH* pole. That is, Mr. B's meaning at this point was not just the denotational content of "in Chicago, at Loyola," but also the moral content of coming out with the truth when the alternative was to commence lying. This hidden content was, I believe, the core of his meaning at this moment and the various parts of this meaning materialized in one or both of the modalities, speech and gesture. The "in" lexical choice brought out ᶜChicago, which is the "Truth" alternative. The "in" – "at" succession arose from the "ᶜ/ᵘChicago" ambiguity that Mr. B had been perpetuating. Having separated the City meaning with "in," Mr. B went on to lay out the University component with "at." The stress pattern, "in Chicágo – át," displays precisely this contrast within a consistent rhythmic pattern (that is, "ín Chicago – át," or "in Chicágo – at Loyóla" – the other possible combinations – lose the contrast that splits out the University concept as something distinct from "ᶜChicago"). The "át," in turn, led to "Loyola" but with hesitancy as if completion of the City–University paradigm had taken on a life of its own and was unfolding somewhat against Mr. B's will or at least with lingering uncertainty.

This extended example is meant to illustrate how GP-style thinking automatically opens routes to the social fabric of interaction, not as an outside force but as an intrinsic element of thought, in this case via a field of meaningful oppositions.

4.1.10.2 Mimicry 1: shared GPs: interpersonal synchrony

Mimicry is widespread in the primate universe and is spontaneous among us as well. Here, we see how Mead's Loop and GPs have co-opted it as part of the social orientation of thinking for speaking. Kimbara (2006) studied gestural mimicry as an interactive phenomenon. She regards it as a process of "interpersonal synchrony," prominent when interlocutors are personally close. Individuals merge gestures out of a sense of solidarity. Figure 4.9 presents such a case. Two friends are having a conversation. The case begins with a gesture by the friend on the right. She is describing the chaotic scene that develops on Tokyo subway platforms during rush hours where multiple lines of waiting passengers form and then disintegrate when the train arrives. Panel 1 depicts the lines; panel 2 is their thickness and leftward direction vis-à-vis the speaker/viewer. The listener is commencing her gesture preparation during panel 2 as well, and panels 3 and 4 are her mimicry. The imagery is the same as the original, including even the same absolute direction, the listener mimicking the speaker's origo, or zero point of the spatial layout (Bühler 1982). From a GP viewpoint, the second

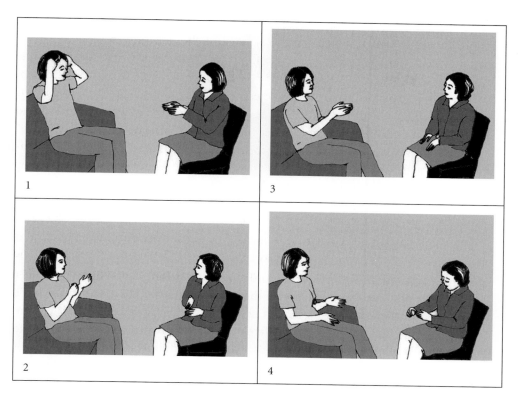

Figure 4.9 Interpersonal mimicry.

Panels 1 and 2 Speaker on right: describing the line as "irregular"; her gesture depicts lines of waiting passengers; the separation of her hands may depict the density of the crowding. Speaker on left: in 2, hands entering the gesture space and preparing to perform gesture in panels 3 and 4.

Panels 3 and 4 Continuous with panels 1 and 2. Speaker on left mimics right speaker's two-lines gesture as she emphatically agrees ("yes, yes, yes, yes"), including absolute direction (in both figures, the hands are moving toward camera). Meanwhile, in (4), right speaker is preparing her next gesture. From Kimbara (2006). Used with permission of University of Chicago Press.

speaker's idea unit included imagery from the first speaker's GP and so was, in this way, a partly mimicked GP.

4.1.10.3 Mimicry 2: shared GPs: joint constructions

Mimicry goes further, providing a kind of mind-merging even with strangers who are not in the same space and time as the mimic. Gesture coders sponta-neously use mimicry in their work, recreating GPs and field of meaningful

Figure 4.10 Scene from Canary Row the individuals shown in Figures 4.11, 4.12, and 4.13 are describing.

oppositions from videos recorded decades before. By replicating another person's gesture and speech, the mimicry imports the gesture into one's own thought–language–hand link. If you ask in what context this gesture could have been a point of differentiation, you also experience an immediate field of meaningful oppositions. The effect is dramatic. The GP and field of oppositions arise before you as if by magic but it is not magic – it is because the original gesture had absorbed this context, and mimicking it recreates it wholly or in part. The exercises below demonstrate that fields of meaningful oppositions and GPs can be brought into one's own experience this way. Mimicry as a product of the evolution of social thinking-for-(while)-speaking may have arisen in small groups, possibly the bands described by Dunbar, where it could have had adaptive value. It recreates the other's gesture–speech unit as if it were a GP of one's own and mimicry now could echo this context in which Mead's Loop also was evolving (cf. a German language translation in McNeill 2010).[23]

In Figures 4.11–13 cartoon narrators are describing an episode where Sylvester, disguised as a bellhop, has run off with what he believes is Tweety in his covered birdcage; he removes the cover and discovers, too late, that it is his nemesis, Granny, instead (Figure 4.10). With each example you are invited to recreate the gesture and speech combination and to introspect whether this clarifies the significance of the gesture. The gestures are chosen because they seem, at first glance, hard to interpret.

1. The gesture (Figure 4.11) occurred with "he's like" and is plausibly a metaphor of alarm – both hands rise upward, palms forward (more broadly, a metaphor of blocking incoming energy; cf. Kendon 2004). The speech is a meta-pragmatic reference to Sylvester's alarm, and the

Figure 4.11 Gesture to be mimicked 1: speaker was saying "he's like" – likely a metaphor of alarm.

Figure 4.12 Gesture to be mimicked 2: speaker was saying "the grandmother // instead of Tweety" and the hands moved in unison upward, downward in small beats – likely highlighting plot twist.

gesture a metaphor of it. However, at first glance, the gesture is ambiguous (it could be the shape of the cage, Granny's location or other interpretations), but with mimicry and the accompanying speech, the "alarm" conception dominates. The hands should start palm down and then rock up once in a quick motion.

2. Beats highlighting the plot twist of "the grandmother // instead of Tweety" (Figure 4.12). The hands are held motionless in the position and location shown except for small up-down beats as the speaker says "instead of," separated from the preceding speech by a pause (the double slashes). The GP concerns Granny's unexpected appearance. Beats,

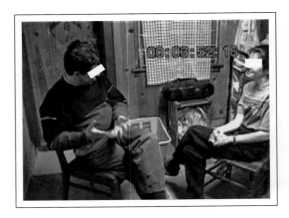

Figure 4.13 Gesture to be mimicked 3: speaker was saying "pulls off // the cover of the cage" – likely metaphor of presenting the dénouement.

especially superimposed beats, in general indicate the relevance of the gesture on which they ride and the speech with which they synchronize to a larger discourse theme, and such appears to be case here as well (cf. beats case 4 in Chapter 1). Raising and extending the two parallel hands "placed" the grandmother in the gesture space. The beats (a kind of miniature reactivation of this gesture) highlight the grandmother's popping up, contrary to expectation.

3. A denouement metaphor, deictically placed, with "pulls off // the cover of the cage" (Figure 4.13). This gesture is also set off by a hesitation (double slashes). The two-handed gesture with "the cover," I find, makes little sense without mimicry, but with it the significance of a denouement emerges clearly (the metaphor is a classic conduit gesture "presenting" the denouement). The position of the gesture in the lower space (reinforced by the speaker's lowered head tilt) links it to several previous gestures (not shown) for the birdcage there in his gesture space.

Materialization through mimicry opens up initially obscure idiosyncratic construals – respectively, something alarming, a plot-twist, a denouement – of the same cartoon episode by different, all unfamiliar narrators.

4.1.10.4 Embodiment in two bodies

Even more dramatic, spontaneous two-body GPs appear in Figure 4.14 from an experiment devised by Furuyama (2000a). The setting was one person teaching a second person, a stranger, how to create

Figure 4.14 Embodiment in two bodies. Used with permission of University of Chicago Press.

Panel 1 Silent mimicry of gesture by learner (on left) synchronized with teacher's speech.

Panel 2 While speaking, learner (left) appropriates teacher's gesture, nullifying usual prohibition of physical contact by strangers. As Furuyama (2000a) observed, the teacher invited contact by turning his body away, giving to his gesture space the same left–right orientation as the learner's.

an *origami* figure. In Panel 1, the learner on the left mimics the teacher's gesture, and again mimicry has social-interactive content. It occurred without the learner speaking but synchronized with the tutor's speech. As the tutor said, "[pull down] the corner," the learner performed the gesture during the bracketed portion. The learner thus appropriated the other's speech, combining it with her gesture, as if they were jointly creating a single GP. The similarities to what Gill (2007) calls entrainment are notable.

The reverse appropriation also occurs. The learner appropriates the tutor's gesture by combining it with her speech. Again, there is inhabitance, this time of gesture, and there is again a kind of joint GP. In Panel 2 of Figure 4.14 the learner takes control of the tutor's gesture and combines it with her speech. She says, "[you bend this down?]," and during the bracketed speech moves the tutor's hand down. As Furuyama observes, the tutor had turned in his chair so that the same left-right gesture space was available to him and the learner, a maneuver that invited the learner to enter his gesture space. It is striking that the taboo normally prohibiting strangers from non-accidental physical contact was overridden, possibly because the hands had become shared symbols no longer seen as hands, actual body-parts, belonging to another person.

Figure 4.15 A dog surveys with its nose, a human with its eyes. Human image from Google (circumstances unknown). Dog image from *Chicago Tribune*, Jan. 6, 2011 (caption says "Sage . . . watches . . . " – watches, that is, with its nose!).

4.1.11 The unlikelihood of language without hands

While gestures take place with all parts of the body, the hands are particularly crucial. Without hands the thought–language–hand link circuitry and the form of language it supported would have been impossible (obviously, this refers to the impossibility of language in a species without hands, not to the acquisition and use of language by humans who happen to lack hands). The hands are special because of their agility and instantiation of gestures in all spatial dimensions, but the feature that made them indispensible for the origin of language lies in the brain; the proximity, in the layout of the motor cortex, of the manual and oral centers, and the role of Broca's area and mirror neurons in organizing actions of both centers (had the human brain lacked this detail language would not have originated, or at least not with Mead's Loop).

It is science fiction to speculate on what an otherworldly alien's language could be like (the problem often skirted by having the aliens speak in robotic English), but we can consider an actual and familiar alien, not one of our primate cousins but a species whose perceptions of the world seem fundamentally different from ours. Despite numerous millennia of domestication, this intelligent alien is the dog. And it is highly unlikely that dogs could ever evolve anything resembling language.

A dog's preference for surveying the world is by smell; its favored perceptual mode is olfaction (Figure 4.15). It is not the nose as such that is decisive; it is the brain behind it. If the perceptually more accessible modality becomes the global-synthetic part of a GP, perhaps another species – dogs, if they evolved a capacity for language – would have non-visual gestures. If we imagine dogs with a language their gestures could be olfactory (leaving aside the delicate problem of how such gestures are produced, but hands are not the only means of creating finely differentiated images). A person on the other hand surveys the world with vision, and we know that his or her gestures are visual-actional, with the hands. However, it seems unlikely there could be a canine Mead's Loop. It would mesh perception (olfaction) and the actions producing odors but would hit an obstacle, in that whatever is the canine analogue to speech – possibly visible actions of moving parts, feet, tail, ears, not necessary barks – would not have mirror neurons in the same brain region as this hypothetical olfactory producer (if dogs have mirror neurons at all),[24] from which it follows that a canine language, independently evolved but comparable to a minimal characterization of human language, would be impossible. Generalizing from this imagined case, it suggests that language could not have evolved without hands because of the requirement for Mead's Loop to carry significances via gestures into the brain areas that orchestrate speech or its equivalents.[25]

4.1.12 Undoing language

It may seem perverse to say that Mead's Loop engenders disorders of language, but that is the assertion of this section: specific disorders that arise from how Mead's Loop originally created the GP, cracks that remain and that, under stress, create the disorders. All but one (on stuttering) of the following brief sections is from a longer paper with Susan Duncan (McNeill and Duncan 2010) that can be consulted for supporting materials.

4.1.12.1 Dysfluent aphasia

Dysfluent (agrammatic) aphasia preserves the psychological predicate character of the GP, the point of newsworthy information differentiated from context. Gestures carry newsworthy content. The aphasia concentrates specifically on the unpacking of GPs via constructions or other syntax. Constructions may also be intact, in part, but are impeded due to motor impediments interacting with the vocal articulators. The evidence for this is that, with catchment support and sufficient time, agrammatic aphasics can develop even multi-clause unpackings. In terms of our brain model, Broca's aphasia, true to its name, is a breakdown of GP unpacking in Broca's area. The area orchestrates vocal and manual actions with significances other than those of the actions themselves. Consistent with such a breakdown, recent reports state that Broca's aphasics have difficulty recognizing other people's actions (Fadiga 2007), pointing to mirror neuron involvement. This can be regarded as the perceptual equivalent of impaired orchestrating capabilities. On the other hand, processes said in the model to be carried out elsewhere in the brain, the posterior left hemisphere, the right hemisphere, and the prefrontal cortex – imagery, the combination of imagery with linguistically encoded categories, and the relating of all this to tailor-made fields of oppositions, as well as prosodic emphasis on the linguistic realization (cf. Goodglass 1993) – all appear intact, evidenced in the continuing ability by agrammatic speakers to synchronize co-expressive speech and gesture, and to differentiate contextually newsworthy information with them.

4.1.12.2 Down's syndrome

Down's syndrome (DS) speakers, children at least, may not experience thinking-for-speaking in anything like the form it takes in normal speakers or the agrammatic aphasic. What is impressive about DS, revealed by work at the Institute of Cognitive Science and Technology, in Rome, is that gestures with speech are mostly *semantically redundant*. In typically developing children of the same mental ages, speech–gesture combinations are "supplementary," as described by Goldin-Meadow and Butcher (2003) – e.g., POINT AT CHAIR+ "daddy" = "daddy's chair." A DS equivalent would be POINT AT CHAIR+ "chair" = "chair." The elements semiotically opposed in DS GPs, being redundant, accordingly have little scope for cognitive movement; are rigid and limited to semantic equivalences; and apply in narrow contexts. The impression one gets therefore is of stasis, immobility, with little potential for fueling a dynamic dimension. Insofar as these features, when present in a normal brain, require prefrontal cortex activity, we can suspect the DS deficit lies in part in this brain region (meager development of which has also been proposed by Wynn and Coolidge 2008 for the Neanderthal brain, suggesting that DS may be the nearest modern human approximation of what, linguistically, it could have achieved – words and redundant gestures with possibly "pivot-grammar" type constructions; cf. Chapter 5).

4.1.12.3 Williams syndrome

As often noted, Down's and Williams syndrome (WS) speakers are mirror images with respect to language. They are similar in being unable to use language as an enriching element of cognition, but the shortfall is for opposite reasons – Down's cannot break out of limited GPs; Williams cannot translate what appear to be robustly active GPs into wider cognition. Williams

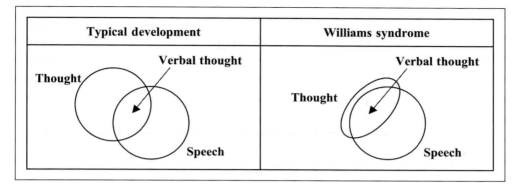

Figure 4.16 Hypothetical "Vygotsky" diagrams for normal and Williams Syndrome overlap of thought and language. Used with permission of the Psychology Press.

speakers seem to have half the normal complement of thinking-for-speaking but are missing the other half. Their GPs are socially engaged but do not pass into thought, possibly because their intellectual deficits (very low IQs) prevent it.

WS poses an interesting puzzle for the GP theory: how, given the theory, does language go so far beyond cognition's offerings? We answer the challenge in the following way. Although it may seem obviously wrong to refer to better-than-predicted language as a "disorder" we shall in fact conclude that, in the WS case, good language arises from disruptions of the GP, namely a disconnect between the social framing of thinking-for-speaking, of which WS clearly are capable, and what Vygotsky (1987) termed "pure thought." Gesture mimicry and other forms of interpsychic collaboration participate in constructing social interactions, as Kimbara showed, and we believe that WS children have similar capabilities. In effect, WS speakers maintain the connection of idea units, GPs, to the social context of speaking, creating with interlocutors (as unimpaired speakers also do) joint GPs and fields of opposition, but are unable to shape thought beyond this social fabric, cannot form idea units on their own, and this is their limitation. Vygotsky visualized thought and speech as overlapping circles, one for thought, one for speech, and the overlap was inner speech. The GP evolved to control this overlap, and what we propose for WS is truncation or inaccessibility of the thought circle from it (Figure 4.16). The result leaves little room for the GP to shape cognition – the reverse of trying to explain how cognition affects language: it is cognition that is not shaped by the ongoing thinking-for-speaking process in WS.

WS is a disorder of the dynamic dimension of language *par excellence*. Language is blocked from shaping cognition online, while it retains what is also usually integrated with thought, the social-interactive fabric. As shown at the earlier mentioned Rome Institute, where WS also has been studied, there is a distinctive gesture profile of WS, in which only certain kinds of imagery take part: iconic gestures and a plenitude of socially constituted emblems (abundant with speakers of Italian in any case, including WS speakers who draw on this lexicon). Both iconics and emblems can engage in social interactions. Gesture metaphors, with discourse significance, however, even the limited kinds that appear with children (Chapter 5), are absent.

4.1.12.4 Childhood autism

Levy (2008, 2009–10, 2011) has developed a method by which to observe the emergence of spoken discourse cohesion over short intervals. A child is shown a classic film, *The Red Balloon*, and tells the story to a listener. Specific to the method is that the child tells the story repeatedly. In this way, changes, which typically are consolidations that increase cohesion, can be tracked as they emerge. Following Levy (2009–10), I concentrate on her case study of a 13-year-old boy with autism. In his first attempts, speech was fragmented and gestures few, responses were "single utterances or utterance fragments, usually in the absence of focused enactment, and often accompanied by diffuse body motion, for example, shifting position, swaying back and forth, rocking, and fidgeting" (p. 45).

Levy documents that from this point fully encoded descriptions emerged along with gestures that look typical for such speech; in other words GPs in what appear to be appropriate fields of oppositions. Coherence increased via catchments: "As D. combined speech with enactment...he created a sequence that was more temporally coherent than the first: All utterances were accurate descriptions of events, and all occurred in accurate temporal sequence" (p. 45). An example analyzed in detail by Levy involves two catchments at early points in the child's narrative attempts – *flying* gestures, and *holding* gestures – that resulted, after several retellings, in a narrated sequence of events corresponding to the film's sequence. Initially, the boy first described flying with balloons, then, immediately following that description, holding onto gesture balloons, a kind of explanation perhaps. Then occurred the performance in Table 4.2.

Although starting with an airborne reference, still out of sequence, he had a holding gesture, and this is in the correct sequence. The GP would be something as suggested in Table 4.2: floating is what happened while holding. Then the child continued with the correct sequence – holding followed

Table 4.2 Speech, gesture and estimated fields of oppositions in an autistic boy's narration. Elena Levy data, used with permission

Narrative order	Speech	Gesture	Field of oppositions and GP something like:
1	he floated	start of holding gesture	What Happened While Holding: floating
2	he hanged on tight	continuation of holding gesture	Still What Happened While Holding: holding tight
3	[no speech]	flying gesture	The Thing That Happened: flying

by flying. Achieving temporal coherence thus stemmed from catchments and, eventually realizing that the catchments interrelate, one continuing what the other began. This is a kind of imagery-enactment version of the logical relationship of an enabling cause/resultant, which the boy perhaps could achieve in this form even if not with a clear insight into the logical connections themselves.

From a GP point of view, autism seems to involve an imbalance between enactment and speech that was overcome with repeated telling. In the brain, we speculate, the imbalance focuses on the pre-frontal and motor cortexes, with the latter initially flooding the former, impairing its return-output to the right hemisphere and Broca's area.[26] But an awakened pre-frontal area eventually creates something like a normal field of meaningful oppositions. In retelling there is something that activates brain regions and leads the autistic speaker toward the realm of the typical. We can imagine that autistic children might seek this kind of cyclic activation on their own – some of the repetitious behavior often remarked upon in the disorder may be an effort to overcome enactment imbalance. At the same time, however, such an effort is a recipe for impaired social communication. What, for an autistic child, may be an effort for eventual enhancement is limited if not actually counterproductive as a kind of social foray. Thus the child would be denied the kind of propulsion from social-enactive cognition that carries WS children so far.

4.1.12.5 Stuttering

We saw briefly in Chapter 2 the close linkage observed by Mayberry and Jaques (2000) of stuttering and gesture. I add now data of an unusual sort, in the hope that someone elsewhere reading with a research iron in the fire with respect to stuttering will take an interest in it. The data stem from an experiment by Richard Mowery and William Pagliuca, at the University of Ottawa, that I was a part of in the late 1980s (described as "DAF Experiment 2" in McNeill 1992; none of us were clinical stammerers). "DAF" stands for delayed auditory feedback – a crucial feature of the experiment. One's own speech was repeated over earphones after a delay. The delays varied from one-tenth of a second up to several full seconds. DAF often causes speech to slow down and even stop, and this is one feature of clinically stuttered speech. But more dramatically, in this experiment, speech continued without interruption but was severely disrupted by multiple repetitions of the just preceding speech elements. At the shortest delays these repetitions were phonetic elements ("t-t-t-t-take" etc); at slightly longer ones syllables ("ta-ta-ta-take" etc.); at the longest words and even phrases ("take the cake-take the cake-take the cake and cut it"). In other words the amount of speech repeated by the subject corresponded to the amount of delay. In the middle range, the speech took on the quality of clinical stuttering (not far from the 300 m interval during which Levelt *et al.* 1982 concluded that speech is encapsulated as it is uttered and not open to reformulation[27]).

Given these observations, Mead's Loop suggests that stuttering is, in part, a *perceptual* effect. Suppose the thought–language–hand link orchestration of speech, for some speakers, is self-mimicked the way DAF mimicked our speech in the experiment. The Mead's Loop "twist" could produce this with pathology, a kind of echo of the orchestration, a re-orchestration. The effect is something like DAF, an involuntary, never-ending private DAF experiment. This hypothesis explains why stuttering disappears when the speaker's voice is masked by music; then one's speech is not heard, is not mimicked, re-orchestration is not triggered, a possible musical GP is activated as well, and one's personal DAF avoided. A musical GP also may be activated in singing, and this too could avoid re-orchestration (musical GPs are discussed in the following section). It also explains why stuttering does not appear in children until age 3 or 4. This is near the age at which Mead's Loop matures in ontogenesis (as explained in Chapter 5) and stuttering may be tied to the GPs emerging at that developmental stage. Also, a second language, acquired later, might be free of it, even if it is present in the first language (two languages acquired concurrently on the other hand may both be prone to stuttering if one of them is).[28] Finally, DAF predicts the possibility of different forms of stuttering, different points where the attack begins, depending on the speaker's personal "delay" interval, much as we ourselves displayed in the Ottawa experiment. In keeping with the close linkage of stuttering and gesture seen by Mayberry and Jaques, or at least the one-half of it where a gesture immediately stops when stuttering begins, our gestures, while not stopping, became wildly disconnected from speech. This means the mimicry-induced re-orchestration did not include our gestures; if this is also the experience of clinical stuttering, any GP would be ripped apart and speech then cycle freely – i.e., it would stammer.

4.2 INDIRECT EFFECTS

"Indirect" in the sense that the topics to be considered next – musical GPs, gestures in written prose – lie outside the spoken discourse realm that has been our topic so far and where it was plausible to say that the domain could not exist without Mead's Loop. Indirect topics feel the touch of Mead's Loop and the GP but are what they are for other reasons, historical and artistic.

4.2.1 Musical GPs (if they exist)

Could there be *musical* GPs? An informant has described to me her experiences with language at a time in her life when she was intensely engaged in music, practicing the Beethoven piano repertoire six or seven hours at a stretch. During these stints she entirely resided in the world of his music and did not engage in any other kind of activity. To her astonishment, after these long musical sessions, she found that she *could not speak*. It was as if speech had switched off. She is always a fluent, highly spontaneous and engaged speaker of multiple languages, so this was quite contrary to her normal self. Could my informant have bundled all her GP resources into the musical mode, with speech becoming literally speechless?

A musical GP would require something like the semiotic opposition of musical forms to gestural imagery, but it would not be language. I am thinking that musical GPs can be found in the *performing* musician organizing actions (performances on an instrument) via imagery, combined with an awareness of music as structure, to create units of meaningful musical (performance) actions. Crucial to this possibility is that performers gesture as they perform. Conductors are obvious instances but instrumentalists also gesture with their instruments where possible. Even pianists can gesture with torso and head movements. A flutist we were shown used her instrument deictically while playing on it, making pointing gestures not to physical locations, including not to the printed page of music she was reading, but to metaphoric spaces similar to those that speakers create as a routine necessity.[29] Perhaps it was equally a necessity for the musician.

She appeared to be organizing two material carriers simultaneously, one the performance itself (a highly structured sequence of actions), the other pointing gestures within a meaningful and non-concrete space. This seems not unlike the dynamic dimension of language but pertaining to musical thought. Not words, but the kind of thinking that – in its linguistic form – fuels language, but in this case fuels a performance of music. I think it is safe to say that musical ideas are a force in structuring a performance. Do musical GPs exist? A GP is an internally complex cognitive package that is created and manipulated to organize motor control as a whole. Can amalgams of gestures and performing actions embody GPs of music? And are these idea units created as differentiations of contexts? What are the fields of oppositions? Zbikowski (2011) lays out this kind of analysis, revealing something that can be taken as both "static dimension" musical content and "dynamic dimension" torso-formed catchments and fields of oppositions. His subject is Fred Astaire playing the piano as he sings "The Way You Look Tonight," in the 1936 Fred and Ginger film, *Swing Time*. Zbikowski's analysis yields insights into the semiotic oppositions that could animate musical GPs: "One way to both describe and hear this melody is in terms of a number of smaller units. There is, for instance, the falling fifth of bars 1 and 2, which is answered by the arch-like rise and fall through a third that occupies bars 3 and 4. The latter motion is replicated (a step higher) in bars 5 and 6, and again in bars 7 and 8" (p. 85). A performing musician, thinking in such terms, together with other specifically musical relationships of keys, accidentals, modulations, tempo markings, etc., could well be creating complex semiotic oppositions to gesture imagery, and so therefore possibly musical GPs, as they perform. A study of pianists' breathing sometimes suggests prosody-like units. King (2006) observed one professional performer always exhaling at the start of musical phrases, an almost exact parallel; not that the pianist was speaking but that, perhaps, his musical actions were structured as prosody in speaking, which in turn maps GPs as they unpack themselves in speech.

What of the non-musician listener? For even untrained listeners music can be a borrowed form of being. It may absorb the person totally who becomes, for the moment, someone or something else, shaped by the music, the performer and composer. In this respect it equals the cognitive being of speech and gesture but without speech of any sort. A listener, non-musically trained, does not have bundles of significant musical oppositions, but still hears melody, tempo, rhythm, volume, etc. that derive from general experiences with sounds, including music, and esthetic responses from who knows where, and these, plus perceptions across time may be experiences of pure speechless thought. They are not the musical GPs of a musician but still they can be a form of being. Foot-tapping, hand-waving, bobbing, moving the torso back and forth and other reflex-like movements while listening to music provide material carriers that embody the music heard in something like gestures. Levitin and Menon (2003) recorded different fMRI responses in Broca's area to music and to scrambled versions of the same music (keeping acoustic parameters constant), concluding that the response to music is in part a motor reaction in this region of the brain affecting temporal coherence; such coherence could be orchestrated by imagery and gesture in the listener.

This whole line of thinking gives fresh meaning to the catchphrase, "the language of music."[30] Mithen (2006) has put forth the idea that singing was a precursor to speech. Music may now be in a condition of *alternation with speech* for infiltrating the GP, as our opening story of speechlessness after intense musical performance suggests. Singing seems special, since it combines linguistic and musical motor orchestrations, and the instrument is the same vocal system as in speech. It could be organized by imagery similarly. Logically, the speech control mechanism had to be orchestrated by meanings other than the meanings of vocal actions themselves. Humming and other musical efforts meet this requirement and could have been in place along with speech, but not before (since Mead's Loop is still necessary). The oldest discovered musical instrument (a flute), pointing to "second language" instruction, dates back 35,000 years, according to news reports (cf. "Magic Flute: Primal Find Sings of Music's Mystery," *WSJ* July 3–5, 2009, p. A9), but that would be nowhere near the dawn of music if it co-evolved with speech. That would have been 1∼2 mya, according to indications of organized communal life.

4.2.2 Written prose (if it incorporates gestures)

Does writing include hidden gestures? Written prose does not necessarily mean that imagery is lacking; rather, it is possible that we write in such a way that gestures are incorporated into the written text. A reader, reading out loud, will often restore the gestures that are in the written text implicitly. We cannot tell if they are reproductions of the author's gestures, but they are readily evoked and seem to the reader to fit the text. *Written prose* thus may contain hidden gestures. Part of learning to write (not forming letters but composing prose) is discovering how to incorporate them. Much of what we sense as the rhythm of written prose, descriptive as well as dialogue, seems gestural. If you read this small bit from a letter by Jane in *Pride and Prejudice* aloud with hand movements, you readily spatialize the text gesturally:

"something has occurred of a most unexpected and serious nature; but I am afraid of alarming you – be assured that we are all well . . . what I have to say relates to poor Lydia . . . "

On the other hand, a verbatim transcript of actual spoken speech, its original gestures lost, strikes one as distinctly unrhythmic and nearly unintelligible (if you read such a transcript and form gestures, the gestures seem to be repeated beats, hitting each stress peak, which alone remains of the original gestures).

Haldeman: Pat does want to. He doesn't know how to, and he doesn't have, he doesn't have any basis for doing it. Given this, he will then have the basis. He'll call Mark Felt in, and the two of them . . . and Mark Felt wants to cooperate because . . .

Writing is traditionally described as decontextualized, as standing on its own. However this tradition may have missed something. If the origin of language was in fact the origin of language and *gesture*, a unified system, there may be gestures hidden in written prose as a matter of its own history. Writing systems that engage the sounds of speech would encounter the gesture imagery that orchestrates speech actions, the moment the writing goes beyond a mere phoneme notation to actual prose.

Literal transcripts, on the other hand, are famously lacking in fluid qualities, and this could be precisely because the manual gestures that originally occurred have been stripped away, and nothing like the hidden gestures of well-constructed prose have taken their place.

Alphabetical writing aims to depict the sounds of speech. Ideographs, Chinese and Japanese characters specifically, relate to conceptual content more than to sound. Nonetheless, ideographs also depict aspects of speech (cf. Daniels and Bright 1996), and the order of characters on the page exactly matches the sequence of speech and this is certainly in the realm of gestures. So there too, fluent "scannable" writing may be gestural.

5 | Ontogenesis in evolution – evolution in ontogenesis

In the language of children we hear echoes of our ancient past. And what we hear is surprising. Signals exist, especially in the early stages, of gesture-first, its supplantation by speech, its extinction, and finally the emergence of GPs, all in sequence – our ancestors turning at the branch points of Figure 3.13, the timeline of hypothetical gesture-first, its extinction, and the dawn of Mead's Loop.

5.1 PHYLOGENETIC ECHOES

Gesture-first may have existed in the two now extinct human lines, Neanderthals and *Denisova hominin*. It could have existed in our line and extinguished as well, but we have survived to evolve a new form of language, Mead's Loop based on speech–gesture equiprimordiality. This new language, as we have seen, could not have emerged from gesture-first and was a *second origin*. The current chapter draws upon the child language literature and in passing makes points about acquisition (in particular, that it is discontinuous because of the two origin echoes), but it is not an overview of children's language. The purpose is not to uncover the intricacies of language development but to scour the literature for hints, clues, signals, anything at all that suggests something of the origin (or origins) of language. This style of argument has often been doubted but there has been a recent revival of interest in it. MacNeilage (2008) has used an ontogenesis-recapitulates-phylogenesis argument to study aspects of speech origin. Such arguments can be useful and heuristic for sorting out steps in phylogenesis.

It is early ontogenesis in fact that suggests that gesture-first may once have existed. Something like a recapitulation of it arises and performs a scaffolding function like that envisioned by Arbib (2005) and others. It dies out and is followed by a transitional period from 2 to 3 years roughly. GPs emerge at age 3 or 4 years, suggesting that gesture-first had existed once phylogenetically but went extinct and was followed by a new form of language in which speech and gesture imagery merged into the unified packages inhabited by thought and being that we ourselves have now.

We can take the recapitulation argument a step further: when something emerges in current-day ontogenesis only at a certain stage we reason (in this way of arguing) that the original natural selection of the feature (if any) took place in a similar psychological milieu in phylogenesis. We exploit the fact that children's intellectual status is not fixed; it is changing. Thus we look for new states that seem pegged to steps in the ontogenesis of growth points and Mead's Loop underlying them, and consider these steps as possible windows onto phylogenesis. Using this argument, we are able to look at the ontogenesis of the GP and formulate possible phylogenetic landmarks.

5.2 SPEECH DOMINANCE

If we say of two stages of children's development that the "age of pantomime and scaffolding" recapitulates gesture-first, and the "age of language–thought unity" does the same for Mead's Loop, with a "dark age of transition" in between, it is important to see that we are not saying too much but too little. The reason is that a modern human infant is dominated by the effects of Mead's Loop before Mead's Loop itself matures – the orchestration of speech actions, once evolved, seems to have become disconnected from inhabitance by thought and control by gesture, moved ahead in time and has been able to color in this way the whole of ontogenesis.

There may have been adaptive advantages to this disconnect, enabling infant vocalizations to secure adult attachment long before the GP becomes possible and also to provide raw materials for the GP when it arises. The unique and apparently universal adult speech register of "baby talk" is an echo of it and itself shows the adaptation of speech forms for securing attachments.

Infants from babbling onward are developing the ability to orchestrate their vocal anatomy for speech. There is evidence that even newborns have distinctive neural responses to the rhythmic patterns of speech (versus speech played backwards), suggesting the perception of rhythmic pulses at this early age (Peña *et al.* 2003). And the birth cries of newborns of French-speaking mothers and those of German-speaking mothers have different "melody contours," rising for the French, falling for the Germans (Mampe *et al.* 2009) – suggesting *intrauterine* speech perception and motor orchestration matches. Although based on Mead's Loop the neural circuitry for orchestrating vocal actions, babbling and melodic-contouring, once disconnected from the Mead's Loop "twist," could take place as a neuromotor program and not require any control by gesture. The "significance" of the vocal action is movement of the anatomy itself and its audible effects. Infant babbling is the result. From the first birthday onward speech does come to be orchestrated by significances other than the movements of the anatomy but gesture still plays no part, as would be the case if the thought–language–hand link of Mead's Loop has not yet matured. None of this is too surprising; children's development is a mixture of different phylogenetic histories that do not tidily sort themselves out, but this does not prevent the "ontogeny recapitulates phylogeny" hypothesis from having heuristic value.

5.3 ONTOGENETIC CONTINUITY/DISCONTINUITY

Probably the most far-reaching assertion of this chapter is that, contrary to a long-standing assumption that children develop more or less continuously (perhaps with stages, but earlier acquisitions still carrying forward), ontogenesis is not cumulative; it is a mixture of continuity and discontinuity. Continuity comes, paradoxically, from the just described disconnect of speech orchestration, which begins before birth and carries ontogenesis through subsequent discontinuities. Discontinuities arise as echoes of the two origins. Origin-1, as we shall call it, is gesture-first, and it dominates at first but then plateaus and ultimately extinguishes after age 2. The phylogenetic extinction of gesture-first is thus recapitulated. Origin-2, Mead's Loop and the GP, arises at ages 3~4. The GP continues with its own development for several more years and lasts the lifespan. In between is a "dark age" of transition, negotiated by the ongoing orchestration of speech but not yet inhabited by thought and being. Speech still has a social and affiliative function which Werner and Kaplan (1963) believe is limitedly communicative (the child "sharing" *with* others but not yet communicating *to* them; see below) and does not engage thought and being. Speech orchestrations and their elaborations, including proto-constructions and proto-GPs, bridge the Origin-1/Origin-2 discontinuity until Mead's Loop, full GPs, and unpacking into constructions become possible. Looking at the "dark age" may capture gesture-first's maximum achievement. Subsequently, thought starts to inhabit speech and the orchestration unit changes to gesture imagery. By far the most direct evidence of the Origin-1/Origin-2 discontinuity is from Levy (2011b). She describes

a changing relationship between gesture and speech:

– During the *age of the single semiotic,* beats (both head and hand) and pantomime/iconic gestures participate in articulating individual utterances . . .

– During the *transitional age*, beats participate in the beginnings of intralinguistic cohesion, by helping to call forth earlier articulations of experienced or observed events . . .

– During the *age of the dual semiotic*, sequences of iconic gestures – gestural catchments – participate in the creation of intralinguistic cohesion . . .

In this proposal, children enter the age of the dual semiotic – a language-thought-hand link – when iconic gestures take on a cohesive function. This begins a dialectic between imagery, encoded as gestures, and the lexicogrammatical categories of speech. (Levy 2011a)

In other words, the relationship between speech and gesture shifts fundamentally at ages 3~4, when we hypothesize that utterances come to be based on a dialectic between contrasting semiotic modes and inhabitance of language and gesture with thought and being begins.

5.4 THREE AGES

So, in sequence: for the first year vocal actions including babbling for the sake of sound and action alone; from age 1 to 2 roughly, pantomime, pointing and scaffolding (*pace* Arbib 2005); from age 2 to 3 or 4 roughly, a transitional dark age with decreased gestures and limited speech complexity as speech supplants gesture-first; and from age 3 or 4 and into school age, thought–language–hand unity based on maturation of Mead's Loop and the first GPs, this age lasting the rest of the lifespan. In this scenario, gesture-first creates what was predicted for it – a limited gesture language that speech supplants, which then disappears.

5.4.1 The age of pantomime and scaffolding

The "essence" of language at this stage is a single, not a dual semiotic. Such also would have been the mental world of the "gesture-first" creature. As might be expected of supplantation, there is not a consistent speech–gesture temporal relationship. Speech may or may not be present. If it is present it may precede or follow the gesture but rarely synchronizes with it (Butcher and Goldin-Meadow 2000, Goldin-Meadow and Butcher 2003; Capirici *et al.* 1996).

Children's first gestures consist of pointing, and appear a month or two before the first birthday. Indexicality seems to be the cognitive mode at this time – connecting oneself to interesting events and objects possibly by way of the interrupted grasping that is shared with other primates (Vygotsky 1987). These steps arise separately from Mead's Loop and prior to the GP. There is evidence that cultural emblems arise around the same time (Acredolo and Goodwin 1990), showing that this end of the Gesture Continuum is accessed long before gesticulation. The positioning of pointing with emblems suggests again that these gesture forms are, underlyingly, similar (metaphoricity is absent; a shared indexicality is the most likely common theme).

Next to appear are the gesture "names" described by Goldin-Meadow and Butcher (2003). "Names" include both indexicality and a range of semantic relationships matching the semantic relations observed with single words during this period (Greenfield and Smith 1976). An example is placing a cup pantomimically to the mouth, not to drink, but to label the action of drinking (summary from Bates and Dick 2002). Goldin-Meadow and Butcher also found speech–gesture combinations (mostly pantomime and pointing) that foreshadow word–word combinations with the same semantic relationships a few weeks later. Something like gesture scaffolding is taking place. A child who pointed at an object and said, "go" would, a couple of weeks later, produce word–word combinations with "go" plus object names. The early gesture–word combinations cover a range of semantic relations: "open" + points at drawer, "out" + holds up toy bag, "hot" + points at furnace, "no" + points at box, "monster" + two vertical palms spread apart (=big) (Goldin-Meadow and Butcher 2003, Table 3). Although such scaffolding presumably exists with children in all linguistic cultures, there is uncertainty over how universal any given pattern is. A review of the early acquisition of more than 50 languages in Bowerman and Brown (2008) makes clear that languages offer widely different openings. But the overall picture is that something like the "language-slotted" locus on the Gesture Continuum emerges in the second year. However, the gesticulation pole is yet to be reached.

The full story of the second year of development thus may be, first, speech and gesture occurring in rough vicinity of each other but not yet synchronizing; then synchrony of speech and gesture in the non-co-expressive semantic relations characteristic of the language-slotted point on the Gesture Continuum; and last, the same relations in word–word combinations showing supplantation, with gestures dropping away.

Rowe and Goldin-Meadow (2009) discovered that children who make many gestures at 14 months turn out to have, at 4 and-a-half years, 40 months later, significantly larger spoken word vocabularies. Rowe and

Goldin-Meadow consider two explanations. A direct role of early child gestures is the practice they may offer at activating meanings that speech later draws on. However, an indirect role is more germane to our quest. The child's gesture elicits speech from the adult (such as, "yes, that's a doll," when the child points at one, providing a word for the object just when the child is focusing on it).

This role fits nicely into a recapitulation of the ancient mother–infant interaction natural-selection scenario. This would be so if mothers, who use their own gestures to orchestrate their speech, were also able, through mimicry, to use their *child's* gestures to orchestrate this same speech, thus providing the "timely speech" models the indirect role of child gestures suggests. The mirror neurons co-opted by the Mead's Loop thought–language–hand link would connect the mother's mimicry of the child's gestures to her speech.[1]

Vocabulary "spurts" at the end of the second year have a new importance from this vantage point. They are growth spurts of disconnected speech ontogenesis – not connected to gesture or, as it appears in research by Parladé and Iverson (2011), to other communicative channels – facial expression, vocalization and previously acquired words, as well as gesture. Vocabulary spurts are purely disconnected speech outbursts, that occur in some children. Spurts in isolation from other communicative actions reveals speech as a disconnected developmental stream at this pre-Mead's Loop stage. After bursts have passed, the varieties of communicative channels settle down and return to their former alignments.

5.4.2 The dark age of transition

"Dark" because so little is known of gesture performance once patterned speech starts; but also "dark" because it is a limbo period during which the initial "gesture-first" language extinguishes but the "Mead's Loop" language with GPs is yet to emerge. It is a period when speech supplants gesture, is configured by patterning, yet is not yet integrated with thought as a unity. Bannard *et al.* (2009), highlight the limited depth of speech at this stage:

children's speech for at least the first 2 years of multiword speech is remarkably restricted, with constructions being seen with only a small set of frequent verbs (Tomasello, 1992) and many utterances being built from lexically-specific frames.[2]

If this line of reasoning is followed we see children's language development not as a continuous process but as a succession of separate paths, later

Table 5.1 Example "pivot" construction
(Braine 1963, p. 5. Used with
permission from the Linguistic Society
of America).

Want baby
Want car
Want do
Want get
Want glasses
Want hand
Want high (= "put it up there")
Want horsie
Want jeep
Want more
Want page
Want pon (= "put on" or "up on" or both)
Want purse
Want ride
Want up
Want byebye car

---

ones overlapping earlier ones, each providing placeholders awaiting later ones yet to come, and the whole tied together by continuing speech but without the ability to inhabit it with thought and being. Finally, using the ontogeny-recapitulates-phylogeny heuristic, we can propose that gesture-first extinguishes (or sequesters itself, to re-emerge briefly during the age of pantomime and scaffolding).

5.4.2.1 Proto-constructions

Some of the supplanting word–word combinations described by Goldin-Meadow and Butcher resemble what Braine (1963) called "pivot grammars." These too have a limited-depth character. A pivot is a word that anchors other "open class" words to make minimal sentences, a kind of proto-construction. It perhaps is something the gesture-first creature could have produced at its maximal level of development. A child may have several pivots each with its own set of open-class words. There is no overall grammar, only a varyingly long list of pivots and open-class mates. Some examples with "want" as the pivot are listed in Table 5.1 (Braine, p. 7). Expressions of desire are possible but nothing else. If this pictures the greatest achievement of Origin-1 it was shallow indeed.

Table 5.2 Pivot-like slots (Lieven *et al.* 2009.) Used with permission of Mouton de Gruyter

Type of slot	Example utterances	Schema (pivot) with slot
referent (REF)	More choc choc *on there.*	REF *on there.*
	Bow's food *on there.*	
process (PRO)	*I want to* get it.	*I want to* PRO *it.*
	I want to roll *it.*	
attribute (ATT)	Pilchard there *he's* hungry a toast.	*He's* ATT.
	He's upside down.	
location (LOC)	*I sit* on Mummy's bike.	*I sit* LOC.
	I sit there.	
direction (DIR)	*Going* under bridge.	*Going* DIR.
	Going down.	
utterance (UTT)	*Mummy,* here go.	*Mummy,* UTT.
	Mummy, what these.	

Observations by Lieven *et al.* (2009) reinforce this description. They also say that children adopt what they call "templates," which seem to be Braines's pivots, into which the child inserts words. For example, "[some reference word] + on there" was a frequent template, as in "more choc choc on there" or "Bow's food on there." The pivot, "on there," indicates the locus of the reference word with a meaning something like "is located at." Table 5.2 (from Lieven *et al.*, p. 486) is organized to show the different classes of Brainelike "open class" words that each takes, and lists several templates. Each has a limited meaning with its own grammar and shows how an Origin-1 supplanting mode might have looked. Templates become less prominent as the child grows older, a decline that would correspond to the beginning of a new dynamic of language – the age of language–thought unity in GPs.

5.4.2.2 Proto-GPs

"Language in the Crib," the title of a famous monograph by Ruth Weir (1962), alludes to speech recorded from a 2-year-old child, Anthony, as he spoke aloud to himself in bed before dropping off to sleep. Nelson and Levy (1987) carried out a study of another 2-year-old, Emily, whose prolific crib talk throws light into the dark age (also cf. Nelson 1989). Besides pivot structures, Emily showed an ability to form cohesive linkages that connected her current speech to earlier speech in the same crib session. Nelson and Levy suggest that a function of Emily's crib talk was to construct "hypotheses" about what she has experienced or expected to experience, and the main structural effects were to tighten internal cohesion. Here are three examples (at 23 months, still within the dark age) – parentheses enclosing the prior speech being cohesively indexed; underlining the pronoun indexing it (as in Nelson and Levy):

(drink p-water) yesterday did <u>that</u> [Nelson and Levy mention that "p-water" is Perrier water]

Daddy Mommy Daddy (put my into bed in my regular bed) actually actually Mommy did <u>it</u>

One morning when (Emmy go Morm in the daytime) <u>that</u>'s what Emmy do sometime

Note that the pronoun always links back to what could have been a point of differentiation in a prior context. That is, cohesion bridged what was newsworthy, and in each case the pronoun-to-newsworthy ensemble can be seen as a kind of proto-GP – "proto-" because the moment of differentiation (the moment of the pronouns "it," "that") is separated from the linguistic segments that would, in an adult or older child, be part of the GP itself. It exemplifies a principle that Karmiloff-Smith (1979) identified over a range of developmental processes, namely, that when a process is just mastered the child tends to treat it as a unit of functioning in its own right. Here points of newsworthiness were separated as things in their own right, seen in how Emily indicated them as if they were entities. The separation interrupted any GP formation, but may show that it formed a "proto-GP." Both cohesion and differentiation were emerging but were not yet unified points in a field of oppositions. Note too that cohesion is essential for fields of oppositions. A meaningful context for differentiation is internally linked, and this also was emerging in Emily's crib talk (her 2-year-old's contexts were water-drinking, being put to bed, etc.). However, still to come was thought and being "inhabiting" speech and gesture.[3]

5.4.3 The age of language–thought unity

On the evidence to be presented now, language–thought unity appears no earlier than age 3~4. Its development continues well into school years, to age 6 or more, when the ability emerges to fit fields of meaningful oppositions to GPs (rather than, as previously, to fit GPs to fields of oppositions). Sekine (2009a) asked children to describe their walking routes to and from school (in Tokyo, where walking to school is common), and noted any gestures as they explained how they went. The 4-year-olds "matched" gestures to actual routes, known geographically, while 6-year-olds "mismatched" – "produced gestures as if making a virtual space in front of themselves, without regard for orientation to the actual environment" (p. 8). In other words, the younger children created gestures to fit into a map, while the older children created a virtual map that fits their descriptions – the beginnings of fitting fields of meaningful oppositions to GPs.

The evidence for the new language dynamic takes several forms – motion event decomposition, meaningful gesture perspectives, a gesture explosion, metaphoricity, and the onset of self-aware agency. Each exhibits an effect of language–thought unity. That a shift in children's relationship to language takes place, as we suppose, when Mead's Loop matures is seen in that correlations in Japanese speech between gesture and codified onomatopoeia ("mimetics"), while appearing for sounds in the "dark age," occurs in non-acoustic ("metaphoric") uses only after about age 4 (Kita *et al.* submitted). We start with (a) the gesture explosion, (b) motion event "decomposition," and (c) gesture perspectives, all occurring at 3 or 4; we end with (d), metaphoricity and (e) self-aware agency. The last is not just a signal but may be the source of the others.

5.4.3.1 The gesture explosion

In keeping with a gesture-first regime in which speech supplants gesture, 2-year olds, once they have begun to combine words, apparently produce few gestures. Output gradually increases during the third year and then, at some point between three and four years, suddenly rises to near adult levels. The upsurge is a signature of the imagery–language dialectic. More than before, gestures are combining with the child's verbal output. The explosion relates to a dialectic in two ways. First, an abundance of gesture makes a dialectic more accessible; there are more gesture–speech co-occurrences in which it can develop. Second, a dialectic itself can cause the upsurge, since an imagery–language dialectic requires, for the first time, that gestures be part of thinking for speaking.

Figure 5.1 shows the output of gestures across a range of ages by 29 monolingual Mandarin-speaking children retelling the usual animated cartoon (data collected in Taiwan by Susan Duncan; figure from McNeill 2005, p. 184). Children speaking other languages – English, Spanish – show similar bursts. One curve shows the number of gestures per clause, the other the number of episodes recalled. Comparing the two curves establishes that

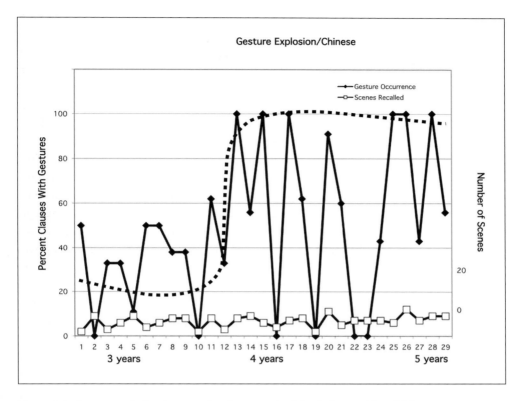

Figure 5.1 Gesture explosion in a sample of twenty-nine Mandarin-speaking children of ages 3 to 5 years. Each child is shown individually in age-order (numbered along the abscissa). Data from Susan Duncan. The occurrence of gestures (shown as the percentage of clauses with gestures) more than doubles at 3 to 4 years. A plausible but, as it turns out, incorrect explanation is that memory for the cartoon improves at that point; however, this is not the case: the number of recalled scenes is constant. The left end of the curve covers the tail end of gesture-first, according to our reconstruction. Gesture is then infrequent, as expected if it is being supplanted by speech, organized presumably by pivot-open-type, mini-constructions. The upsurge at age 3~4 marks the shift to the new form of language with GPs and inhabited by thought and being. Used with permission of University of Chicago Press.

the upsurge of gesture is not due to improved recall of the stimulus – while gesture surges, recall remains flat. We observe, in other words, a *gesture explosion.*

5.4.3.2 Motion event decomposition

The second clue is a reduction in the complexity of gestures depicting motion events. This follows the dark age, in which the same child's gestures

Table 5.3 Gestural viewpoints of English speakers at three ages.[†] Used with permission of the University of Chicago Press

	Viewpoint	M+P Combined	M Decomposed	P Decomposed
Adults	**CVPT**	0%	5%	0%
N=28	**OVPT**	34%	0%	51%
	Dual VPTs	0%	0%	11%
7–11 years	**CVPT**	3%	25%	17%
N=25	**OVPT**	4%	12%	31%
	Dual VPTs	0%	0%	9%
3–6 years	**CVPT**	5%	24%	2%
N=47	**OVPT**	9%	10%	47%
	Dual VPTs	0%	0%	4%

[†]Values are percentages. M = Manner; P = Path. Dual viewpoint gestures have some features in O-VPT, other features in C-VPT (see Parrill 2008). Table from McNeill (2005).

"apparently" carry motion events in their full complexity (the scare-quotes, to be explained shortly).

Decomposition, while seemingly regressive, is actually a step forward. It shows that the gesture has moved beyond pantomime and has developed analytic power, distinguishing motion event components. It thus hints at a new relationship of gesture and thought. Still, the process is incomplete because the analyzed events are not reassembled.

Animated cartoon motion events often are comprised of a simultaneously present Figure, Path, and Manner (using Talmy's 2000 terms). A scene depicting Sylvester rolling down the street with the bowling ball inside him includes, in one event, a Path (along the street), a Manner of motion (rolling), as well as the Figure (Sylvester). Adults speaking a range of languages (English, Spanish, Mandarin) tend to describe such scenes with two kinds of gestures, either Path only (the hand moving down) or Manner and Path together (the hand rotating as it goes down) (Turkish and Japanese are exceptions; see Kita and Özyürek 2003). However, adult speakers of these languages almost never have a gesture depicting Manner only without Path (the hand just rotating). Children of 3~4 match adults in having Path-only gestures but, unlike adults, they have a large number of pure Manner gestures and very few Path + Manner gestures. All of this is shown in Table 5.3. Confirming data from a wider sample of narrators are provided in Parrill (2011). In other words, children "decompose" motion events to pure Manner or pure Path (plus Figure), and tend not to have gestures that combine Path and Manner. Yet, adult speakers of the same languages fuse Path with Manner with high frequency.

Figure 5.2 shows a Mandarin-speaking, a Spanish-speaking and two English-speaking 4-year-olds producing gestures in which Path + Manner cartoon events are decomposed into Manner alone. The first and second panels (Mandarin-speaking and Spanish-speaking) depict Sylvester climbing the drainpipe with pure clambering but no upward motion for the Path; the third panel, English-speaking, depicts Tweety in another episode flying with pure wing-flapping but no Path; in the fourth panel, also English-speaking, a child is imitating an adult model who combined Path + Manner (his hand moving forward and the first and second fingers wiggling for Sylvester running on overhead wires, another episode) with pure Manner (rotating hands, no Path component). It is interesting to observe the imitating child's extended forefingers, echoing the adult's extended two fingers, but without the function they have in the model. In every case, including this direct imitation, the child's gesture decomposed Path + Manner into pure Manner.

Younger children, however, do not show motion event decompositions. Figure 5.3 is a 2;6 (a two-and-a-half) year-old English-speaking girl depicting Sylvester as he rolled down the street with the bowling ball inside him (she concludes that it is under him). The important observation is that she does not show decomposition. In a single gesture, the child combines Path (a sweeping arc to the right) and Manner; this latter in two forms – an undulating trajectory and an opening and closing of her hand as it sweeps right, suggested by the up-and-down arrow.

Is this an adult-like combined Manner–Path gesture? Probably not. A key difference is the child's redundant Manner; an adult would include one but not two (and the opening-closing of the hand is also unlikely). The double Manner is suggestive of pantomime, since redundancy then would heighten the effect. In gesticulation, redundancy muddles the gesture–speech co-expressiveness (which manner is co-expressive?). Werner and Kaplan (1963) observed that the symbolic actions (in this case, gestures) of young children have "the character of 'sharing' experiences *with* the other rather than of 'communicating' messages *to* the other" (1963, p. 42). Sharing with, as opposed to communicating and representing to, is well served by pantomime and could be what we see in the 2;6-year-old's gesture. Her two versions of manner (lower case) offer a lively dramatization, in which the more moving parts the better.

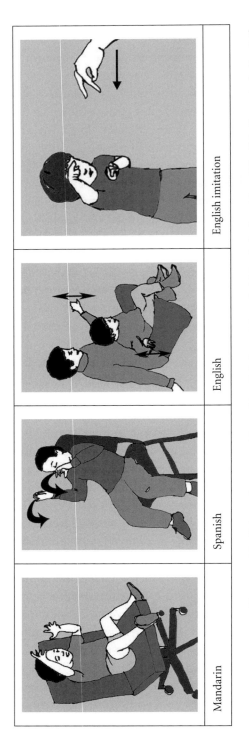

| Mandarin | Spanish | English | English imitation |

Figure 5.2 Motion event "decomposition" shown by 4-year-olds speaking (in left-to-right order) Mandarin, Spanish, and English. Events including Path and Manner (e.g., "Sylvester was climbing [manner] up [path]") are reduced to Manner alone. If Path appears at all, it appears as a separate gesture. Used with permission from University of Chicago Press.

Figure 5.3 A 2;6-year-old appears to combine Path and Manner in a single gesture (Path = her sweeping arc to the right; Manner = undulating trajectory and an opening-closing of her hand, suggested by the up-and-down arrow). See text for explanation. Used with permission from University of Chicago Press.

5.4.3.3 Viewpoint

A correlated phenomenon is the segregation of viewpoints. In observer viewpoint, or O-VPT, the speaker's hands are a character or other entity as a whole, the space is a stage or screen on which the action occurs, and the speaker's body is distanced from the event and is "observing" it. In character viewpoint, or C-VPT, the speaker's hands are the character's hands, her body is its body, her space its space, etc. – the speaker enters the event and becomes the character in part. Unlike pantomime, C-VPT is synchronized and co-expressive with speech and creates psychological predicates (see Parrill 2008 for extensive discussion of viewpoint combinations).

Segregation comes with viewpoint decomposition and also signals a new relationship of thought and gesture. As we see in Table 5.3, young children rigorously separate roles: C-VPT is for Manner, O-VPT is for Path. Adult gestures, including Path + Manner combinations, in contrast are overwhelmingly O-VPT. Distinguishing viewpoints, as segregation reflects, implies that the child has become aware of taking different perspectives on events. It also implies that he knows that he is telling a story (in contrast to

sharing interesting sights with the other), and so sometimes takes the character's role, other times the observer's. Like motion event decomposition,
viewpoint segregation indicates that children are starting to fuse aspects of
thought (here vantage point) with speech but the viewpoints are now seg-
regated. For these children the role of an observer is exclusively to register
Path, that of a character is for Manner.[4]

5.4.3.4 Metaphoricity

Empirical studies of when children's metaphor comprehension first develops agree with a rough 3~4 years date (e.g., Gardner 1974). This also points
to the emergence around then of Mead's Loop. Mead's Loop, as we saw in
Chapter 3, builds into GPs the potential to experience one thing in terms
of another. However, a complication is the many examples of so-called
"children's metaphors." These appear well within the "dark age" (cf. Vosniadou 1987 for a review) and long before Mead's Loop has appeared –
a 24-month-old saying "cup swimming" as he pushed a cup along in his
bath water or "I'm a big waterfall" as he slides down his father's side while
wrestling (from Carlson and Anisfeld 1969, cited by Vosniadou). But do
these "metaphors" depend on metaphoricity, the ability? Carlson and Anisfeld and Vosniadou hold that they are metaphors in the sense that the child
is juxtaposing similar ideas belonging to different categories. That they do
so is evident but does this also imply that the child is actually experiencing
one thing (sliding over his father's side) in terms of something else (a waterfall)? This seems far-fetched. Instead, these verbal expressions could be the
equivalent of the 2-year-old's double manner pantomime: a piling on of
descriptions that are being "shared with the other." That these expressions
happen to spark metaphoric understanding in adults, who unquestionably
possess metaphoricity, is not evidence of course.

5.4.3.5 Self-aware agency

Underlying all these changes is a growing sense of the self as an agent, as
capable of acting in the world, a dimension of experience beyond needs,
demands, sharings, and excitements. Awareness of the self as agent opens the
way to distinguish self as an observer and as a character, and hence to both
the decomposition effect and viewpoint segregation. It gives one a sense
of inhabitance, entering language and gesture and entering is what you do
yourself, as opposed to language and action as display with the other (who
is not seen as "other" either). Self-aware agency is an ability we imagine the

Mead's Loop creature had to have in order for the adaptive advantages of the Mead's Loop "twist" to be felt. If the origin of language included adults giving instruction to infants, and the advantage was in seeing one's own gestures as socially meaningful, awareness of self as agent seems a necessity. GPs then would have been tied to self-aware agency phylogenetically and would tend to emerge ontogenetically now just when this awareness emerges. There seem to be no developmental studies of it, and the best we can do is to say that we predict the first glimmerings of self-aware agency at ages 3∼4.

Susan Hurley (1998) wrote of the link between perspective in a social context and self-awareness as follows: "[H]aving a unified perspective involves keeping track of the relationships of interdependence between what is perceived and what is done, and hence awareness of your own agency" (p. 141).

The concept of self-aware agency is a cousin of the idea in Tomasello (2008) of "shared intentionality," which he argues is fundamental to the ontogenesis of social attachment and the discovery and acceptance of social norms and morality. Like self-aware agency, shared intentionality gives the agent purpose and direction in a self-reflective form, and one can envision a comprehensive ability in which both agency and shared intentionality develop more or less in tandem.

Theory of mind is likewise related to self-awareness. Theory of mind, so called, is really, in its experimental demonstrations by Wimmer and Perner (1983), awareness that self and another have different perspectives on a shared visual field and would not seem possible without awareness of one's self as an independent agent.

These developments all seem to occur at the critical ages of three to four years and the linkage of Mead's Loop to self-awareness helps explain why the GP emerges then too, more or less.

5.4.3.6 Advent of gesticulation

This is the final step in our survey of the "age of language–thought unity," the child's arrival at the gesticulation pole of the Gesture Continuum.

I am indebted to Gale Stam (pers. comm.) for the examples in Table 5.4 of pantomime-to-gesticulation transitions by a second precocious 2;4-year-old recounting the bowling ball episode. The listeners were his mother and grandmother. The gestures on lines (4), (10) and (12) commence in gesture-first manner without speech-synchrony. In (10) and (12), however, two changes occur: (a) gestures and speech become synchronized, and (b) viewpoints emerge. In microcosm, pantomime is being exchanged

Table 5.4 Gestures and speech by 2;4 year-old boy describing the bowling ball episode. Gale Stam data, used with permission.

(1)	Mom	what did the rabbit do?
(2)	Evan	he just go away for the man
(3)	Mom	\<yeah\>
(4)	Evan	and h[e* he went \<a\>and<u>\<d\></u> <u>\<uuhm uuh\></u> // **down** /]

a   b

(a) pantomimic: full body, both arms rise, hold overhead, and then body goes down with one hand landing on the floor,
(b) gaze down and retracts to sitting. \<falling down\>

(5)	Grandmother	he went down?
(6)	Evan	yeah
(7)	Grandmother	did you see * remember the ball?
(8)	Evan	yeah
(9)	Grandmother	what happened with the ball?
(10)	Evan	a\<a\>nd he did dunk ⌈it in to<u>\<o\></u> **the**\<e\>]\<uhm\>

iconic: right hand raises and then lowers \<Tweety dropping ball into drainpipe\>

(11)	Mom	what did he do with the ball?
(12)	Evan	he\<e\> d[u* dunk **it** in]

iconic: right hand raises and then lowers \<Tweety dropping ball into drainpipe\>

for gesticulation. The (a) and (b) steps occurred together, as they should if emerging viewpoints and speech-synchronized gesticulations are two signals of the GP.

Further insight comes from the role of cohesion, or its lack, in the genesis of the hallmarks of language–thought unity. Levy (2008, 2009–10, 2011b) observed in her repeated narrations experiment an inverse relationship of pantomime and discursive fluency – as fluency increased, pantomime decreased. (This in itself suggests that pantomime is not involved in speech orchestration.) Decreased pantomime was the case with a 13 year-old autistic boy and is also true of normal development. What drives pantomime into its own Gesture Continuum slot is the emergence of dynamic speech–gesticulation *cohesion*, a particular property of orchestrating speech with imagery, the imagery unifying the utterance and linking it to the context, that cannot be formed with pantomime. All the features that we have studied – the gesture explosion (triggered by gestures metapragmatically indicating themes), decomposition and viewpoint (directly increasing cohesion and so motivated by it), metaphoricity (also increasing cohesion and so motivated by it) – are linked to increasing cohesion, either as cause or effect. It completes the package of features we consider to herald the dawn of the GP and maturation of Mead's Loop.

Cohesion shows up in another form that suggests the last gasp of gesture-first and supplantation with speech, mixed with and overlapping the onset of gesture–speech unity. Özçaliskan and Goldin-Meadow (2009) discovered that gesture is also a groundbreaker in establishing new constructions, not simple pivots and open words but two-argument constructions. However, gesture does not foreshadow adding a third argument. A two-argument example, one argument in gesture and the other in speech, is "I paint" + GIVE, with a conventional extended upright palm to request a crayon (Özçaliskan and Goldin-Meadow, Table 1, note *h*). The speech + gesture combination introduces an enablement request that is followed, later, by the same construction in speech alone ("I want to draw with a crayon" or such).

Three-argument constructions ("I cook bunny for suppertime") however appear in speech and gesture at the same time; combinations with speech + gesture that have separate constituent functions do not pave the way.

The two-argument and three-argument constructions seem to arise in a child's development at the same time, which suggests that some of the time a child is in pivot mode. Speech is naturally then limited to just two arguments, since the gesture is pivot or open and speech is the other. But when the two-argument combinations in speech are GPs, plus their unpackings, the two-argument constructions are unified with gestures. They are now *gesticulations*, no longer pantomimes. There is no pivot-like gesture–speech combination, and into these proper GPs third arguments readily fit. Their non-forecasting character is thus another indication that the dark age is closing and the age of inhabiting speech beginning.

By age 5 inhabitance in language is solidly established. We saw at the end of Chapter 3 its grip on children as young as 5, a grip so strong that children that age consider it less likely that an English-speaking child they had just met would grow up speaking French than that the same child would change its race (Kinzler and Dautel, 2012).

5.4.3.7 Consciousness, developmentally

A prediction (as far as I know not formulated before) is that focal attention at L-centers should not be possible until thought-inhabited language develops at ages 3 or 4, and would not be fully developed for several years more (cf. Sekine 2009a who finds, as described above, examples at age 6 of children starting to shape fields of meaningful oppositions to make differentiations within them possible). Without GPs, there is no unpacking and no core versus peripheral consciousness; everything is in a panorama with any focus determined by external events. Similarly, pre-Mead's Loop creatures (including current-day chimps) would not control their own awareness via symbols, even though they are able to focus on events in the world. The ability to control one's own awareness is yet another result of Origin-2. That chimps (they standing in here for all the pre-Mead's Loop creatures) cannot focus attention with the use of symbols is testable in an experiment proposed at the end of Chapter 6.

5.5 SEMANTICS OF THE SCENARIO

What can we infer from observations of current-day children's development about the mother–infant scenario and the selection pressures brought to bear within it? A number of things, it turns out.

The creatures in which language originated experienced two origins. Origin-1, or gesture-first, led to pantomime and pointing and was supplanted by limited, shallow speech structures, like pivot grammars and is echoed in the speech produced around the second year of life by contemporary children. Origin-1 in our ancestors "extinguished" and is recapitulated in ontogenesis within even the same sentences on occasion, and in general in how pivot-grammars dead-end to nowhere. Origin-1 in our ancestors however "extinguished" in the sense of reaching a plateau (and did literally extinguish with the other two human lines, Neanderthals and *Denisova hominim*). Origin-2 provided the dual semiotic, a new form of gesture capable of merging with co-expressive speech, of which the gesture became the orchestrator. This scenario bears broad similarity to the origin scene described by Bickerton (1990). With the final step came speech–gesture synchrony, the gesture explosion, viewpoints, inhabitance by thought, and L-center focal awareness. Pantomime and pointing, the gestures of gesture-first, moved into their own places on the Gesture Continuum, itself a product of the second origin, with pointing undergoing cultural anchoring. The mental world of the second-origin creature was shaped in situations where value attached to unifying complex actions under imagery and regarding them as social, and this became possible with the advent of awareness of the self as an agent, a scenario to which specifically the adult–infant interaction situation gave adaptive value.

The dual semiotic and hence GPs arose because they were adaptive in unifying actions during the induction of infants into culture by adults (chiefly mothers). In turn, the GP created its own selection pressures to find ways to stabilize this dialectic. It is this step, along with growing discourse cohesion, which altered gesture from pantomime to gesticulation, since pantomime is incapable of unifying gesture and speech and of unifying speech cohesively.

6 | Alternatives, their limits, and the science base of the growth point

6.1 ALTERNATIVES

It is admittedly unorthodox to present major hypotheses – the GP and Mead's Loop – and the evidence for them before discussing alternatives and their limits, but I have had little choice. With a few exceptions, including gesture-first, which was integral to presenting Mead's Loop and the possibility of two separate origins of language, to explain alternatives and to say why they come up short or deal with other topics, the reader must already understand the GP and Mead's Loop, and this has determined the order of our discussion. This order also better reflects the actual history of this book than would a fantasy picture of surveying the field in advance, finding in it gaps, and now plugging them. More realistically I have proceeded from the GP and Mead's Loop and then discovered how other approaches resembled or differed. So with this acknowledgment we take up major alternatives, their resemblances, differences, and limits.

6.1.1 Gestures – are they supplements?

A supplement, as used here, is when speech and gesture cover different ideas that, although related, cannot form a single idea unit. The phenomenon is distinct from co-expressiveness, where speech and gesture express possibly different sides of one idea at the same time. Supplements can be discerned on different levels – semantic (as in the "firehose" next) and pragmatic (as in gestures in silence after that) – and the status of the two, vis-à-vis the GP, differs.

6.1.1.1 The "firehose"

In a formulation twenty-five years ago by Bill Eilfort and Suzanne Markel Fox (never published), the gestures-as-supplements hypothesis was likened to a firehose in which water pressure, crimped at one place (a breakdown of speech), causes a bulging out someplace else (a gesture); a recent version, called the "trade-off" hypothesis, has been proposed by de Ruiter (2007) and tested by de Ruiter *et al.* (2012). We can use the firehose metaphor to show how supplements differ from co-expressivity. According to co-expressivity speech and gesture express the same idea in unlike semiotic modes, rather than gestures supplementing speech with a new idea.

The problem is to distinguish the firehose and co-expressivity empirically. A gesture and utterance are co-expressive if they cover the same idea unit. This doesn't mean they have the same content; in fact often they do not. Idea units are multifaceted, with some facets expressed better in language and others in gesture. Indeed, given multifaceted co-expressiveness, non-redundancy is to be expected. Still, gesture and speech share the same underlying idea. De Ruiter *et al.* (2012) have performed the first experimental test of the firehose of which I am aware, and find evidence against it: "iconic gesture rates were not affected at all by codability [= the ease with which one or more words express some reference]. If gesture indeed facilitated speech planning, it is hard to explain why codability affected the length and planning times of referring expressions, but had no effect at all ɪɪ the gesture rate" (ms. p. 244). This is not anything like the firehose bulge.

Other arguments against the firehose are derived from the GP and Mead's Loop. I have three that support co-expressivity over the firehose.

1. The positive correlation between speech and gesture with communicative dynamism (as noted earlier, speech and/or gesture "pushing the communication forward"; cf. Firbas 1971). I refer back to Figure 4.4. We see there that over the full range of materializations, from zero to full, speech and gesture respond to the variable of CD together and *in the same direction.* This is the reverse of the negative correlation the firehose expects.
2. Gestures depict rhemes – the novel departure, the point of differentiation in the utterance. This too is clear in Figure 4.4. If, as on the firehose principle, the gesture expresses what is left over from speech, it should be anything but the rheme (unless the speaker is being deliberately uncooperative). But gestures express rhemes specifically.
3. The gesture stroke coincides with the co-expressive part of the linguistic utterance but the preparation for the stroke precedes this segment. That is, the gesture has already started before it "observes" what speech does not express.

So the theory of a semantic "firehose" supplement does not hold; instead speech and gesture are co-expressive and synchronous.

6.1.1.2 Pragmatic silence

Gestures in silence, in contrast, do supplement speech but at the same time move one or more steps away from gesticulation on the Gesture Continuum. To quote a study of the rhetorical uses of silence, "[S]ilence . . . is an integral element of discourse, and constitutes a socially significant act when it is voluntarily performed during a conversation. Such acts are generally intended to address some aspect of the relationship between the parties involved in the interaction, by way of establishing, maintaining, curtailing, or clarifying the personal connections that exist between them" (R. McNeill 2010, pp. 69–70). While these silences leave broad rhetorical gaps, gestures appear in silences with similar pragmatic effects. Such gestures lack co-expressivity and, indeed, that is their function. They create a context in which *to be silent is felicitous.* In this narrower silence, speech halts, the gesture takes over, and this is done for pragmatic effect. Gestures move over one notch to the language-slotted position and become part of the sentence structure, occupying an unspoken slot, e.g., "the parents were [a gesture suggesting distraction]." The gesture becomes a predicate adjective; there is no speech, and indeed that is the point. Silence-filling gestures have socio-pragmatic functions that arise from enabling speech to stop. In my constructed example there is a sense that a felicitous use implies rapport with the interlocutor. Insofar as speech-supplementing gestures fulfill pragmatic functions, understanding them requires taking into account the social interaction between speaker and listener and that the gesture is part of a deliberate communicative event (rather than the unwitting imagery component of a dialectic with speech at the gesticulation pole).

6.1.2 Gestures – are they asynchronous?

The claim that gestures are asynchronous with speech is surprisingly persistent and takes numerous forms, yet is incorrect as a general description (asynchrony has specialized domains of application, such as organizing silences, as just described). Exact synchrony is not essential to the GP so long as the same underlying idea is represented in two unlike semiotic modes and this triggers dialectic activity. But the point of the alternative is that there is a systematic lack of synchrony.

6.1.2.1 Illusory asynchrony

Butterworth and Beattie (1978) are often cited as asserting that gestures tend to be launched during brief pauses and anticipate speech. However

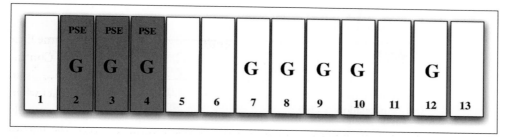

Figure 6.1 Hypothetical gestures during pauses and phonations. Diagram conceived and constructed by Fey Parrill. Used with permission of University of Chicago Press.

this is a misrepresentation of their paper. Two issues must be considered. First, the phases of gestures must be identified. It is one thing to say that gesture preparations precede speech and may occur during hesitations (as they sometimes do), and quite another to say that gesture strokes do (they rarely do). The second issue is with what these strokes do synchronize.

Butterworth and Beattie filmed college tutorial sessions and looked where gestures began. Presumably, although they do not say so, the beginning of a gesture was for them the onset of preparation. Concentrating on the "fluent" phases of speech (utilizing the definitions of fluent and hesitant phases from Goldman Eisler 1968: "fluent" speech, while indeed fluent, contains brief pauses as well), they found that gestures, *per unit of time,* started during pauses about three times more often than during phonations. This is the factoid that has become part of the folklore of gesture–speech timing. It is often repeated in the following stronger form: gestures tend to take place during pauses, not during speech.

The shift in meaning from the original to the legendary claim, highlighted by my italicization of the phrase "per unit of time," is the crucial error. Butterworth and Beattie did not demonstrate that gestures occur during pauses. This would be false – most gestures, by far, occur during phonations. What they said is that the probability, *per unit time,* of a gesture launch is greater during pauses than during phonation. This may or may not be so (see below), but without doubt it is a fact that far more time is spent phonating in fluent discourse than pausing, and therefore that more gesture onsets also occur during phonations than pauses, and this would be so even if (contrary to fact in some circumstances) it were true that more gesture occurs per unit time in pauses. To see this point, imagine that Figure 6.1 represents a series of units of time, with the gray boxes representing pauses ("pse") and the white boxes phonation. In such a situation, the claim could be made that a gesture (G) was initiated in 100 percent of all pause units, but in only 50 percent of all phonated units. However, it is also the case that

Table 6.1 Gesture rates (onsets per 1000 s) in fluent speech compiled from Nobe 2000

	Butterworth and Beattie (phases unknown)	Nobe (onsets of preparation phases)
During silent pause	280.1	321.7
During phonation	106.9	372.3

almost twice as many gestures occur during phonations as pauses. Thus, because pause units of time are less frequent than phonation units of time, examining the initiation of gesture by comparing units of time can lead to a deceptive result.

Furthermore, the probability per unit of time of a gesture launch during a pause may not, in fact, be higher than during phonation. Using the same definitions of fluent speech and pause, Nobe (2000) compared onsets in pauses and onsets in phonations in the narrations of six subjects delivering a narration of our standard cartoon stimulus, with the results summarized in Table 6.1.

Contrary to the near 3:1 predominance of pauses in the Butterworth and Beattie column, Nobe finds a slight predominance of gesture initiations during *phonation* (though non-significant). In Nobe's case, we know these are the onsets of preparations. The strokes to which the preparations led occurred during phonations to an even greater degree – 90 percent.

To explain the difference between the studies, Nobe speculates that the original Butterworth and Beattie result could have related to the specific speech situation from which their data came (tutorials). His hypothesis is that this dialogic situation resulted in a higher occurrence of "turn attempt-suppression signals" (Nobe 1996, p. 45, quoting Duncan and Fiske 1977). A gesture with a turn-attempt suppression function is obviously more likely during a pause. Given the ambiguity of what the pause signifies, a listener may incorrectly think a turn has ended, and the speaker then starts a gesture to keep the floor. Such a gesture would also automatically precede the linked speech – and hence both aspects of the Butterworth and Beattie result are explained by Nobe's ingenious argument. This turn-holding strategy would rarely be evoked in cartoon narrations.

6.1.3 Gestures – are they based on practical actions?

This alternative was discussed at length in Chapter 4, §4.1.1, with the conclusion that it does not distinguish the "new-actions" of gestures from the "old-actions" of practical action. It is mentioned again here as a reminder and cross-reference. Mead's Loop and the thought–language–hand link created new forms of action, where significances other than those of the actions themselves orchestrate the motor areas over a thought–language–hand link in the brain. While using the same motor neurons, schemas, and musculature as practical world-directed actions, the "gesture–action" path diverges from that of "action–action." The divergence is shown most directly in the IW case (Chapter 3, §3.8.1), where, under no-vision conditions, practical actions cannot occur but speech-synchronized, co-expressive gestures are normal. And with unafflicted speakers, gestures like "up through" that may look like practical actions (lifting up in this case) contain no such action but are orchestrations of the motor system around images (in this example) like "rising hollowness."

6.1.4 Gestures – are they grammatical?

Some gestures are partly grammatical. The emblem and the point have standards of form, conventional meanings and functions, and are socio-culturally constituted and maintained. They do not have combinatoric potential however, and thus fall short of an essential feature of language. And, as explained in Chapter 1, when they enter into dialectics with speech it is because they have been absorbed by and can ride on gesticulations. Enfield (2004) however has presented examples of speech-synchronized gesticulations that he describes as combinatoric. Such combinations, should they exist, would have major significance for the concept of an imagery–language dialectic. It would be necessary then to study the possibilities of a dialectic of lessened semiotic oppositions involving two combinatoric systems, one the syntax of speech, the other the putative syntax of gesture. Such a combination might even point to some other mechanism than a dialectic. However, although Enfield uses the term "syntax," it is in a broad style that equates it with anything structured and hides the semiotic opposition of gestures to linguistic form that constitutes the dynamic in GPs. The gestures he describes seem familiar – they are global, synthetic, and *non*combinatoric, in that they do not produce syntagmatic values and larger units. What he has discovered, in fact, appears to be *another means of forming catchments* – those discourse segments carried in gesture (cf. Chapter 2). We have seen three kinds of catchments so far, one based on the speaker's own field of meaningful oppositions (the contest of opposed forces in Figure 2.8), one based on an elaboration of imagery (elaboration in answer to a listener query in

Figure 2.2), and one based on prolonged gesture holds (McCullough 2005, Park-Doob 2010, cf. note 15, Chapter 2). Enfield's examples illustrate a fourth, based on the structure of the objects being described, plus the speaker's intention to explain them. The discourse segment reflects this referential information, filtered by this explanatory goal (possibly metapragmatically organized). There is no gesture structure apart from these discourse segments, and no "syntax" of gesture.

The example from Enfield (2004) in Figure 6.2 is accompanied by a repetition of the elaboration example in Figure 2.2 from one of our English speakers. Enfield's speaker, a Laotian fisherman, is explaining how the mouth of a fish trap is flared open, then narrows and then expands again, and how a fish, passing through the opening, is trapped inside. The first gesture depicts the shape of the mouth; the next its smallness (a microscope effect, not unlike Figure 4.6); and the last the fish inside. "Symmetry-dominance" is the presumed gesture construction and is modeled after an actual syntactic pattern of the same name in sign languages of the deaf (e.g., Sandler 1993, Engberg-Pederson 1994).

In the gesture version, a two-handed gesture is performed with the hands arranged *symmetrically* (first panel); then, one hand becomes *dominant* and the other passive relative to it (third panel). Enfield regards this as a syntactic pattern with the third-panel gesture dependent on the first-panel gesture (the second panel would be an interpolation). The pattern recurs across speakers whenever an entity (like a trap) is being described and the focus shifts from the entity as a whole to a detailed or functionally dependent part. But this is not a recurring pattern of gesture forms; it is a recurring kind of discourse segment. Enfield himself states the discourse pattern: "Typically, speakers start an artifact description by introducing the overall shape and size of the artifact.... Having established the overall size and shape of an artifact, a speaker then has a context for making finer specifications" (Enfield 2004, p. 60). Here he describes exactly a discourse segment and not a gestural construction. The continued "dominant" hand is in fact a gesture catchment. In the English speaker's gesture, there was no symmetry phase, the discourse segment began with a one-handed gesture and then became a two-handed gesture in which one hand was dominant. This is again a discourse pattern but contrary to the presumed construction. Again, a catchment is in force – here, space carried the cohesive theme.

Among catchments, then, we have four sources of cohesion (not to say there are not more):

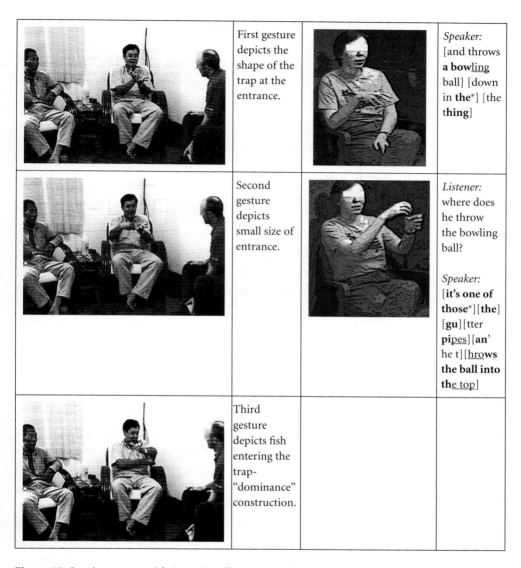

Figure 6.2 Laotian gesture with (questioned) grammatical construction from Enfield (2004) compared to image elaboration (Figure 2.2 repeated). See text for interpretation. Laotian images used with permission of de Gruyter Press.

Fields of meaningful oppositions, the "it down" bowling ball as a force for good, the most basic kind.

Elaborations, the example in Figure 2.2.

Artifacts described at two levels of detail, the discourse approach of starting large and moving on to details.

Prolonged holds, comments on and/or additions to the theme embodied in the hold.

Sweetser (2007) presented an example that also seems to reveal something like a static dimension structure of gesture. However, it is impossible to separate this dimension from the dynamic. Sweetser wrote:

> In one example, a lecturer says he will stop talking, and metaphorically cuts off the talking process with a cutting gesture parallel to the front of his body . . . But he cuts with a pointing hand, pre-formed for a following indexical point at the audience as he says "interact with you," and then for a temporal point at the floor as he says "I'll do that here" (= "now"). This STOP gesture has rich conventional componential structure, even though its interpretation depends on accompanying speech. (from the abstract)

Consider how this gesture–speech combination could have emerged. The speaker (we suppose) was getting late for his plane. His GP (the "stop" emblem, absorbed by pointing that was itself used metaphorically for the temporal moment of speaking, combined with either "interact with you" or "I'll do that now" or both – the description is unclear on timing) differentiated a field of meaningful oppositions that we can sketch as *TIME IS GETTING SHORT: STOP NOW TO INTERACT* (as usual after academic talks). If we are right, this utterance and gesture entered into an imagery–language dialectic and comprised at least one GP. The static dimension is important for describing constraints and outcomes of this emergent process. The dynamic dimension gives insight into the thinking, speaking, and their mutual impacts. Certainly how we picture dialectics of gesture and language can be enriched by further insights along these lines.

True syntactic combinatory in gestures, with morphs and syntagmatic values, appears only in the *absence* of speech – sign languages and the experiments with speech-denial in Chapter 3, the "birth" of novel morphs and syntagmatic values; but when speech is present gesture retains its imagery semiotic and enters into a dialectic relationship with it. In sign languages, there is a real system of grammar, evolved in the absence of speech, and the symmetry-dominance pattern found there is a true grammatical phenomenon.

6.1.5 Modules

The concept of a mental module dates to Fodor (1983). A module is a hypothetical self-contained mental "device" that carries out specific (not necessarily simple) functions. Its inputs are from a restricted set of the other devices (possibly just one) and its outputs go to a restricted set of different devices (again possibly just one). The input/output contacts are formed in advance and do not change as a result of the module's own activity. The parallel is with the modular design of computers and stereo equipment, although the idea of separate "faculties" of the mind, as Fodor points out, goes back to the nineteenth century and phrenology. Like their electronic exemplars, modules are said to have self-containment such that, when a breakdown occurs, the damage is limited and repairs, including self-repairs, can be accomplished on a limited scale. Because of this supposed advantage modules are thought to have had a selective advantage in evolution and thus have come to permeate the mind/brain. In Fodor's original form, it was an inspired idea with which to explain how certain illusions are impervious to correction (such as the Müller-Lyer). Which is longer? We know that tip-to-tip the lines are equal, and yet they look different and refuse to look otherwise. Perhaps a module is tapped:

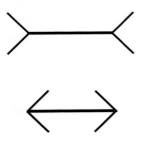

Such are some of the a priori arguments for modularity. It is equally clear however that, outside of persistent illusions, modules of language and thought are contradicted by the synchrony of co-expressive speech and gesture in forming psychological predicates. Whatever one may think of modularity in general, gesture and speech fly in the face of any modular scheme. Anything on the dynamic dimension that combines imagery and linguistic form and is inseparable from context also contradicts it. The GP, this unity of imagery and language form differentiating fields of meaningful oppositions, is the flat opposite of it. Speech–gesture unity, psychological predicates, and the inclusion of context into the GP are further contradictions. The "inhabiting" of language and gesture with thought and being are still more contradictions. Another equally telling difference is that modular theories impose a rigid thought-first, symbolic expression-after order, and this too the GP contradicts. I can cite two modularity hypotheses pertaining to gesture, the Information-Packaging Hypothesis (IPH) due to Kita (2000), and the Postcard Hypothesis (PCH) due to de Ruiter (2007, which his latest experiment, summarized under the "firehose," seems to contradict). IPH and PCH are not identical but both are modular and neither can explain the imagery–language dialectic.

The IPH and PCH were devised with a clear appreciation that gesture and speech are psycholinguistically bound, and must be dealt with jointly. For this reason they are instructive of how modularity blocks explanations and even descriptions of an imagery–language dialectic.

In the IPH, gesture and speech are said to be two independently running streams. Imagery is the path-breaker, preparing the way for the linguistic stream, and this is observable when speech hesitates for some reason. The streams meet at an "interface," where information (including timing information) flows between them, but there is otherwise no contact.

In the PCH, gesture and speech originate together and divide the communicative stream between them, part going to speech and another part to gesture (it is thus a "firehose" type model, contradicted as noted by the experiment described earlier). From then on they are independent (the modular feature). Mead's Loop could have produced the joint speech–gesture stage of the PCH, before the division, but after that it is incompatible with a dialectic and could not have been part of its origin.

One telling difference is how each of these theories explains speech–gesture synchrony. In the GP synchrony is a matter of thought. It is a necessity, an *inherent* feature. In the IPH and PCH, synchrony is *external*, a mechanical effect produced by signals passing between the gesture and speech modules. It is not a necessity in either theory, and neither has an intrinsic reason for it; it is to them arbitrary, requiring attention because it *is* a fact, but it could just as well have been asynchrony.

Indeed, in the IPH, speech–gesture *a*synchrony is the necessity (it is then that the gesture finds a path for the next output of speech). In keeping with the IPH such asynchronies do occur. Some gesticulations do occur out of step with their speech (and these are real gesticulations, not the gestures of silence discussed earlier). The IPH explains them as preparing information for the speech module which then formulates the next bit of output. But in the examples of this process that Kita cites the gestures have a more intimate connection to speech than asynchrony implies.

In fact, what look like path-breakers in these examples were components of psychological predicates, and the "path" they laid out was actually a field of meaningful oppositions. The gesture created this field and a second gesture, synchronous with speech, then differentiated it. This function of the asynchronous gesture predicts that it should be followed by such a

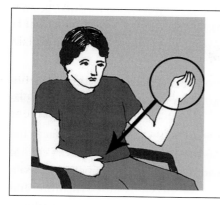

Figure 6.3 Gesture "pathfinder." The first gesture, in silence, created a field of meaningful oppositions; the second, with speech, differentiated a GP within this field, meaning *THE WEIGHT FALLS* (= field of oppositions): *HE GETS CLOBBERED* (= the GP). Used with permission of University of Chicago Press.

second gesture that is co-expressive and synchronous with speech. It also predicts that the asynchrony would be reserved for new fields of meaningful oppositions. In Figure 6.3, there first is an isolated gesture and then, second, a speech-synchronous co-expressive gesture (the example was first analyzed by Kita 2000). The second gesture looks like a miniaturized version of the first, but the two gestures are in fact not the same: the first is establishing a field of meaningful oppositions which the second is differentiating. In the cartoon, Sylvester throws a weight onto the opposite end of a board balanced on a box. The board catapults Sylvester to Tweety's window and he grabs him. As he comes back down, Tweety in hand, he lands on the end of the board from which he was catapulted. Now the weight on the opposite end is catapulted up, over and, as such things go in the cartoon world, finally lands on *him*. The first panel of Figure 6.3 is the large downward gesture of the weight falling. It occurred in silence. Possibly this silence had the earlier mentioned pragmatic function of drawing attention to the gesture as it set up a field of meaningful oppositions. It was immediately followed by the second, smaller gesture, probably a beat, that was exactly synchronized with the co-expressive speech, "gets clobbered." This second gesture and its synchronized speech comprised a GP differentiating the field of meaningful oppositions created with the first gesture.

The GP idea unit was thus about the impact of the bowling ball. The reduced gesture size was perhaps a beat, as mentioned, or could have been metaphoric for the achievement aspect of the GP, focusing on the climax of the arc, not the whole but the moment of impact. The GP then was: the large gesture = *BOWLING BALL FALLING DOWN* which the small gesture plus speech differentiated = *CLOBBERS HIM.*[1]

> [//**first gesture**// <u><and></u>] / [and **he get**<u>s clobbered by the weight</u>]
> (silence)

Bringing this discussion back to modularity, the first gesture, far from belonging to a separate module, was part of the same psychological predicate that included the GP.

When two theories – here modularity and GP – cover the same facts, the differences between them point up areas that one or the other theory cannot reach. The IPH applies when speech and gesture are out of phase. However, it does not have any organic explanation of speech–gesture synchrony and does not show how gesture and speech jointly absorb context (and, hence, how the first and second gestures relate): these are the domain of the GP.

6.1.6 Models

While modules can be likened to electronic devices, this section argues that purpose-designed artificial devices of any kind do not model GPs and their evolved global-synthetic semiotics (for arguments against the computer model metaphor, see Gigerenzer and Goldstein 1996). As a result, they do not model an imagery–language dialectic.[2] Instead, these systems model gestures (as in conversational agents and physical robots), in a bottom-up, features-to-whole, language-like way that, even if synchronized with speech, is incapable of forming a dialectic.

The problem is not just adjusting models to include imagery. Mead's Loop is beyond their reach basically because action, which speech fundamentally is and which the linguistic system evolved in part to orchestrate, does not exist as a unit in these artificial systems. They instead construct actions using a feature-based mode wherein the features are the units and the actions the outcomes (in a GP, features are outcomes, actions are the units).

We can consider proposals for bringing artificial systems within the Mead's Loop orbit – most importantly, having coordinative structures attracted to idea units, and analog devices – but they create problems of their own, suggesting some sort of fundamental incompatibility of systems designed for artificial devices and the evolved biological system of language on its dynamic dimension.

6.1.6.1 The global requirement

Foremost of these difficulties is the global-synthetic imagery of the GP, essential for its dialectic. The problem is that the use of features in computational models forces the process of gesture creation to be combinatoric, to move from parts to whole rather than whole to parts; and this is the opposite semiotic from that of imagery. Once created we can usually identify form and meaning features, e.g., enclosure means interiority, and so forth. But we must not conclude from this observation that composition was the process of creation; it is the result of our analysis. Features are products. This is the paradox of natural gestures – they work in the opposite direction from modeling based on features.

6.1.6.2 Coordinative structures

Coordinative structures may provide a partial way out. They are "flexible patterns of cooperation among a set of articulators to accomplish some functional goal" (anonymous Yale linguistics handout found on Google; accessed 02/14/07). The approach would be to exploit the inherent flexibility of coordinative structures in such a way that the significance of gestures and speech activates and shapes them.

This process could indeed work from global meaning to forms. It seems however that form features still need meanings of their own. Form features need their own meanings in order for the global meanings above to locate them. These meanings would be things like "spherical," "interior," "downward," and "effort." Such a requirement again conflicts with the global property.

Here is a sketch of what such a model might try to do to skirt the problem:

1. Suppose that global significances ("thrusts-bowling-ball-down") trickle down and the author of "it down" improvised something that, after the fact and upon examination, we observe to mean "spherical," "downward," and "effort" – what does she need in order to do this?
2. She needs to perform *an action that embodies the global meaning.* Does this imply form–meaning features? Or is it enough to "act"? Is the idea of propelling a bowling ball downward sufficient to generate a gesture with the significance that we are after, without positing a preexisting "spherical" feature?
3. *A stab at resolution*: given a thought–language–hand link, *ideas or significances can be the "attractors" of coordinative structures;* coordinative structures then zero in on these attractors, the properties of the attractor bringing out features in the coordinative structures interactively: in this way, *gesture features are outcomes, not initial conditions,* with significances that derive from the action as a whole: and this is the global property. There is no lexicon of feature–meaning pairs (no "facing down → force

downward" and the like). The features arise during the action itself. Each coordinative structure is an "action primitive," but the critical difference from a feature (or morpheme) is that coordinative structures do not in themselves have significances like a standard feature (rounded shape = spherical).

4. So far then, so good. While coordinative structures with ideas as attractors may avoid the bottom-up problem they create a new problem. A weakness of the coordinative structures approach is that it imposes a distinction between "image" and "gesture" (the attractor is the image and coordinative structures fashion a gesture to embody it). This distinction creates a new contradiction, now with the concept of a gesture as a material carrier. The gesture *is* the image – the image in its most material form; it is not a copy of it. Thus we have merely exchanged one contradiction for another, and are no closer to a model of the GP and imagery–language dialectic.

6.1.6.3 Analog?

One may think that a hybrid analog–digital machine with self-defining, self-segregating imagery would do the trick. The most effective approach would be to build in a self-responding Mead's Loop and then attempt to have the machine evolve a language. Robots capable of limb and hand motion may be the nearest approximation to such a machine. A hybrid device may be able to model growth points and how they differentiate fields of oppositions. An analog device meeting the following requirements may provide something like an image in a dialectic. Information needs to be:

1. in 3D, that is, embody variation as in gesture space
2. with correct orientation, as in gesture space
3. in the correct direction, as in gesture space
4. with texture, as in gesture space
5. as a spatial array, as set up in gesture space
6. with local identity in space (in all 3Ds), as set up in gesture space
7. with memory of past configurations, as in catchment space
8. and organized by action.[3]

No doubt the list can be extended but it is already a substantial departure from what I understand to be current modeling practice. Its feasibility is far from assured and a global analog device is at present more a *deus ex machina* than a realizable thing. This counts as *its* limitation vis-à-vis the GP.

But there is a more profound difficulty. None of this is actually imagery, global-synthetic and meaningful. Meaning is totally absent, so a hybrid machine is no closer to the imagery–language dialectic than the presumed digital one.

6.1.6.4 Summary of modeling

So, we learn from these thought experiments that artificial models do not in several areas match an evolved biological/psychological process, or head in the right direction to reach the GP – most crucially, that the semiosis must include a global component (to drive the dialectic), that there *is* a dialectic, and that finally the process is embodied in and tied to action (specifically coordinative structure units), and requires accordingly a "body" that is the embodiment of meaning. Further, the whole differentiates a context and the context and its differentiation are "a meaning." Finally, all these models conflict with Quaeghebeur's "all-at-onceness," in that in their logic they are sequential. Conversational agents can simulate many of these properties, but the basic difference between an artificial system, designed by rational intelligence, and what has naturally evolved remains a root fact in the contrast of the GP with modeling schemes.[4]

6.1.7 The lexical affiliate

The lexical affiliate is the word in the co-occurring speech to which a gesture corresponds most closely in meaning. It has been used to link gestures and speech by a number of researchers (e.g., Morrel-Samuels and Krauss 1992, Butterworth and Hadar 1989; cf. McNeill 1989 for comments). Schegloff introduced the concept in his 1984 paper, "On some gestures' relation to talk," to identify, via a gesture, upcoming topics in conversations. Like the growth point, the lexical affiliate posits a tight speech–gesture linkage. However, unlike the GP, the lexical affiliate is independent of context. It is discovered from the semantic content alone of the word the gesture is identified with, in contrast to the GP where the linguistic component can be identified by reference only to the field of meaningful oppositions that it along with the co-expressive gesture differentiates.[5] In *Gesture and Thought* (2005), to demonstrate this distinction, I analyzed in GP terms one of Engle's (2000) examples, where she applies the lexical affiliate concept. It also helps clarify the limits inherent in the lexical affiliate concept:

A clear illustration of the lexical affiliate/co-expressive speech distinction appears in Engle (2000). A gesture anticipated a lexical affiliate, consistent with Schegloff's original observation, but the immediate context of speaking suggests that the gesture and the *co-expressive speech* were actually synchronous. This is the example: Attempting to explain how a lock-and-key mechanism works, the subject said, "lift them [tumblers] to a // height, to the perfect height, where it [**enables**] the key to move," and appeared to turn a key as he said, "enables." The lexical affiliate is "key" or "key to move" and the key-turning gesture clearly occurred in advance of it. But from the vantage point of what would be newsworthy content in context, the synchrony of "enables" with the key-turning gesture embodies an idea this speaker might be expected to highlight – that by lifting the tumblers up, you are *able to turn the key*, and this thought is what the combination of a turning gesture plus "enables" captured. (McNeill 2005, pp. 37–38)

Another illustration of how the GP differs from the lexical affiliate is the "it down" example in Chapter 2, where it excluded exactly the lexical affiliate ("drops") of the thrusting gesture.

6.1.8 Comparative semiotics

In recent writings and presentations, Adam Kendon has questioned the entire tradition in which "gesture" is distinguished from other forms of kinesis (e.g., Kendon, 2008a, where the challenge is formulated in relation to sign languages of the deaf, but I believe he intends to include spoken language in its scope as well), proposing instead a continuum where,

Visible action, for all humans, is a material out of which symbolic forms of expression can be crafted. *How* this is done, what forms are crafted and when, depends upon whether or not it is used, and how it is used in conjunction with other symbolic systems. . . . studies must take into consideration what other modalities are available and are being used and what the ecological circumstances are in which these available modalities have been and can be elaborated. In this way, I think, we could work toward a comparative semiotics of kinesic expression. (pp. 359–360, emphasis in original)

If I understand the thrust of Kendon's aim here and elsewhere, it is to achieve, as he says, a comprehensive explanation of a comparative semiotics of *kinesic expression* (my emphasis). This is in no way incompatible with the arguments being developed here but our aims are not the same, and it is important to observe the difference. Rather than "kinesic expression," as such, I am attempting to explain the *nature of language*, when it is understood to include kinesic expression as an integral part, and particularly (since I also argue that gesture was involved in the origin of language) when it includes the kinds of kinesic expressions we defined in Chapter 1 as "gestures." A theory of "the comparative semiosis of kinesic expression" that obliterates the special status of language and conceals gesture within the general category of kinesic expressiveness would obscure rather than clarify what we are trying to do, define the role of "gesture" in the origin of language.

6.1.9 Representationalism

6.1.9.1 Quaeghebeur and Reynaert's critique of cognitive (and other) linguistics

A first-person, non-representational point of view is natural to the dynamic dimension. The philosophical foundations for such a perspective are in Merleau-Ponty's (1962) phenomenology. Quaeghebeur and Reynaert (2010) take phenomenology as their point of departure for an analysis of "representationalism," the doctrine that meanings, thoughts, percepts, etc. are not the thing itself but a "re-presentation" of it to a viewer. A word "represents" a meaning, a gesture "represents" whatever it means. In all cases, there is an implicit viewer to whom the thing is being "re-presented." Quaeghebeur and Reynaert focus on cognitive linguistics (and beyond on all third-person approaches in general) and say that it is forced to perceive "a gap between the 'rich' intended meaning (the thought, the cognitive content) and the 'poor' communicated meaning (the verbal material) which both speaker and listener must (unconsciously) bridge in a process of cognitive/mental encoding and decoding" (2010, p. 18). The gap engenders complex theories of how to fill it. A further problematic assumption is that "the thought somehow precedes its own material (verbal) externalization" (also p. 18), an assumption shared by modular models like the IPH and PCH.

They propose a theory based instead on Merleau-Ponty (1964) that is non-representational (analyzing language as situated instead) whereby thought and language are two sides of one "thing" (only it is not now a *thing* but a mode of being in the world). There is the previously mentioned "all-at-onceness" principle, whereby language, thought and body are engaged *all at once* in the phenomenon of language, not sequentially or causally. Meaning now turns out to be *overdetermined*, in contrast to the seeming underdetermination faced by the isolated, unsituated third-person speaker envisioned in synchronically based accounts.

Quaeghebeur and Reynaert's project envisions a *non-synchronic* linguistic paradigm. The spirit of cognitive linguistics has always been to enlarge the conception of language with an array of "cognitive" and "embodied" tools, but it has remained committed to the synchronic axiom. In *Gesture and Thought* (McNeill 2005) I was pessimistic about the chances of escaping any tight one-dimensional synchronic embrace, but Quaeghebeur and Reynaert may have found a way out through their phenomenological program, plus the idea of direct perception, familiar from Gibson as far back as 1950. Meaning, they say, is *directly perceived* in an embodied/situated performance, "served on a platter," and the gap filled by a complex theory vanishes. This is possible because, basically, the need for this theory is a self-created illusion: "C[ognitive]L[inguistic]'s third-person methodology leads to the *postulation* rather than the *discovery* of a subpersonal cognitive system [the inner steps of a causal chain] of an isolated subject which solves linguistic problems in a race against the clock" (p. 34, italics in original).

6.1.9.2 Improved correlations of static and dynamic

Whatever the ultimate fate of their revision of the synchronic conception of language and how far it can be extended, a phenomenologically inspired approach has other implications for linguistic analyses that do not depend on rejecting the century-old synchronic method or rejecting the static dimension and a linguistics devoted to studying it. To illustrate how, we can reanalyze a Langacker (2000) example of the integration of shifting attention and grammatical formulation. The reanalysis shows how a static approach can be adapted to foster a dynamic one. Langacker writes (pp. 363–364), "Invoking a reference point is thus an inherently dynamic process involving a shift of focus from the more readily accessible reference point to a target accessed through it," and provides invented examples such as, "in the kitchen, on the counter, next to the toaster, sat a cute little mouse," which requires constantly shifting foci and reference points.

There is in this a succession of reference points but note where the locus of change lies: it is not at the level of the emerging forms; the forms are still treated as static objects (as Langacker recognizes); an example is the "canonical event representation." Forms can be matched with communicative intentions but there is nothing of the forms themselves emerging or of an imagery–language dialectic fueling them. The concept of a blend in Fauconnier and Turner (2002) is a kind of snapshot on the static outcome of a dynamic process (for a recent extension of blending theory to gesture, in which the snapshot quality of the blend is explicitly put to use, see Parrill and Sweetser 2004). I consider these analyses to address the engagement of linguistic objects with perception but not the dynamic dimension itself. The metaphor is still "use" rather than "inhabitance." Cognitive grammar is unique among linguistic models in that it characterizes the static dimension with prepared (synchronically determined) cognitive templates. It also has shown itself to be interested in gesture and how it relates to the static dimension. The caused-motion construction in Chapter 3 demonstrated a meshing of such a template with a GP – a preformed structure with a slot for agent and one for object – that with minimal fuss and maximal speed unpacked the "it down" GP and its field of meaningful oppositions, with its built-in associations of significance the GP itself could activate.

Taking a dynamic viewpoint, we say that instead of shifting attention (Quaeghebeur and Reynaert's "racing the clock"), each GP/L-center is an *updating of cognitive being* (both the speaker's and an engaged listener's). Updating automatically shifts attention, which is now an aspect of linguistically geared consciousness rather than a force on its own. The job of the linguistic code, in this view, is to provide the categorial segments of L-centers. Languages do this with a minimum of fuss, and how they do it is a proper topic of linguistic analysis. Also, the language system opens fast paths to unpack GPs, and this too needs to be analyzed linguistically, with an updating-of-being functionality in mind.

These goals are purely linguistic and synchronic, but now are tied to the functions of the static system in a dialectic. So doing shapes the kinds of things on which the analyst focuses – patterns (seen synchronically) not solely because they contrast with other patterns or capture linguistic intuitions (respectively, the Saussurian and Chomskian legacies), but because they intersect the dynamic dimension, provide L-centers and make fast unpackings possible. None of this presumes that the system of patterns the static dimension encapsulates models the procedures the speaker and listener follow (the target of Quaeghebeur and Reynaert's critique). The basic "instinct" to form analytic atoms and combine them under shareability may have its own laws, arising when high levels of internal complexity have been reached, and a purely static analysis applies to uncover them. This possibility leaves linguistics much as ever. What is needed beyond tradition is a framework in which the linguistic system is regarded as action-patterns shaped by shareability and adapted first to triggering, and then to stopping dialectics by unpacking, and to do so "all at once." The embodiments that cognitive linguistics captures are not steps in the generation of speech (what Quaeghebeur and Reynaert call "subpersonal" steps) but are functions to be carried out by the linguistic forms paired with imagery in this dynamic process.

6.2 SCIENCE BASE

Why language, on its dynamic dimension, is a dialectic of imagery and linguistic form; why a meaning is irreducibly a differentiation of a field of oppositions; and why both are tied to action – these "whys" of language are explained by the "hows," that at the origin of language they were tied together. In this respect, the totality of explanation is a kind of confirmation of the separate hypotheses, the parts. But the GP hypothesis as a whole has its own justifications, and this section explains them.

6.2.1 Falsifiability – meeting the dictum

Growth points are inferred from the totality of communicative events with special focus on speech–gesture synchrony and co-expressivity.[6] A GP requires:

a. That speech and gesture be co-expressive.
b. That speech and gesture jointly differentiate newsworthy information in context.
c. That they shift their timing jointly depending on context; and
d. That they co-vary in materialization depending on communicative dynamism.

Missing any of these requirements, the hypothesis that is the GP in any instance can be falsified or at least shown to require modification. There are many avenues for falsifying a GP in keeping with Karl Popper's doctrine of scientific hypothesis testing. But one must be careful in formulating falsifications. For example, the out-of-synchrony gestures cited in Kita's (2000) paper presenting the IPH also help create conditions for GPs, so in fact work together with the GP hypothesis (see discussion in §6.1.5 of this chapter). "Data," it is often said, is interpretation as well as observation, and must be evaluated with awareness of the full texture of the hypothesis under test.

6.2.2 Coding as hypothesis formulation and test

Meeting the falsifiability test requires a way to collect and evaluate data. Each GP is an empirical hypothesis concerning the momentary cognitive being of an individual speaker. To detect GPs requires coding speech and gesture jointly, contrary to the common practice of coding gesture without the accompanying speech, to avoid "contamination." To code gestures without speech hides the very thing to be coded, the gesture–speech unit, the GP.

Another departure from standard practice is that a growth point can be inferred only for individual cases. Although samples can be compiled, a GP cannot be found from them; the concept does not apply to collections; this is because the concept has *an intrinsically individual perspective and is meaningful only in relation to a field of oppositions (which is local).* Aggregating GPs into samples inevitably includes mutually cancelling viewpoints and fields of meaningful oppositions, which again destroys the things to be studied.

If you take the following steps with care and rigor for each putative GP, you will find idea units that reside in two semiotic modes at once and jointly differentiate a context. Each idea unit is judged to be a minimal chunk of imagery–language dialectic, or a growth point:

1. Start with an exact transcription, including hesitations (filled and unfilled) and "errors": find the linguistic segment(s) and/or non-speech features coinciding exactly with the gesture stroke and any poststroke hold (excluding any prestroke hold). The speech–gesture timing must be within a syllable, which requires use of synchronized and immediate sound with a slow- and stopped-motion sound movie (since the demise of video, we have used Apple Corp's FinalCut© technology, which provides these essential features; convenient control is by a Contour Shuttle©).
2. Determine that the gesture and speech content are co-expressive of an idea unit (not necessarily the same aspects), such that the linguistic content brings the imagery content into the system of language categories. The linguistic and imagery content may be on different discourse levels. The linguistic segment may or may not be the lexical affiliate.
3. Crucially, determine that the speech–gesture combination comprises a psychological predicate embodying the "newsworthy" in its field of meaningful oppositions. The field of oppositions it differentiates can be identified through catchments and/or use of gesture–speech mimicry (cf. Chapter 2, §2.5.1 and Chapter 4, §4.1.9.3). There may be several

GP hypotheses each with its own version of the core idea unit and field of meaningful oppositions. Judgment inevitably enters into the coding process and a flexible attitude is essential.

As long as the same idea exists in two modes, exact synchrony is not essential. The synchrony question, at this point, is a matter of data purity. A combination of unlike semiotic modes is the critical factor and the clearest examples have exact synchrony. At some amount of temporal separation, I think about 2 s, to consider gesture and speech as one "thing" becomes untenable. Obviously, this requires judgment but it can be tested, explained, and justified.

The above does not capture all aspects of the dynamic dimension; in particular, it does not uncover the discourse direction and the speaker's goals. An analysis of the linguistic track for the pattern of metapragmatic indexicals (Silverstein 2003) can partially pin down this aspect. With narrations, the story content provides a large share of the overall direction, and is known to the coder. Often something in the discourse at some later time clarifies earlier points, and a kind of back-and-forth takes place. Goals impact how fields of oppositions form, what is newsworthy and how growth points relate to each other, and all of these factors need to be identified as well. All these steps are seen in action in the following extended example of gesture coding and GP analysis.

6.2.3 Tautology – shunned

In a 2006 article Geoffrey Beattie and Heather Shovelton wondered if the GP is not arbitrary and tautological, a view that others may also hold. [7] However, this view pays insufficient (or no) attention to the dependence of the GP on context. The GP, as pointed out more-than-often in this book, is a psychological predicate; it is not independent of its context and only exists as a point of differentiation within it. In a slightly different misunderstanding, which may or may not also have been on the minds of Beattie and Shovelton, some may suppose that a GP is inferred from the gesture – that whatever this gesture conveys is the GP, which is indeed tautological. However, while the gesture is part of the GP that is not how the GP is identified.

A GP is inferred from multiple information sources, and whatever is inferred must be shown, within the immediate context, to be the point of differentiation: it is this requirement to incorporate context that the Beattie and Shovelton queries overlook. Contexts differ, and are created by speakers. Part of figuring out the GP is an analysis to determine this context.

Catchments play a major part, as does mimicry, which can bring out both the GP and the field of meaningful oppositions as well. Taking these steps we ward off tautology.

Beattie and Shovelton write: "So according to McNeill for one speaker 'clambering' was salient, for another 'interiority' was important and for another both 'interiority' and 'manner of movement' were crucial. . . . But how can McNeill support such conclusions? How can he validate the interpretations he makes – interpretations about the mental state of the participants? What evidence do we have that the various speakers held different semantic properties to be the crucial ones in their actual communication?" (p. 66).

To ask, as Beattie and Shovelton do, how different "semantic properties" are "salient" and "crucial to communication" changes the terms of analysis in subtle but crucial ways. These are questions whose answers can be given *without context*. "Salience" in their query seemingly refers (although one cannot be sure) to selective attention to the outside world (whereas in GP terms salience depends upon how the speaker differentiates the field of meaningful oppositions that she/he has at least partly constructed as part of the meaning). "Semantic properties" pertain to words or gestures as objects on their own. "Crucial for communication" is a function answerable by reference to the recipient of the communication. These are not questions addressed to the GP itself (nonetheless I believe that communication questions can be answered in GP terms, and in doing so we change the questions: not to say that the speaker is thinking about what is "crucial" for communication but how the speaker attempts to get the interlocutor to share his/her GPs, field of meaningful oppositions, and in general state of being; see the McNeill *et al.* 2010 paper for several analyses of conversational interactions along these lines). The GP, fortified by the idea of a catchment and use of mimicry, breaks out of the tautological trap Beattie and Shovelton believe they have found; the circle is broken by reference to the context the speaker has constructed, registered through catchments, mimicry, and text-based clues.

6.2.3.1 Breakout example – the tautology non-issue

It is important to establish that the picture in this book of what evolved is plausible as a first approximation. Beattie and Shovelton's queries appeared in the primary journal dedicated to the gesture field. I shall take some time to show that GPs and fields of opposition are derived from careful observation and close reasoning. The best way to reply to "how does McNeill know?"

is with examples that show both "how I/we know" and, indeed, what it means, "to know." The demonstration in Figure 6.4 is the moment-by-moment unfolding of verbal thinking in GPs and successively updated fields of opposition. I reconstruct the successive GPs and fields of opposition of one speaker as she narrates Sylvester's experiences after Tweety dropped the bowling ball into the pipe.

I have retained the full transcription by Susan Duncan, plus a good portion of her notes, to which I have added GP notes. My purpose is to provide a detailed illustration of how gesture and speech are actually examined and analyzed, in the confident belief that any reasonable person reading this transcript will see that while there is always room for debate and decisions are sometimes left unresolved (with alternatives laid out), interpretations are not arbitrary. They are motivated by empirical evidence without guesses or circularity of reasoning. I justify this lengthy (approximately 11 seconds) example on the ground that only in its entirety can it show a doubting critic how gesture analysis and GP discovery are actually carried through. It incidentally is also a good illustration of gesture coding practice, as Susan Duncan has developed it at our University of Chicago gesture lab. Her method of instructing in gesture coding relies heavily on going through just such detailed examples.

Note on first- and third-person perspectives: We are aiming to reconstruct a speaker's momentary states of cognitive being, to show how, GP-to-GP, she differentiates psychological predicates within created and updated contexts, and how these have come to be. The goal, that is, is to recover a first-person perspective. But we are limited to the third-person perspective of the observer, which means that our own steps at evidence gathering and evaluating are not good models of the speaker's first-person cognitive steps. For example, we conclude that the initial gesture belongs to a catchment whose theme is *WHAT THE BOWLING BALL DID.* We conclude this in part because we can look ahead at later gestures with similar two-handed downward moving formats that also carry this theme. The speaker of course did not do this. *She* created gestures on the fly, while thinking that the bowling ball was causing all this drama, and reactivated the two-hands image (iconic for the ball) with updates whenever she came back to this theme.

The example: The speaker creates two catchments, the first immediately interrupted by the second on a metanarrative level; she then returns to the first with successive updates and on one occasion backtracks to the original form. So a complex picture emerges of the speaker's construal of contexts and the GPs that differentiated them. Context and GPs track her thinking-for/while-speaking.[8]

[/ and it **goe**s_dOWn]

Both hands (BH) mirroring each other in tense spread C-shapes, palms toward center (PTC), and move down from upper central periphery to lower central periphery, <u>slightly</u> rightward at the end to low right central periphery; sudden stop.

01:04:14

GP notes: The field of meaningful oppositions (itself emerging out of what the speaker had said just previously, "and he drops a bowling ball into the rainspout") was WHAT THE B-BALL DID and the GP was WENT DOWN. The hallmark of this catchment is the use of two similar hands throughout, iconic for the bowling ball. The slight rightward tilt at the end probably is iconic for the shape of the drainpipe at the bottom. So the gesture synthesizes a number of elements. The abrupt cessation suggests a new level of discourse merging with its own field of meaningful oppositions, leading to the following metaphoric interlude in which there is a new catchment, use of a single hand, a new meaning of space, and GP formations on both a narrative and a metanarrative level.

and it* [/ <u><ah></u>

Spatial metaphor; left hand (LH) loose curved spread-5 palm turned up hits left knee during hesitation ("/").

01:06:01

GP notes: a GP is not discernible due to absence of linguistic categorization, but this is much like the earlier IPH example as a field of meaningful oppositions was being created: Looking at the following use of the same gesture space, we can say that the theme is AMBIGUITY. Thus begins a spatial catchment (above the left knee) for this theme.

Figure 6.4 Extended example from a narration of the bowling ball episode illustrating hypothesis formulation and test in reconstructing GPs.

<u>you ca</u>] [[**an't tell**]

Iconic & spatial metaphor; LH cupped spread-5 palm turned down @ lap; and the LH is the <bowling ball>. The b-ball TRAJECTOR is in its "<u>under</u> Sylvester" location.

01:06:16

GP notes: AMBIGUITY (the catchment just started) due to the cartoon's unclarity about the b-ball's movements rather than, say, one's own indecisiveness. The imagery is that the b-ball is "under" Sylvester, which is one pole of the ambiguity. It is immediately exchanged in the following for its alternative – the b-ball inside him. The GP here is thus AMBIGUITY: ONE POLE IS UNDER SYLVESTER, which explains why the gesture was glossed by "you can't tell" (i.e., the 'under' image is so glossed).

[if the **bow**<u>ling ball</u> /]]

Iconic & spatial metaphor; LH cupped spread-5 palm turned up between the speaker's abdomen & her left knee. The TRAJECTOR <bowling ball> in its "<u>inside</u> Sylvester" location.

01:07:17

GP notes: still the AMBIGUITY catchment with iconic and deictic additions conveying the b-ball's possible location inside Sylvester. The field of meaningful oppositions and GP are understood as AMBIGUITY: ONE ALTERNATIVE IS B-BALL IS INSIDE, that is, the situation is ambiguous, and one possibility is that Sylvester has swallowed the bowling ball. The GP is the straightforward differentiation of the ambiguity field of meaningful oppositions with inside imagery glossed as "the bowling ball."

[is un* <u>L</u>]

Iconic & spatial metaphor (aborted altered repeat); LH cupped spread-5 palm turned up hesitantly prepares to hit the speaker's left knee in the "<u>under</u> Sylvester" location.

01:08:01

An IPH-style anticipation of "under" (speech and gesture are aborted for reasons unknown), followed immediately by the "under" GP. However, a possible reason for aborting is described in the next panel

Figure 6.4 (*cont.*)

[[is **und**er Sylvester]

Iconic & spatial metaphor (repeat); LH cupped spread-5 palm to body @lap; LH is the <bowling ball>. The b-ball TRAJECTOR in its <u>under</u> Sylvester location.

01:08:18

GP notes: the AMBIGUITY catchment continues in another full imagery–linguistic combination. The significance is AMBIGUITY: ONE ALTERNATIVE IS UNDER. The spatial locus is closer to her belly, in contrast to the next gesture, still in the AMBIGUITY space, which is farther out. These self-generated spatial values subdivide the catchment space. The faltering in the preceding speech pulse, at 01:08:01 above, with the start of "under," could be due to the poles of the ambiguity being glossed here in non-parallel syntactic forms. At 01:06:16 the gloss was with "the bowling ball" while here it is "Sylvester," yet the two are parallel in the sense of alternative options in the same field of meaningful oppositions. So with this explanation the speaker hesitated at 01:08:01 with an unpacking that was also not grammatically parallel. The problem is immediately resolved in the following

[or **ins**i**d**e of him]]

Iconic & spatial metaphor; LH cupped spread-5 palm turned up between the speaker's abdomen & her left knee. The TRAJECTOR <bowling ball> in its "<u>inside</u> Sylvester" location.

01:09:21

GP notes: AMBIGUITY: ONE ALTERNATIVE IS "INSIDE." The semantic opposition of "under"/"inside" is now settled with parallel frames.

END 6-PART SPATIAL METAPHORIC SEQUENCE

Two gestures in immediate succession:

Figure 6.4 (*cont.*)

but [[it **rOll**]

1. iconic; MANNER, PATH, FIGURE; 2 similar hands
cupped spread-5s palm turned right & down, fingers
away from body; move from lower left central to lower
central center, hands rotating on wrists; O-VPT.;
<Syl.+ bowling ball roll out>
NB: The cupped LH hand shape (1) continues to
suggest the rounded shape of the trajector. When
the fingers start to wiggle in the next pulse, this
feature diminishes.

01:10:19

[s him **OUt***]]

2. Iconic; 2SH bent-5s palm turned right & down,
fingers away from body; move from low central center
to low right periphery, fingers wiggling; O-VPT.
NB: MANNER+PATH in gesture time with a MANNER-
encoding main verb and its PATH satellite in speech.
The pronoun ('him') representing FIGURE comes
in between these two, so there's no way to tell if the
stroke was meant for it. Syl.+b-ball down the street>

01:11:01

Susan Duncan noted: The first gesture (01:10:19) seems to be about *across the street*,
rather than about *out the drainpipe as* is the case with speech. Is this some kind of
"mismatch" or, is it gesture getting ahead of speech? Or does this gesture refer
specifically to the final, horizontal, portion of Sylvester's journey through the
drainpipe? This production has been coded as self-interrupted (the *), on the
thinking that the speaker has Sylvester rolling *out* of the drainpipe before she rolls
him *down* in her narration, making it necessary to back up, and this back-up could
account for the slight disfluency and lexical search problem that the Spkr exhibits
trying to get out the word "drainpipe," next. Another interpretation (to S. Duncan
from D. Wilkins) is that this is not a self-interrupt at all, but rather that the speaker
is saying the equivalent of, "It rolls him out *by* rolling him down the drainpipe".

*GP notes: The combination of a diagonally down-horizontal path, low periphery (deictic
for the street-level), gestural manner (wriggling fingers) and the linguistic categorization
of "rolls" could be the return after the 6-part metaphoric interlude to the original WHAT
THE B-BALL DID field of meaningful oppositions, updated by AT THE BOTTOM.*
GP1: WHAT THE B-BALL DID AT THE BOTTOM OF THE PIPE: ROLLED
SYLVESTER (i.e., caused his motion, "the b-ball caused Sylvester to move by rolling" –
adopting the D. Wilkins interpretation, on the grounds that it explains the GP
differentiation). An updated catchment: the evidence is the lower space with a left-right
and downward orientation. It retains the two-handedness of the What the B-ball Did
catchment, and so is deemed "updated" rather than"new".
GP2: WHAT THE B-BALL DID AT THE BOTTOM OF THE PIPE: EXPELLED
SYLVESTER (still caused-motion, but now the salient information is the outcome, rather
than, as before, the motion caused by rolling: in effect, "the b-ball CAUSED Sylvester TO
LEAVE the pipe by rolling".
The updated catchment structure has this evidence: the low space is deictic for action at
the bottom of the pipe, at street level, which is thematically evaluated as events that took
place at the bottom of the drainpipe.

Figure 6.4 (*cont.*)

[[dOwn the /⌐]]

Iconic (interrupted); **velocity** MANNER, PATH, ¿FIGURE;
2SH bent-Ls palms to center fingertips turned down
move down from central head-level; O-VPT:S;
<Syl+b-ball down spout> N.B.: path in gesture skips
the path satellite to time with a speech pause. The
speaker hesitates in getting the word "rainspout" out.
The gesture is correspondingly interrupted and then
continued to completion in the next pulse. Speech
disfluency/lexical search problem, or backing up from
the previous production could account for weird
timing here; i.e., gesture "wants" to time with the
ground component coming up in the second
production?

01:11:16

*GP notes: the two-handed catchment continues with another update possibly to register
the metanarrative fact that this utterance is an emendation. The speaker had already
said the b-ball rolled Sylvester "out," and is now adding that it was also "down." We
posit that the context has reverted to its initial form, WHAT THE BOWLING BALL
DID, since the space is back to head-level now. The handshape change to bent-L –
forefinger extended and bent at first knuckle, other fingers curled in – from bent-5 is
perhaps purely formal, marking that the emendation GP is not the preceding
down-the-pipe GP. Or, alternatively, bent-L could be motivated as a signal of meta-level
commentary: the bent-L signaling precision (imagery suitable for emendation). These
alternative interpretations – form contrast, precision metaphor – remain open in the
absence of other bent-L gestures for comparison.*

[/ **rain**spo]][ut

iconic (reduced repeat); **velocity** MANNER, PATH; 2SH
bent-Ls palms to center fingertips turned down move
down from right center; Repeat due to lexical search
glitch?; O-VPT:S; <Syl+b-ball down spout> NB: PATH
in gesture times with GROUND in speech. A post-stroke
hold extends to cover most of the remainder of the
GROUND NP that isn't covered by the stroke. **NB:** ENDPT =
rather abrupt stroke termination. $spatial: resumes,
reduced; next gesture marks exit from rainspout at
lower right periphery; next one to extreme right
periphery for vector into bowling alley (consistent with
cartoon image orientation for the various angles
viewing the scene as well).

01:12:12

*GP notes: the same as above with the same WHAT THE BOWLING BALL DID
catchment, plus end-marking for the termination of the meta-level emendation, in effect
a closing of parentheses.*

Figure 6.4 (*cont.*)

/ **out**_i_][nto

iconic; 2SH 5-hands palms turned down fingers away
from body fingertips turned down flick down @ lower
right; rebound; O-VPT:S; **velocity** MANNER, PATH,
PATH**border** (hands pop open), P-to-Ggoal; <Syl+b-ball
drop out of spout> **NB:** path in gesture times with
path satellite in speech. **NB:** ¿ trajectory here is Syl's
free fall between the mouth of the pipe and the surface
of the street below it. Code it as landmark (boundary)-
expressive because the fingers pop into a more spread
position, suggesting coming out of the mouth of the
pipe. Speaker's use of the preposition "into" here is
unusual. Is it a usage like, "he went out into the street"?

01:12:24

GP notes: return to the narrative line with an updated WHAT THE BOWLING BALL
DID AT THE BOTTOM catchment. The GP is a new differentiation within it: sent
Sylvester "out" explosively (as in the gesture imagery – high velocity "popping out"). Note
how these interpretations stay close to the visual and linguistic evidence.

the sidew][alk

iconic: <Syl rolling> RH 5-shape FAB PTD @ lower
right periphery moves to center then away from center
with fingers wiggling; NB: How to indicate: away from
center motion encodes trajectory but not to center
motion? Can we break things down: finger wiggling:
MANNER. Away from center motion: trajectory instead
of breaking it down by articulators? Maybe different
kinds of motion can be different articulators?

01:13:07

GP notes: new catchment. The right hand moves as described with the addition of
manner, via finger wiggling; the left hand is static but maintains the form it had in the
preceding two-handed gestures (where it was moving), and then relaxes into a kind of rest
position at the end of "sidewalk", occupying the gesture space with the right hand alone.
This shift to one hand marks the new catchment. It is no longer focused on the bowling
ball (consistently two hands) but seems instead to be WHAT HAPPENS TO SYLVESTER,
with the GP being MOVES WITH ROTATING FEET ON THE SIDEWALK – the "feet"
interpretation being based on our knowledge of the cartoon itself, the "sidewalk"
interpretation coming from the linguistic categorization and the lower periphery imagery.
There is room here however for a layering of catchments, the earlier WHAT THE
BOWLING BALL DID AT THE BOTTOM catchment continuing in this lower space.
Then the GP at this point is a differentiation within a field of meaningful oppositions,
which is itself within another field of meaningful oppositions. The weak point of this
interpretation is that the lower space could be deictic on its own (not a continuation of the
old catchment imagery), since in the cartoon the action actually does take place at the
bottom of the frame

Figure 6.4 (*cont.*)

into a]

iconic; RH spread-5 palms turned down fingers away from bodt slices LtoR and away from body at lower right periphery; O-VPT:S; **velocity** MANNER, PATH, **PATH-to-GROUND**goal; <Syl.+b-ball roll into the bowling alley>; PATH in gesture times with speech pause just prior to PATH in speech; a post-stroke hold extends to cover the PATH satellite to the verb. NB: Consider this production separate from the previous four, because it is one-handed and seems to have its own launch; however, in makes use of the same integrated gesture space exploited by the others. Marks extreme right periph for vector into bowling alley (consistent with cartoon image orientation for the various angles viewing the scene as well).

01:13:24

GP notes: continues the new "Sylvester" catchment: ENTERS being the new information.
Two gestures in immediate succession:

[bowling **alley** / <u>and he knOcks over</u>]

1. iconic+metaphoric;RH;5; palm to center; fingers away from body at periphery; elbow pivots to R periphery, flips palm up, away from body, H=S M=knocking pins; O-VPT:S: general action vector resumed, palm flip codes metaphoric conduit for result as object: (knocking over the pins).

01:14:22

2. RH;5; palm to center; fingers away from body; hand moves down @ lower R periphery, fingers may point to location of pins or possibly a superimposed beat. all the ^**pins**<u>*</u>]

(next panel shows end of downward stroke)

01:15:10

Figure 6.4 (*cont.*)

End of stroke

01:15:23

GP notes: GP 1: motion and space are much like the preceding gesture, but the orientation of the palm upward suggests a metaphoric upshift within WHAT HAPPENS TO SYLVESTER, the GP is an outcome: discursive presentation imagery categorized as "knocks all the pins".

GP 2: if deictic, the point of differentiation is something like LOCATED BELOW; if a superimposed beat, it is to relate the lexicalization ("the pins") to the outcome metaphor, and the GP is something like 'this bit of speech is important in relation to the field of opposition.'

Figure 6.4 (*cont.*)

6.2.4 Non-tautology summary

To wind up this lengthy example, a coded gesture transcript is something like a lab log, a record of observations carefully made and recorded, hypotheses proffered, evaluations and alternatives weighed, and a careful acknowledgement of when and for what reasons questions are, after all, still unanswered. There is nothing circular or tautological in this; just the normal scientific practice of hypothesis formulation, evaluation and test guided by informed judgment.

6.3 MEAD'S LOOP AND GP TESTS (SOME WHEN TECHNOLOGY PERMITS)

Experiments would be important for various claims in this book, the origin of Mead's Loop in particular. Two kinds of tests are described. The first looks for effects that Mead's Loop says should be found; however, they await technological improvements to current brain imaging. The second looks for effects that should result from the absence of Mead's Loop; they are possible now with the right animals (I envision chimps) but test a negative proposition.

6.3.1 Currently inaccessible (positive) brain imaging tests

The most basic prediction of Mead's Loop is that, in the human brain, there is a special form of mirror neuron that responds to one's own gestures as if from another. This section provides predictions that can theoretically be tested with brain imagery. These experiments test "positive" predictions: what the Mead's Loop circuit should be able to do. If technology finds a way to negate movement artifacts and record brain activity while someone is performing manual gestures, the predictions could be tested with fMRI using the techniques presented in Hasson *et al.* (2004) that avoid blocking or repeating events (since any test of GP/Mead's Loop, by its very nature, requires continuous discourse sampling with newsworthy psychological predicate formation, not isolated and no repeated events).

Mead's Loop predicts the activation of mirror neuron circuits in Broca's Area during one's own gestures with speech. Growth points specifically predict orchestrations involving the right and left hemispheres, anterior and posterior left hemisphere, and prefrontal cortex. Such activation creates a unique signature. Seven predictions deriving from Mead's Loop are the following:

- First, because gestures are material carriers of imagery there should be mirror neuron activation whenever thinking requires the global-synthetic semiotic enabled by the thought–language–hand link of Mead's Loop.
- Second, since gestures are carriers of imagery but are not the only form that imagery takes, the fMRI activation pattern is predicted, but weaker, when speaking whether or not one performs gestures.
- And third, if there is a gesture, it strengthens the materialization and the activation will be greater.
- Fourth, since in the Mead's Loop "twist" one's own gestures have the feel of social otherness, "social circuits" of the brain should be activated by one's own gestures.
- Fifth, if a gesture materializes consciousness the effect should appear as a blip of activation at the moment of differentiation.
- Sixth, this differentiation is possible only through the interaction of multiple brain areas, so there should be concomitant prefrontal, posterior left hemisphere and right hemisphere activation.

A seventh prediction is inspired by a study of human subjects by Skipper *et al.* (2007) who tested the (perceptual) fMRI response of Broca's area to a video of continuous speech and gestures performed by a speaker recounting a story. Compared to a second stimulus tape constructed with equal numbers of non-informative "adaptor" movements (scratching, adjusting glasses, etc.), gestures triggered *less* fMRI activation in a brain area independently identified as selecting among alternative semantic interpretations (a section of Broca's area known as the *pars triangularis* or PTr). Skipper *et al.* conclude, "the meaningful information that speech-associated gestures convey reduces semantic ambiguity and thus reduces the need for semantic retrieval/selection" (p. 260).[9] (The PTr is not the area where, in the brain model, fields of meaningful oppositions form – that is the prefrontal cortex.)

In GP terms, gestures also "reduce ambiguity" by the differentiation of psychological predicates. Only a linguistic meaning that is co-expressive with the gesture and with it jointly able to differentiate a field of meaningful oppositions could be active; hence less pressure to refine meanings further – they are already as precise as context allows – and the PTr is less active.

- This process provides the seventh prediction, parallel to the Skipper *et al.* perceptual results for a future production experiment: Mead's Loop/GP predicts that if a speaker (rather than a perceiver) makes a speech-synchronized gesture the multiple brain areas of the GP should be active and the PTr be *inactive*; if there is no gesture and these areas are also inactive (implying that a GP has not formed), PTr should be *active* (and speech itself should show signs of disruption since orchestration is weak, e.g., when the speaker cannot recall the next event in a cartoon story); and if there is no gesture but the areas involved in the GP are *active* (implying that the GP has formed but has not been fully materialized), PTr activity should be intermediate (and speech possibly disrupted as well).

6.3.2 Currently accessible (negative) primate tests

The following tests could be conducted with non-human primates (I envision chimps). They are accessible tests to those working with such animals, and predict what a brain lacking Mead's Loop should not be able to do (hence "negative"):

- **Mimicry.** The experimenter first waits for a chimp to gesture toward some prize just out of reach and, when it occurs, immediately mimics it. But the prize is not handed over until the chimp mimics the experimenter's gesture in return. It is important that the chimp's second gesture should occur immediately after the experimenter's. The question now is, does the chimp regard this second gesture as repeating its own gesture or does it see the gesture as a social response to the experimenter? If the chimp's own gesture has a social Other value, as Mead's Loop provides, it could understand (a) that it was mimicked in the first place, and (b) that the chimp, in turn, in its second gesture, had mimicked the experimenter. In this case, it would understand that the experiment is about mimicry. To determine which is the case, the experiment continues with a slight change. In the next phase, the experimenter gestures and waits until the chimp mimics this gesture before delivering the prize. The chimp will presumably learn to do this readily (it could be by operant conditioning). But now, crucially, does the chimp from now on gesture and then wait for the experimenter to gesture, and then gesture back? If so the chimp has the idea that mimicry is involved. Or does it just gesture as before and show no expectation that the experimenter will do something? In this case, we can say that the exchanges of mimicries have no meaning for it. The animal may still mimic the experimenter's gesture in this case, showing that conditioning was a factor.

- **Gesture protects memory.** Something like the chimpanzee equivalent of the "gesture protects memory" effect described earlier can be tested by comparing performance on a task while some other information (such as the location of a hidden prize) has to be kept in memory. Is retention of this other information better if the animal happens to gesture and vocalize together during the first task? Hopkins and Cantero (2003), as mentioned earlier, observed more right-handed gestures by chimps when they vocalize, suggesting some sound–hand connection in the animal's left hemisphere. Given the explanation earlier of "gesture protects memory" in terms of GPs, the effect, should it appear, would be a clue that the chimpanzee uses gestures for organizing consciousness. But, without GPs, it should not have this ability.
- **Social flavor A.** A behavioral test that may reveal a social flavor to gesture in primates is to conduct a variant of the above mimicry experiment with now a second chimp present. As before, chimp A makes a gesture toward a just-out-of-reach prize and the experimenter mimics it. It is not that chimp B has to make a gesture, although if one occurs the test is even better. Does chimp A now react to the other chimp in any way that suggests rivalry? From examples of two chimps focused on an out-of-reach prize (from the video recorded by William Hopkins), there is joint focus but it is parallel and non-interactive. However, if chimp A

considers its own gesture to have the flavor of a social Other, as would be the case if the chimp has something like Mead's Loop, it may consider that chimp B has mimicked it as well, and this could result in an interaction display of some sort. If B sometimes gestures after A and sometimes not, or gestures before A, we have more useful comparison trials. According to Mead's Loop, A's gesture should simulate an "Other" and so it should not make a difference in terms of interaction whether B does or does not also gesture, and we expect no difference in A as a function of B's behavior, some rivalry response in any event.

- **Social flavor B.** Another observational test for the virtual Other aspect of Mead's Loop would be to see if non-human primate mothers ever show evidence of monitoring the infant's response to the mother's own demonstrations, especially deixis. Orangutan mothers do monitor infant imitations of their actions (Erica Cartmill pers. comm.) but do they monitor whether and how the infant responds to their gestures? (A human adult will certainly be aware that she has made a communicative effort even though perhaps unaware that it was her gesture that did it, and would monitor its effect.) If chimps do, this also would suggest Mead's Loop and its absence the absence of Mead's Loop.

These "negative" experiments test a predicted absence of result, indicating absence of Mead's Loop. Of course a negative result always has other explanations, but the test can be suggestive when a positive test is not available (waiting until brain imaging tests with gesture movement become possible).

Notes

Notes on Chapter 1

1. A sign of the new respectability is that so many recent books have taken up the challenge to explain language origin wholly or in part. I list here a sample: Allott 2001, Anderson 2004, Armstrong and Wilcox 2007, Armstrong, Stokoe, and Wilcox 1995, Bermúdez 2007, Burling 2005, Clark 1997, Corballis 2002, De Waal 2001, Deacon 1997, Dessalles 2007, Donald 1991, Dunbar 1996, Fitch 2010, Gamble 2007, Hurford 2007, Jackendoff 2002, 2007, Lieberman 2006. MacNeilage 2008, Mithen 2006, and Tomasello 2008.
2. With essential help from Nobuko B. McNeill.
3. I adopt "gesticulation" reluctantly and use it only when I sense that ambiguity looms. I prefer simple "gesture" partly for brevity but more crucially because "gesticulation" carries an image of windmilling arms that is false to the reality we are aiming to explain. Equally misleading, it allows that gestures occur with or without speech, contradicting the sense of speech-synchronized gesture pursued in this book (both unwanted senses appear in its *OED* definition: to gesticulate is "To make lively or energetic motions with the limbs or body; esp. as an accompaniment or in lieu of speech.")
4. The timing of signs with speech by hearing ASL/English bilinguals is described in Chapter 3, §3.2.1.2.2.
5. Simone Pika (email 05/07/11) raises an interesting point: where on the Gesture Continuum do ape gestures fall? I do not mean that ape gestures are not "gestures," but the Gesture Continuum, as a whole, is organized by dimensions that come from human evolution. We should not expect to find ape gestures easily fitting onto it. They probably come closest to pantomime – extending a hand, not to actually grasp something, but to indicate grasping with the same goal-directedness as the full action; an "action stub," symbolic but only partially differentiated from full actions and limited to pragmatic goals. As we shall see in Chapter 3, starting from pantomime could not have gotten to human language.

Notes on Chapter 2

1. The phrase is from Kendon (2008a), who also argues against the view.
2. A rhyme signals that lines linked by recursion, the rhyming lines, have a paradigmatic contrast; for example, "His big tears, for he wept full well/Turned to mill-stones as they fell" (Shelley, "The Masque of Anarchy"). (Thanks to Randall L. B. McNeill.) The rhyming "-ell"s, on the axis of combination, project a new

semantic opposition, on the axis of selection – "well" to "fell" – cluing us to seek meaningful linkages (possibly ironic). The rhyming function obeys this principle on the level of sound, but 'rhymes' of phrases, clauses, and in our case, gestures, also occur (Furuyama 2000b).

3. The terms "transformational" and "generative" sound dynamic but the grammars bearing these names in fact are static. See my *Gesture and Thought* (McNeill 2005) where this is discussed.

4. Stills of videos comprise roughly half the illustrations of this book. The videos have been the subject of study for many years, have been transcribed and annotated fully, and are the source of much insight but they are, by now, of low quality as images; the illustrations, moreover, are screenshots, further diminishing quality. Recognizing these limitations I have attempted to bring out features critical to each example by Photoshop©, even though the resulting images have a slightly acromegalic look. The enhancements add emphasis to edges but do not add features, and only make the murky clearer. Figures 1.2 and 2.1 are examples and many others follow.

5. An example I can suggest that may look like a syntagmatic value from the combination of gestures is the following: one hand points to a gesture made in the other hand. Does the second gesture become the object of the pointing gesture, a value it would not have had outside the combination? Perhaps, but there are complicating factors: first, while pointing may in some respects be like an emblem, the second gesture need not be emblem-like, even though it must be in the focus of awareness; pointing is not then an emblem–emblem combination from which syntagmatic values emerge. Second, the reason the second gesture need not be an emblem is that it need not be a gesture at all. The gesture is the target of the point and has all the properties of an indicated entity in a deictic field – no different than when the target is a sunset, a shoe, or anything at all. Emerging syntagmatic value is the wrong concept in these situations.

6. An example of speech and gesture delivering their own aspects of a single idea unit is this (many such are found in storytelling):

[to j*ust go*] [o *in the* front door of the] [ho*tel* #

      1   2   3

1. iconic; Left Hand flat "B" shape, Palm Turned Down, moves rapidly R to L <Syl *to* bldg>
2. iconic; Left Hand flat "B" shape, Palm Turned Down, small hop R to L <S *into* bldg>
3. beat on poststroke hold

Focusing on 2, speech conveys motion and locus of motion; gesture conveys path and manner of motion (a hop "over the threshold"); yet they certainly belong to one idea unit. Real mismatches are seen with children at the brink of, but not yet over, some learning threshold. For example, while saying the number of marbles has increased when the experimenter spreads them apart, a child points at each marble successively, as if counting them; here one idea does not encompass both speech and gesture without contradiction.

7. Wallace Chafe suggested the term "newsworthy" (pers. comm.).

8. That meaning and context are indissolubly linked bears comparison to a philo-sophical approach known as "dynamic semantics," where the emphasis is on adding to context. In both, context is changing. They differ in that with dynamic semantics the focus is on information reception, while with the GP it is on pro-duction. The two approaches nonetheless seem complementary.

9. Susan Duncan discovered the logic of this natural experiment. It is now the basis of a designed experiment that she and Dan Loehr are conducting. They are comparing gestures after participants have watched the standard outside–inside order to the gestures of different participants who have watched it in the reverse inside–outside order. They find interiority in gesture for the outside–inside order but not for inside–outside, showing that interiority, while percep-tually present, is not significant when it does not contrast to outside.

10. Thanks to Susan Duncan for this observation.

11. Thanks again to Susan Duncan.

12. The thumb is also extended, which reinforces the conclusion that what we see here is a modified sign (extension of the thumb is part of the canonical sign form). It is not clear why the fourth finger was extended, but perhaps this was compensation for the gestural use of the first and second fingers, to maintain something of the "extended-fingers" feel of the canonical sign.

13. Frank Bechter (2009) comments that skilled ASL storytelling (a culturally highly valued form) uses what he terms a "diagrammatic/cinematographic style" of orchestration. He regards this style to be true "deaf language," as opposed to the linear "grammatical" style invoked in many linguistic analyses of ASL, which he suggests may owe its existence more to English than to sign.

14. The metaphor comes from the land area, a "catchment" (= "*a field of mean-ingful oppositions*") that drains into (= "*is incorporated by*") a body of water (= "*a GP*"). The flaw of the metaphor is that in it the GP ends up a static entity, while in reality it is a dynamic process. Still, the flow of context into GP is captured.

15. McCullough (2005) and Park-Doob (2010), building further, have pointed out an independent function for extended holds covering multiple GPs, namely, to embody *discourse continuity* – also a kind of catchment: one or both hands held in space indicating the continuing relevance of whatever significance the discourse has attached to the location and/or the gesture form. While these authors perceive something basically different between extended holds and catchments, just one difference seems important. The hold is continuous while the catchment allows breaks and interpolations. Whether a discourse segment runs continuously over some stretch of speech or recurs intermittently may

find prominence in different speech styles ("paragraphs" versus "episodes"), but I do not believe this changes the dialectic picture we are developing here.

16. More precisely, Tweety was the original antagonistic force that the caused-motion construction, "and (Tweety) drops it down," transferred to the bowling ball.

17. Thanks to Nobuhiro Furuyama for discussing this analogy with me from Vygotsky (1987).

18. I am grateful to Kamala Russell for alerting me to this diagram. Figure used with permission.

Notes on Chapter 3

1. Thanks to Liesbet Quaeghebeur for coining this marvelous word.

2. Armstrong and Wilcox, in *The Gestural Origin of Language* (2007), imply supplantation by, as it were, omission. They do not consider how speech came into being after sign language (as they identify gesture-first); but so skipping the question does not solve the mystery of how speech supplanted gesture and still ended up being integrated with it. For other points, see Adam Kendon's review (2009).

3. "We speculate that having segmented structure in the oral modality as we currently do leaves the manual modality free to co-occur with speech and to capture the mimetic aspects of communication *along with* speech. Thus, our current arrangement allows us to retain along with a segmented representation, and in a single stream of communication, the imagistic aspects of the mimetic that are so vital to communication ..." (Goldin-Meadow *et al.*, 1996, p. 52, emphasis in original).

4. Or further back: Fogassi and Ferrari (2004) have identified neural mechanisms in monkeys for associating gestures and meaningful sounds, which they suggest could be a pre-adaptation for articulated speech.

5. The iconicity may have been somewhat "accidental" if the bonobo on the left started her swing gesture after the bonobo on the right had already started to move. Her hand moved without actually touching the other but still may have been meant as a shove; but even a failed shove can be a precursor.

6. Our Lucky Charm coined this phrase that captures everything.

7. Adult–infant "instruction" by New Caledonian crows has been observed by Holzhaider *et al.* (2010), and takes place in strikingly similar circumstances to those envisioned for the evolution of Mead's Loop. But unlike the instruction enabled by Mead's Loop, where the adult's own communicative actions are felt as social and are rearranged for the benefit of the infant, the crows rearrange the physical environment. There is nothing symbolic and nothing in the manipulations that is social, and learning appears to be by observation and imitation not by the adult's self-aware instruction. Some aspects of the Mead's Loop selection are thus present but not all.

8. Claudia Sowa transcribed and organized the SW morph data in Figures. 3.4–3.6 and the later Canary Row proto-morph data in Figure 3.7.

9. An insight due to Amy Franklin, pers. comm.: If the same gesture appears in different combinations, and has different values, this could be evidence of syntagmatic value.

10. All the more striking, then, that gestures *with* speech are global and synthetic – resisting these construction-like tendencies.

11. Recent fMRI studies by Menenti *et al.* (2011) find that the areas of the brain specifically associated with syntactic decisions overlap in speaking and listening, and this overlap includes areas of the motor cortex. A thread of other experimentation has tended to show that the perceptual understanding of manual action verbs includes activation of the hand areas of the brain (see Willems *et al.* 2011 and references therein). However, "new actions" would encompass a far wider range of linguistic comprehension than the "old action" responses of throwing, grasping, squeezing, etc. these experiments have measured.

12. And now bolstered by increasing genetic diversity along presumed coastal migration routes during the populating of Asia (The HUGO Pan-Asian SNP Consortium; see HUGO 2009).

13. Perniss writes (email 11/11/10, quoted with permission), "I might be speaking English and suddenly can think of a particular word only in German. Knowing the German word, however, does not necessarily make it easy to come up with the English counterpart, since it's not a matter of simple translation between entries in my mental lexica. Instead, I find myself conjuring up a scenario or situation in an English-speaking context in which that word might be more salient and thus then accessible to me again."

14. For a vivid description of this kind of experience, see the introductory section of "Speaking in Tongues," by Zadie Smith, *NYRB*, 02/26/09, pp. 41–44.

15. The role of multiple factors seems particularly germane to Kanzi's spoken English comprehension. While the tests Savage-Rumbaugh conducted took great pains to exclude extralinguistic cues that could steer Kanzi to correct choices (such as the human handler's gaze), we nonetheless see in the "Bonobo People" video some cases of Kanzi reaching for the correct item *in advance* of hearing the critical word identifying it, so other cues seemingly were available to him despite all precautions – we know neither what nor how many. Given the multifaceted character of speech comprehension, this is perhaps not too surprising even with conscientious control efforts. I am grateful to R. L. B. McNeill, who first noticed this temporal anomaly in Kanzi's responding.

16. The "IW project" is a collaboration with neuroscientist Jonathan Cole and philosopher Shaun Gallagher, with participation by University of Chicago gesture lab members Susan Duncan, Amy Franklin, Mischa Park-Doob, Karl-Erik McCullough and Nobuhiro Furuyama, plus our colleague Bennett Bertenthal. IW was the subject of a 1998 BBC *Horizon* program, "The Man who Lost his Body."

17. IW is seated under a blind that allowed visual contact with the room while blocking vision of his hands. The blind was conceived by Nobuhiro Furuyama and constructed by David Klein.

18. Bennett Bertenthal (pers. comm.) proposed a possible mechanism for this tandem reduction. Speech and gesture, slowing together, could reflect the operation of a "pacesetter" in the brain that survived IW's deafferentation; for example, his hands moved outward each time at speech stress peaks, and this motion–stress association was maintained over a range of speeds. Thanks to Mead's Loop, such a pacesetter can be co-opted by significances other than the action of rotation itself – in this case the metaphor of a process – and be controlled by it over the thought–language–hand link. Metaphoric control is displayed in IW's timing, since his hands rotate only while he was saying, "I'm starting to . . . " (and did so both times) and stopped between the first normal speed and second reduced speed rotations as he said, "and that's because," indicating that the rotation and stress point linkages were specifically tied to the process as rotation metaphor.

19. Another deafferented patient in a private film featuring IW had not at the time of filming developed any of his strategies for achieving movement control, but nonetheless preserves speech–gesture synchrony at points of co-expressivity. This patient's arms and legs seem to float cloudlike in space but his gestures in the midst of these floating limbs are timed precisely with co-expressive speech (for example, closing his hands just as he said "clamp **down**"). This patient prefers privacy and cannot be described further. Jonathan Cole has recently encountered another case like IW, who also reveals the thought–language–hand link. After deafferentation, gestures returned before most pragmatic movements, suggesting that gesture and practical action depend in part on separately recovering circuits. Cole writes, "[the patient] is so vibrant and alive that it was inspiring. Of interest is that she remains ataxic so does not use a cup and has trouble raising food to her mouth. She has gesture. She said it returned on its own, within months, i.e. without her consciously doing it, though she has to tell it to stop if she is insecure in a chair. Whereas Ian's gestures are precise and orchestrated to an extent hers appear far more free and expressive (she is freer and more expressive too!). There is a huge difference between these and her movements when they have to be spatially accurate. I asked why gesture was so much better and she immediately replied, 'Because they don't have to be placed accurately.' I asked her to make a square shape in the air when gesturing and her free expressive movements were replaced by conscious ataxic movements. So, firstly, she maintains her gestures reappeared on their own quite soon and when her other movements were poor. Secondly her gestures are quite big and relatively uncontrolled but not ataxic compared with her smaller slower spatial accurate(ish) ataxic ones." (email from Jonathan Cole, received 08/22/2010, quoted with permission).

20. Broca's area sends axons to the primary motor cortex but not to the spinal cord (Ana Solodkin, pers. comm.).

21. Thanks to Ana Solodkin, Department of Neurology of the University of Chicago, Tae Kunisawa, Department of Linguistics of the University of New Mexico, and James Goss, Department of Comparative Human Development of the University of Chicago, for bringing many of these references to my attention.

22. Consistent with this role of the prefrontal cortex as part of the thought–language–hand link, Lin *et al.* (2012), comparing RNA traces of genetic activity at different stages of life in postmortem-examined macaque, chimp, and human brains, single out the prefrontal cortex as one of the areas in which human activity begins earlier, continues longer, and is greater.

23. And hand-axes dating to nearly 1 mya have been discovered in Spain (Scott and Gilbert 2009).

24. Another crucial factor would have been the physical immaturity of human infants at birth and the resulting prolonged period of dependency giving time, for example, for cultural exposure and GPs to emerge at leisure, an essential delay pegged to the emergence of self-aware agency. Neanderthals, in contrast, may have had a short period of development (cf. Rozzi and de Castro 2004).

Notes on Chapter 4

1. We are thus not stumbling into the "movie-in-reverse" fallacy appearing in much evolutionary psychology, of playing the evolution movie backward from some current-day linguistic or other function to a hypothetical selection of this very function. There are too many branch points leading to the past for this to be possible. We work in the reverse direction. We have identified an adaptation and scenario in which it could have been naturally selected, and look for current-day functions that plausibly descended from it.

2. The discovery of the FOXP2 gene points to the centrality of action control at the foundation of language. The gene has undergone accelerated evolution (see Konopka *et al.* 2009) and when implanted into engineered mice changes vocalization (Enard *et al.* 2009). It is not a "language gene" but appears to code for a transcription factor affecting the expression of possibly many other genes (which transcription differs in the human version compared to that in chimps, Konopka *et al.* 2009). The mutation in the KE family that led to its discovery affects fine motor control, speech articulation, and other actions, as well as syntax, which, as we saw in Chapter 3, can be regarded as a set of culturally maintained action schemas. As a gene affecting fine-tuned action control, it would influence the raw material on which Mead's Loop and its new form of action worked (the Mead's Loop innovation itself would be something else genetically). For an accessible and clarifying discussion of the FOXP2 discovery, see Mac Andrew (www.evolutionpages.com/FOXP2_language.htm, accessed 12/02/11).

    The Neanderthal genome project (Pääbo and colleagues; cf. news focus in *Science* 2009 323:866–871) shows that this extinct form of human also had

FOXP2, and also may have been capable of fine motor control. Whether this control covered the vocal tract is unknown but speech seems not impossible (and points to **Version A** in Figure 3.13). Some have suggested that the Neanderthal brain, although large, had a different developmental time course (much briefer, cf. Rozzi and de Castro 2004) and did not sustain robust activity of the prefrontal cortex (Wynn and Coolidge 2008). A short ontogenesis meant less time for Mead's Loop development (which does not appear before age 3 or 4 in contemporary human children; see Chapter 5). An early critical period cutoff in Neanderthals would have truncated any GP-like developments. The prefrontal cortex, among its other functions, arranges and selects alternatives. The formation of fields of oppositions is a place in language where this ability is tapped. Weakened fields of oppositions could have yielded cognitive inflexibility and repetitiveness (not unlike the picture for Downs syndrome described later in this chapter). Other than this rigidity, which appears in many contexts, including hunting methods that never developed throwing spears and required close-in stabs of large, dangerous prey, adaptive intelligence was also present (as described by Wynn and Coolidge 2011; their attempt to capture the Neanderthal mindset reveals both qualities). Such a creature would have had little chance against the *H. sapiens* mode of cognition, not necessarily because of massacres, although these may have occurred, but because of mental inflexibility.

3. Careful experiments by Sahin *et al.* (2009) reveal detailed features of these vegetative actions as co-opted for speech. Taking clues from Levelt *et al.* (1999), they recorded directly from brain areas of patients undergoing open skull surgery, and found temporal segmentations of brain activity built around the lexical and morphological infrastructure of words. Patients were shown printed nouns or verbs either alone or after a sentence with a blank space: "Every day they ____ " or " Yesterday they ____ " for verbs (other frames for nouns elicited singular or plural). They found that lexical, grammatical, and phonological steps occurred with distinctive delays of about 200 ms, 320 ms, or 450 ms, respectively, in accord with the Levelt *et al.* sequential model. In other words, the vegetative action system, co-opted by Mead's Loop, may have split up layers corresponding to the logical steps that successively orchestrate the motor system and which are quite different from the original vegetative use. However it is not known how imagery affects this timing. If differentiating in a field of meaningful oppositions a past time, say, the idea unit may *begin* with an inflected verb plus imagery. Does the GP's onflashing then have to wait 320 or 450 ms? These kinds of questions have not been asked. Delay seems unlikely (although would be fascinating to find).

4. Thanks to Gale Stam for this translation.

5. Müller views metaphor dynamically, as a *process* by which the speaker and her listener generate metaphoricity in the context of the speech event; clearly a conception in alignment with the position of this book.

6. The word "experience" is from Cornelia Müller and replaces the "understand" of the original formulation by Lakoff and Johnson 1980 ("one understands one

thing in terms of another"). In the same formula, "being one thing in terms of another" anticipates the "cognitive being" in the next essay of this chapter.

7. Some odd phonetic tags, like the "sn-" nasal words, "snot," "sniff," "sneeze," and others may be similar (the "imagery," a "snout gesture" that orchestrates a closing of the vocal tract at the alveolar ridge, as a reflex action when air actually is expelled through the nose), but since all these examples are actual words a historical source can't be ruled out; cf. Rhodes and Lawler 1981 for a pioneering linguistic study of such terms, and www-personal.umich.edu/~jlawler/ (accessed 12/09/11) for much recent work, including extensive word lists; all actual English words.

8. This is not reference; not the gesture referring to the antagonistic force (or vice versa); it is the gesture as a metaphor of the force.

9. That thought and language are imbued with metaphoricity gives rise to comical hybrids like "all these people bit off my head and started breathing down my neck" (overheard by Nancy Dray) or "we need all this new blood coming down the pipe" (overheard on a different occasion by the author). That they occur at all shows how much is metaphoricity at the center of mental life.

10. As mentioned briefly in Chapter 1, some emblems start instead from metonyms but otherwise meet similar cultural form standards. For example, Payrató (1993) cites the 2-fingers-up "V" shape at the lips to request a cigarette. Both metaphor-based and metonym-based emblems show a kind of recalibration of motor acts (here, holding a cigarette to the mouth) around cultural standards of form and function. Unlike emblems based on metaphors, however, metonym-based ones are pantomimic at the source. It is an open (and interesting) question whether emblemizing pantomime also enables it to become absorbed by gesticulation; or whether, instead, the resistance of pantomime to gesticulation continues, and these emblems also are not absorbed; a future study might look into this.

11. The "conduit" name itself refers to the "channel" along which the "container" with its "cargo of meaning" is sent to a "recipient" (still other uses of the same conduit metaphor).

12. Thanks to Josef Stern of the University of Chicago Department of Philosophy.

13. Whereupon the properties enumerated in Chapter 1, §1.4.1 would emerge – repeatable, listable, reportable; adhering to standards of form/function; containing extra form elements to distinguish it as an emblem, and sociocultural standing defined and maintained.

14. Pointed out to me originally by Elena Levy. The quote (recovered by Tae Kunisawa) is: "That which is specific to this particular form of sound has remained unexplored. As a consequence, this research has not been able to explain why sound possessing certain physical and mental characteristics is present in human speech or how it functions as a component of speech. In a similar manner, the study of meaning has been defined as the study of the concept, of the concept existing and developing in complete isolation from its material carrier. To a large extent, the failure of classic semantics and phonetics has been a direct

result of this tendency to divorce meaning from sound, of this decomposition of the word into its separate elements" (Rieber and Carton, 1987, p. 46).

15. Merleau-Ponty's quotation is from Gelb and Goldstein (1925, p. 158).

16. I am indebted to Jan Arnold for this quotation.

17. The "H-model" avoids the homunculus problem encountered by the third-person perspective inherent to the concept of a "representation" and with it the "theater of the mind" problem highlighted by Dennett (1991). The theater of the mind is the presumed central thinking area in which representations are "presented" to a receiving intelligence. The possibilities for homunculi – each with its own theater and receiving intelligence –spiraling down inside other similarly endowed homunculi in this theory are well known. In the H-model, there is no theater and no extra being; the gesture is, rather, part of the speaker's momentary mode of being itself, and is not "watched."

18. This is why the material carrier and communicative dynamism concepts are opposite to the economic, costs-minimizing/benefits-maximizing, "least effort" = "best result" dictum. The economic model, for those fond of eponymous acronyms, can be called the "Summer Lazing on the Beach" or SLOB model of speaking (SLOB: "Uhh!" – Jeeves: "Would you care for a cool drink, sir?"– maximizes benefit at the minimum of cost).

19. I am grateful to Zenzi Griffin for alerting me to this passage.

20. I am grateful to Kazuki Sekine for first raising this question.

21. Relatedly, Oberauer (2005) noted that briefly presented contents not used in ongoing processing can be held in the background and, while there, do not interfere with operations in working memory itself.

22. Using Silverstein's notation and transcription: Q = question, R = reply; A = by Mr. A, B = by Mr. B; numerals = position in sequence in Silverstein (1997) with subdivisions of R_B7 to indicate gesture space uses.

23. And it offers an explanation (suggested to me by Liesbet Quaeghebeur) of a frequently experienced but never remarked upon contagion in tip of the tongue states – when someone speaking unexpectedly cannot recall a common word whose meaning is clear to everyone, often the interlocutor is also unable to recall it. If the interaction includes "mind merging," it could also include "tip-of-the-tongue merging" through involuntary mimicry.

24. According to a BBC online science report (07/28/10), Fredericke Range of the University of Vienna has shown something like mirror neuron responses by dogs. If an owner demonstrates how to open a box with her hand, the dog far more quickly learns the trick if it uses a paw, compared to having to use its mouth; and if the owner uses her mouth, the dog is much faster to use its mouth, compared to having to use a paw. The experiment however did not test combining paw and mouth actions, the domain of Mead's Loop, so we do not know if the dog's brain is able to forge such bonds.

25. Dogs show every sign of understanding some human speech, and experiments demonstrate an ability to follow deictic gestures (Soproni *et al.* 2002), in contrast

to chimps who seem oblivious to them (Hare *et al.* 2002), but these achievements do not show anything like growth points as opposed to stimulus-response, and there is no indication that the same dogs ever make gestural motions of their own ("pointers," game dogs, may not understand they are pointing, as opposed to reacting in a ritualized manner to (probably) olfactory and auditory cues).

26. In support of this idea, mice with cortico-stiatal circuit deficits (affecting motor regions of the cerebral cortex) show autistic spectrum disorders (Peça *et al.* 2011), self-injurious grooming and poor social interactions. A further important discovery by Voineagu *et al.* (2011) points specifically to gene expression that is "significantly disrupted" in autism affecting the frontal areas (among other areas).

27. Thanks to Susan Duncan for alerting me to the relevance of this constant. If, during the 300 ms capsule, the process of orchestration cannot be altered and is running ballistically, and it is then self-mimicked and perceived, another 300 ms capsule is sealed, and repetition – stuttering – begins.

28. The idea that there may be less stuttering in a second language was suggested to me by Our Lucky Charm. I have added Mead's Loop and the GP.

29. This draws on a seminar on music and gesture at the University of Chicago at which Lawrence Zbikowski and Ric Ashley, music theorists and performers in their own right, presented eye-popping examples of spontaneous, unrehearsed gestures by performing musicians as they proceeded with their performances.

30. Children of Mozartian precocity who from exposure and ability have knowledge of significant musical oppositions and perform one or more instruments while very young, would be extremely interesting to observe from a musical GP point of view. Is their music acquisition anything like their own speech acquisition, the beginning of musical thinking being timed, as with the GPs of language, to the dawn of self-aware agency, around age 3 or 4, and developing from there? This could show itself in the kind of musical gestures that we have been identifying suddenly surging upward. I am not aware of any evidence pertaining to this question, but such a correlation would be convincing evidence in itself of musical GPs.

Notes on Chapter 5

1. By the same token the urge of current-day mothers to provide a spoken gloss to the objects a child indicates in gesture can also be seen to depend on Mead's Loop, this being the link the child's gesture taps.

2. Abstract found on the International Cognitive Linguistics Conference web page before the site was removed, accessed 03/18/09.

3. I am grateful to Elena Levy for alerting me to the relevance of the crib language studies to the "dark age."

4. The 2;6-year-old in Figure 5.3, in her redundant manner inclusions, seem-ingly also combined viewpoints: the opposite of the slightly older children of Table 5.3 – her sweeping undulating arm is O-VPT for Manner and Path; the opening and closing hand is C-VPT for Manner alone (reproducing what the child imagines Sylvester was experiencing) but it is questionable that she had viewpoints at all. Instead, recalling Werner and Kaplan's point, she may have been simply displaying interesting things – both felt and seen – to her listener (her mother) with pantomime.

Notes on Chapter 6

1. A second example analyzed in Kita (2000) also displayed an "echo" with co-expressive speech, after a full-size gesture performed absent speech, and it too seems to have been reshaped to constitute a psychological predicate in the context. Other narrators also produce such examples, suggesting that the phenomenon of speechless gestures followed by speech-synchronized gestures is a general one.

2. In a book published in 1968, Herbert A. Simon made the case for a science of what he called the artificial. However the origin of language was not "manmade" in a purposeful, goal-directed sense.

3. These points were originally presented at the 2007 MLMI (Machine Learn-ing, Machine Intelligence) meeting, in Bethesda, MD. I am unaware of any follow-up.

4. A radically different approach may provide a way to make the GP computable. The approach, as described to me by Michita Imai, computer scientist and robot-designer at Keio University, Japan, is based on a form of logic being explored by Yukio Pegio Gunji of Kobe University. While I cannot evaluate the technical limits of the following, I mention it as a new and remarkable idea. It is based on a form of logic described as "True and False," which may open a way to the mathematical expression of a dialectic opposition (not True or False, which is tautology). Imai is currently applying this logical form as an exploration of GP computation (Imai in progress). He writes: "When we try to prove the logical form of 'True and False,' an eternal proving loop appears. It never stops. The calculation is as follows. If we take the position that a GP can be expressed as a symbol, it is not a GP because a GP cannot be completely written by a symbolic expression. If we take the position that the GP exists without symbolic expressions, there may be some way to express it as a symbol. And then we go back to the first position that we can write the GP with a symbol but it is not the GP . . . This loop continues forever. [DM: Thus capturing instability. However, this is not a dialectic opposition. Its chief difference from the GP is that the spontaneity of the system does not differentiate contexts or have a place for any field of oppositions. It is without meaning. Still, such a system could be used with the Mead's Loop, language-evolving robot described in §6.1.6.3 "Analog?".] The cycle of 'I'/'me'

[from Mead's 1974 theory of the self, applied to GPs in *Hand and Mind* 1992] may come from this kind of unsatisfied interaction. The logic of 'True and False' is never satisfied and never stops because it includes a contradiction in itself." Imai goes on to say: "I have tried to implement Gunji's model on robots to generate spontaneous behaviors...My motivation...is not to control the robot but for spontaneous behaviors. I think that we can consider a calculation model of the GP based on Gunji's model," which Imai is now developing in the cited work. Among other germane properties, the resulting agent has creative flexibility such that "it does not employ a way of selecting a behavior which is prepared prior to execution" (from the paper in progress). This is in contrast to other autonomous agents. Susan Duncan (pers. comm.) once contrasted such an agent to the GP as follows (and it is this Imai's approach promises to overcome): "Max [the autonomous agent] works as follows – looks ahead, sees what the linguistic resource will be, calculates how far back the preparation will have to be in order for the stroke to coincide with this. Then speech and gesture are generated on their own tracks, and the two assembled into a multimodal utterance. In contrast, in the GP the gesture image and linguistic categorization constitute one idea unit, and timing is an inherent part of how this thought is created. The start of preparation is the dawn of the idea unit, which is kept intact and is unpacked, as a unit, into a full utterance."

5. For a GP-based understanding of turn-exchange see McNeill *et al.* (2010).
6. Phrasing originally from Susan Duncan.
7. Beattie, however, is clearly not opposed to GP analysis. In a recent work, "Why Aren't We Saving the Planet? A Psychological Perspective" (2010), he ingeniously undertakes what I regard as context-sensitive GP analyses to uncover un-"green" biases in speakers who, in their speech, espouse green verities, but in their gestures reveal more "brown" attitudes – of which the speakers themselves seem unaware.
8. As far as I know no other approach in the psychology and linguistics of thought and speech provides anything like the degree of continuity and delicacy that we have in our analyses here, which is in no way an exception and is typical of many of other descriptions.
9. The gestures, however, were performed by an actor and this clouds the validity of the results. To quote Susan Duncan: "A member of our lab went back and analyzed the gestures on the stimulus videos, using our techniques, and found that they synchronized oddly with speech and were unlike typical gesturing in several other respects. So, in other words...the gesturing was unlike anything a participant would ever have encountered in real life." (pers. comm.).

References

Acredolo, Linda P. and Goodwyn, Susan W. 1990. "Sign language in babies: The significance of symbolic gesturing for understanding language development," in Vasta (ed.), pp. 1–42.

Allott, Robin. 2001. *The Great Mosaic Eye*. Sussex: The Book Guild.

Anderson, J. R. (ed.) 1981. *Cognitive Skills and Their Acquisition*. Hillsdale, NJ: Erlbaum.

Anderson, Stephen R. 2004. *Doctor Dolittle's Delusion: Animals and the Uniqueness of Human Language*. New Haven: Yale University Press.

Arbib, M. A. 2005. "From monkey-like action recognition to human language: An evolutionary framework for neurolinguistics." *Behavioral and Brain Sciences*, 28: 105–124.

Armstrong, David F. and Wilcox, Sherman E. 2007. *The Gestural Origins of Language*. Oxford University Press.

Armstrong, David, Stokoe, William F. and Wilcox, Sherman E. 1995. *Gesture and the Nature of Language*. Cambridge University Press.

Atkinson J. M. and Heritage J. (eds.) 1984 *Structures of Social Action*. Cambridge University Press.

Atkinson, Quentin D. 2011. "Phonemic diversity supports a serial founder effect model of language expansion from Africa." *Science* 332: 346–349.

Baars, B. J. 1988. *A Cognitive Theory of Consciousness*. Cambridge University Press.

Bachelder, Bruce L. 2001. "The magical number 4 = 7: Span theory on capacity limitations." *Behavioral and Brain Sciences* 24:116–117.

Baddeley, A. and Hitch, G. J. 1974. "Working Memory." In G. Bower (ed.), pp. 49–89.

Bahktin, M. M. 1981. *The Dialogic Imagination*. (M. Holquist, ed.; C. Emerson and M. Holquist, trans.). Austin, TX: University of Texas Press.

Baker, Mark C. 2001. *The Atoms of Language: The Mind's Hidden Rules of Grammar*. New York: Basic Books.

Bannard, C., Lieven, E., and Tomasello, M. 2009. "Evaluating constructivist theory via Bayesian modeling of children's early grammatical development." Abstract posted on the International Cognitive Linguistics Conference website, accessed 03/30/09.

Bates, Elizabeth and Dick, Frederic. 2002. "Language, gesture and the developing brain," in Casey and Munakata (eds.), pp. 293–310.

Bavelas, Janet B., Coates, Linda, and Johnson, Trudy. 2000. "Listeners as Co-narrators." *Journal of Personality and Social Psychology* 79: 941–952.

Beattie, Geoffrey. 2003. *Visible Thought: The New Psychology of Body Language.* New York: Routledge.

Beattie, Geoffrey and Shovelton, Heather. 2006. "When size really matters: How a single semantic feature is represented in the speech and gesture modalities." *Gesture* 6: 63–84.

Bechter, Frank Daniel. 2009. Of deaf lives: Convert culture and the dialogic of *ASL* storytelling. Unpublished Ph.D. Dissertation, University of Chicago.

Berkeley Linguistic Society, Proceedings of the 13th Annual Meeting. 1987. Berkeley, CA: Berkeley Linguistics Society.

Berkeley Linguistic Society, Proceedings of the 27th Annual Meeting. 2006 [Meeting in 2001]. Berkeley, CA: Berkeley Linguistics Society.

Bermúdez, José Luis. 2003. *Thinking Without Words.* Oxford University Press.

Bertenthal, Bennett, Longo, Matthew R., and Kosobud, Adam. 2006. "Imitative response tendencies following observation of intransitive actions." *Journal of Experimental Psychology: Human Perception and Performance* 32: 210–225.

Bickerton, Derek. 1990. *Language and Species.* University of Chicago Press.

Binkofski, Ferdinand, Amunts, Katrin, Stephan, Klaus Martin, Posse, Stefan, Schormann, Thorsten, Freund, Hans-Joachim, Zilles, Karl, and Seitz, Rüdiger J. 2000. "Broca's region subserves imagery of motion: A combined cytoarchitectonic and fMRI study." *Human Brain Mapping* 11: 273–285.

Black, Max. 1962. *Models and Metaphors.* Ithaca: Cornell.

Bloom, Ralph. 1979. Language creation in the manual modality: A preliminary investigation. Unpublished Bachelors thesis, Department of Behavioral Sciences, University of Chicago.

Blumenthal, Arthur (ed. and trans.) 1970. *Language and Psychology: Historical Aspects of Psycholinguistics.* New York: John Wiley and Sons Ltd.

Bonda, Eva, Petrides, Michael, and Evans, Alan C. 1994. "Frontal cortex involvement in organized sequence of hand movements: evidence from positron emission tomography study." *Society for Neuroscience Abstracts* 20: 353.

Botha, Rudie and de Swart, Henriette (eds.) 2005/2006. *Restricted Linguistic Systems as Windows on Language Evolution.* Utrecht: LOT (Netherlands Graduate School of Linguistics Occasional Series, Utrecht University). http://lotos.library.uu.nl/publish/articles/000287/bookpart.pdf (accessed 05/02/11)

Bower, G. (ed.). 1974. *Recent Advances in Learning and Motivation, Vol. III.* New York: Academic.

Bowerman, Melissa and Brown, Penelope (eds.) 2008. *Crosslinguistic Perspectives on Argument Structure: Implications for Learnability.* New York: Taylor and Francis.

Braine, Martin D. S. 1963. "The ontogeny of English phrase structure: The first phase." *Language* 39: 1–13.

Brennan, M. and Turner, G. (eds.) 1994. *Word-order Issues in Sign Language.* Durham: International Sign Linguistics Association Publications.

Bressem, J. 2010. "Pounding the verbal utterance: Forms and functions of beats." *International Society of Gesture Studies*, Conference Talk, Frankfurt/Oder, Germany.

Browman, Catherine P. and Goldstein, Louis. 1990. "Tiers in articulatory phonology, with some implications for casual speech," in Kingston and Beckman (eds.), pp. 341–376.

Brown, Terrence A. 2010. "Stranger from Siberia." *Nature* 464: 83.

Bühler, Karl. 1982. "The deictic field of language and deictic words," in Jarvella and Klein (eds.), pp. 9–30.

Burling, Robbins. 2005. *The Talking Ape: How Language Evolved.* Oxford University Press.

Butcher, Cynthia and Goldin-Meadow, Susan. 2000. "Gesture and the transition from one- to two-word speech: When hand and mouth come together," in McNeill (ed.), pp. 235–257.

Butterworth, Brian and Beattie, Geoffrey. 1978. "Gesture and silence as indicators of planning in speech," in Campbell and Smith (eds.), pp. 347–360.

Butterworth, Brian and Hadar, Uri. 1989. "Gesture, speech, and computational stages: A reply to McNeill." *Psychological Review* 96: 168–174.

Call, Josep and Tomasello, Michael (eds.) 2007. *The Gestural Communication of Apes and Monkeys.* Mahway, NJ: Erlbaum.

Campbell, R. N. and Smith, P. (eds.) 1978. *Recent Advances in The Psychology of Language: Formal and Experimental Approaches.* New York: Plenum Press.

Capirici, Olga, Iverson, Jana M., Pizzuto, Elena and Volterra, Virginia. 1996. "Gestures and words during the transition to two-word speech." *Journal of Child Language* 23: 645–673.

Carlson, Patricia and Anisfeld, Moshe. 1969. "Some observations on the linguistic competence of a two-year-old child." *Child Development* 40: 569–575.

Cartmill, Erica and Byrne, Richard W. 2007. "Orangutans modify their gestural signaling according to their audience's comprehension." *Current Biology* 17: 1345–1348.

Cartmill, Erica A., Beilock, Sian, and Goldin-Meadow, Susan. 2012. "A word in the hand: Action, gesture, and mental representation in human evolution." *Philosophical Transactions of the Royal Society, Series B* 367: 129–143.

Cartmill, Erica and Maestripieri, Dario. 2012. "Socio-cognitive specializations in nonhuman primates: Evidence from gestural communication," in Vonk and Shackelford (eds.), pp. 166–193.

Casey, B. J. and Munakata, Y. (eds.) 2002. Special issue: Converging Method Approach to the Study of Developmental Science. *Developmental Psychobiology* 40.

Chafe, Wallace L. 1994. *Discourse, Consciousness, and Time: The Flow and Displacement of Conscious Experience in Speaking and Writing.* University of Chicago Press.

Chalmers, David J. 1996. *The Conscious Mind: In Search of a Theory of Conscious Experience.* New York: Oxford University Press.

Chase, W. G. and Eriksson, K. A. 1981. "Skilled memory." In Anderson, J. R. (ed.), pp. 227–249.

Chomsky, Noam. 1965. *Aspects of the Theory of Syntax.* Cambridge, MA: MIT Press.

Cienki, Alan. 2008. "Why study metaphor and gesture?" In Cienki and Müller (eds), pp. 5–25.

Cienki, Alan. 2010. "Language as a variably multimodal phenomenon." *International Society of Gesture Studies*, Plenary Talk, Frankfurt/Oder, Germany.

Cienki, Alan and Müller, Cornelia. 2008. *Metaphor and Gesture.* Amsterdam and Philadelphia: John Benjamins.

Clark, Andy. 1997. "Being there: Putting brain, body, and word together again." Cambridge, MA: MIT Press.

Clark, Andy. 2008. *Supersized Mind.* Oxford University Press.

Cohen, Akiba A. 1977. "The communicative function of hand illustrators." *Journal of Communication* 27: 54–63.

Cohen, James, McAlister, Kara T., Rolstad, Kellie, and MacSwan, Jeff (eds.) 2005. *Proceedings of the 4th International Symposium on Bilingualism.* Somerville, MA: Cascadilla Press.

Cohen, Ted. 2008. *Thinking of others: On the Talent for Metaphor.* Princeton University Press.

Connolly, K. and Bruner, J. (eds.) 1974. *The Growth of Competence.* New York: Academic Press.

Corballis, Michael C. 2002. *From Hand to Mouth: The Origins of Language.* Cambridge, MA: Harvard University Press.

Cowan, Nelson. 2001. "The magical number 4 in short-term memory: A reconsideration of mental storage capacity." *Behavioral and Brain Sciences* 24: 87–185.

Custers, Ruud and Aarts, Henk. 2010. "The unconscious will: How the pursuit of goals operates outside of conscious awareness." *Science* 329: 47–50.

Danesi, Marcel. 1993. *Vico, Metaphor, and the Origin of Language.* Bloomington: Indiana University Press.

Daniels, Peter T. and Bright, William. 1996. *The World's Writing Systems.* Oxford University Press.

De Jorio, Andrea. 2000. *Gesture in Naples and Gesture in Classical Antiquity. A Translation of La mimimca degli antichi investigata nel gestire napoletano (1832). Translated with an Introduction and Notes, by Adam Kendon.* Bloomington and Indianapolis: Indiana University Press.

Deacon, Terrence W. 1997. *The Symbolic Species: The Co-evolution of Language and the Brain.* New York: Norton.

Decety, Jean, Perani, Daniela, Jeannerod, Marc, Bettinardi, Valentino, Tadary, B, Woods, Roger, Mazziotta, John C., and Fazio, Feruccio. 1994. "Mapping motor representations with positron emission tomography." *Nature* 371: 600–602.

Deng, Li. 1998. "A dynamic, feature-based approach to the interface between phonology and phonetics for speech modeling and recognition." *Speech Communication* 24: 299–323.

Dennett, Daniel C. 1991. *Consciousness Explained.* Boston: Little, Brown and Co.

de Ruiter, J. P., Bangerter, Adrian, and Dings, Paula. 2012. "The interplay between gesture and speech in the production of referring expressions: Investigating the tradeoff hypothesis." *Topics in Cognitive Science* 4: 232–248.

de Ruiter, J. P. (2007). "Postcards from the mind: the relationship between thought, imagistic gesture, and speech." *Gesture,* 7, 21–38

Dessalles, Jean-Louis. 2007. *Why We Talk: The Evolutionary Origins of Language.* Oxford University Press.

de Waal, F. (ed.) 2001. *Tree of Origin: What Primate Behavior Can Tell Us about Human Social Evolution.* Cambridge, MA: Harvard University Press.

Dewey, John. 1896. "The reflex arc concept in psychology." *The Psychological Review* 3: 357–370.

Donald, Merlin. 1991. *Origins of the Modern Mind: Three Stages in the Evolution of Culture and Cognition.* Cambridge, MA: Harvard University Press.

Dray, N. L. and McNeill, D. 1990. "Gestures during discourse: The contextual structuring of thought," in Tsohatzidis (ed.), pp. 465–487.

Dreyfus, H. 1994. *Being-in-the-World: A Commentary on Heidegger's Being and Time, Division I.* Cambridge, MA: MIT Press.

Dunbar, R. I. M. 1996. *Grooming, Gossip, and the Evolution of Language.* Cambridge, MA: Harvard University Press.

Duncan, Starkey Jr. and Fiske, Donald W. 1977. *Face-to-Face Interaction: Research, Methods, and Theory.* Hillsdale, NJ: Erlbaum.

Duncan, Susan D. 1996. Grammatical form and 'thinking-for-speaking' in Mandarin Chinese and English: An analysis based on speech-accompanying gestures. Unpublished Ph.D. Dissertation, University of Chicago.

   2005. "Gesture in signing: A case study in Taiwan Sign Language." *Language and Linguistics,* 6: 279–318.

   2006. "Co-expressivity of speech and gesture: Manner of motion in Spanish, English, and Chinese," *Berkeley Linguistic Society, Proceedings of the 27th Annual Meeting,* pp. 353–370.

Duncan, Susan D., Cassell, Justine, and Levy, Elena T. (eds.) 2007. *Gesture and the Dynamic Dimension of Language.* Amsterdam/Philadelphia: John Benjamins.

Duncan, Susan and Pedelty, Laura. 2007. "Discourse focus, gesture, and disfluent aphasia," in Duncan, Cassell and Levy (eds.), pp. 269–283.

Dunn, Michael, Greenhill, Simon J., Levinson, Stephen C., and Gray, Russell D. 2011. "Evolved structure of language shows lineage-specific trends in word-order universals." *Nature on-line* www.nature.com/journal/vaop/ncurrent/full/nature09923.html (Accessed 19 April 2011).

Duranti, Alessandro and Goodwin, Charles. 1992. "Rethinking context: An introduction." In A. Duranti and C. Goodwin (eds.), pp. 1–42.

Duranti Alessandro and Goodwin, Charles (eds.) 1992. *Rethinking Context: Language as an Interactive Phenomenon.* Cambridge University Press.

Eliasson, Stig and Jahr, Ernst Hadon (eds.) 1997. *Language and Its Ecology: Essays in Memory of Einar Haugen.* Berlin: de Gruyter.

Emmorey, Karen, Borinstein, Helsa B., and Thompson, Robin. 2005. "Bimodal bilingualism: Code-blending between spoken English and American Sign Language," in Cohen, Rolstad and MacSwan (eds.), pp. 663–673.

Emmorey, K. and Reilly, J. (eds.) 1995. *Sign, Gesture, and Space.* Hillsdale, NJ: Erlbaum.

Enard, Wolfgang *et al.* 2009. "A humanized version of FoxP2 affects cortico-basal ganglia circuits in mice." *Cell* 137:961–971.

Enfield, N. J. 2001. "'Lip-pointing': A discussion of form and function with reference to data from Laos." *Gesture* 1: 185–211.

    2004. "On linear segmentation and combinatorics in co-speech gesture: A symmetry-dominance construction in Lao fish trap descriptions." *Semiotica.* 149–1/4: 57–123.

Engberg-Pedersen, Elisabeth. 1994. "Some simultaneous constructions in Danish Sign Language," in Brennan and Turner (eds.), pp. 73–87.

Engle, Randi A. 2000. Toward a theory of multimodal communication: Combining speech, gestures, diagrams, and demonstrations in instructional explanations. Unpublished Ph.D. Dissertation, Stanford University.

Evans, Patrick D, Gilbert, Sandra L., Mekel-Bobrow, Nitzan, Vallender, Eric J., Anderson, Jeffrey R., Vaez-Azizi, Leila M., Tishkoff, Sarah A., Hudson, Richard R., and Lahn, Bruce T. 2005. "*Microcephalin,* a gene regulating brain size, continues to evolve adaptively in humans." *Science* 309: 1717–1720.

Fadiga, L. 2007. Report in *OMLL (Origin of Man, Language and Languages), ESF EUROCORES Program Highlights* (Dec. 2007), p. 13.

Fauconnier, Gilles and Turner, Mark. 2002. *The Way We Think: Conceptual Blending and the Mind's Hidden Complexities.* New York: Basic Books.

Ferrari, Pier Francesco, Gallese, Vittorio, Rizzolatti, Giacomo, and Fogassi, Leonardo. 2003. "Mirror neurons responding to the observation of ingestive and communicative mouth actions in the monkey ventral premotor cortex." *European Journal of Neuroscience* 17: 1703–1714.

Fillmore, Charles J. 1987. *Fillmore's Case Grammar: A reader* (René Dirven and Günter Radden, eds.). Heidelberg: J. Groos.

Firbas, Jan. 1971. "On the concept of communicative dynamism in the theory of functional sentence perspective." *Philologica Pragensia* 8: 135–144.

Fitch, W. Tecumseh. 2010. *The Evolution of Language.* Cambridge University Press.

Fodor, Jerry A. 1983. *Modularity of Mind: An Essay on Faculty Psychology.* Cambridge, MA: MIT Press.

Fogassi, Leonardo and Ferrari, Pier Francesco. 2004. "Mirror neurons, gestures and language evolution." *Interaction Studies* 5: 345–363.

Freyd, Jennifer J. 1983. "Shareability: The social psychology of epistemology." *Cognitive Science* 7: 191–210.

Furuyama, Nobuhiro. 2000a. "Gestural interaction between the instructor and the learner in origami instruction," in McNeill (ed.), pp. 99–117.

2000b. De-syntacticizing theories of reference maintenance from the viewpoint of the poetic function of language and gesture: A case of Japanese discourse. Ph.D. Dissertation, University of Chicago.

Furuyama, Nobuhiro and Sekine, Kazuki. 2007. "Forgetful or strategic? The mystery of the systematic avoidance of reference in the cartoon story narrative," in Duncan, Cassell and Levy (eds.), pp. 75–81.

Gallagher, Shaun. 2005. *How the Body Shapes the Mind.* Oxford: Clarendon Press.

Gambarara, Daniele and Givigliano, Alfredo (eds.) 2009. Origine e sviluppo del linguaggio, fra teoria e storia. *Pubblicazioni della Società di Filosofia del Linguaggio.* Rome: Aracne editrice s.r.l.

Gamble, Clive. 2007. *Origins and Revolutions: Human Identity in Earliest Prehistory.* Cambridge University Press.

Gardner, R. A. and Gardner, B. T. 1969. "Teaching sign language to a chimpanzee." *Science* 168: 664–672.

Gardner, B. T. and Gardner, R. A. 1971. "Two-way communication with an infant chimpanzee," in Schrier and Stolnitz (eds.), pp. 117–184.

Gardner, Howard. 1974. "Metaphors and modalities: How children project polar adjectives onto discrete domains." *Child Development* 45: 84–91.

Gelb, A. and Goldstein, K. 1925. "Über Farbennamenamnesie." *Psychologische Forschung* 6: 127–186.

Gentilucci, Maurizio and Dalla Volta, Riccardo 2007. "The motor system and the relationship between speech and gesture." *Gesture* 7: 159–177.

Gershkoff-Stowe, L. and Goldin-Meadow, S. 2002. "Is there a natural order for expressing semantic relations?" *Cognitive Psychology* 45: 375–412.

Gibson, James J. 1950. *The Perception of the Visual World.* Boston: Houghton Mifflin.

Gigerenzer, Gerd and Goldstein, Daniel G. 1996. "Mind as computer: Birth of a metaphor." *Creativity Research* 9: 131–144.

Gill, Satinder. 2007. "Entrainment and musicality in the human system interface." *AI & Society.* 21: 567–605.

Givón, Talmy. 1985. "Iconicity, isomorphism and non-arbitrary coding in syntax," in Haiman (ed.), pp. 187–219.

Glucksberg, S. and Keysar, B. 1990. "Understanding metaphorical comparisons: Beyond similarity." *Psychological Review* 97: 3–18.

Goldberg, Adele. 1995. *Constructions: A Construction Approach to Argument Structure.* University of Chicago Press.

Goldman Eisler, F. 1968. *Psycholinguistics: Experiments in Spontaneous Speech.* London: Academic Press.

Goldin-Meadow, Susan. 2003a. *The Resilience of Language: What Gesture Creation in Deaf Children Can Tell Us About How All Children Learn Language.* New York: Taylor & Francis.

   2003b. *Hearing Gesture: How Our Hands Help Us Think.* Cambridge, MA: Harvard University Press.

Goldin-Meadow, Susan and Butcher, Cynthia. 2003. "Pointing toward two-word speech in young children." In S. Kita (ed.), pp. 85–107.

Goldin-Meadow, Susan, Nusbaum, Howard, Kelley, Spencer D., and Wagner, Susan. 2001. "Explaining math: Gesturing lightens the load." *Psychological Science* 12: 516–522.

Goldin-Meadow, Susan and Sandhofer, Catherine Momeni. 1999. "Gestures convey substantive information about a child's thoughts to ordinary listeners." *Developmental Science* 2: 67–74.

Goldin-Meadow, Susan, Goodrich, Whitney, Sauer, Eve and Iverson, Jana. 2007. "Young children use their hands to tell their mothers what to say." *Developmental Science* 10: 778–785.

Goldin-Meadow, Susan, McNeill, David, and Singleton, Jenny. 1996. "Silence is liberating: Removing the handcuffs on grammatical expression in the manual modality." *The Psychological Review* 103: 34–55.

Goodglass, H. 1993. *Understanding Aphasia.* San Diego, CA: Academic Press.

Goren-Inbar, Naama, Alperson, Nira, Kislev, Mordechai E., Simchoni, Orit, Melamed, Yoel, Ben-Nun, Adi, and Werker, Ella. 2004. "Evidence of hominid control of fire at Gesher Benot Ya'aqov, Israel." *Science* 304: 725–727.

Greenberg, Joseph H. 1970. *The Languages of Africa.* The Hague: Mouton.

Greenfield, Patricia M. and Smith, Joshua H. 1976. *The Structure of Communication in Early Language Development.* New York: Academic Press.

Gritten, Anthony and King, Elaine (eds.) 2006. *Music and Gesture.* Farnham: Ashgate.

   (eds.) 2011. *New Perspectives on Music and Gesture.* Farnham: Ashgate.

Guendouzi, Jacqueline, Loncke, Filip, and Williams, Mandy J. (eds.) 2010. *The Handbook of Psycholinguistic and Cognitive Processes: Perspectives in Communication Disorders.* New York: Psychology Press/Taylor & Francis.

Guo, Jiansheng, Lieven, Elena, Budwig, Nancy, Ervin-Tripp, Susan, Nakamura, Keiko, and Özçaliskan, Seyda (eds.) 2009. *Crosslinguistic Approaches to the Psychology of Language: Research in the Tradition of Dan Isaac Slobin.* New York: Psychology Press.

Haiman, J. (ed.) 1985. *Iconicity in Syntax.* Amsterdam: John Benjamins.

Hale, Ken. 1983. "Warlpiri and the grammar of non-configurational languages." *Natural Language and Linguistic Theory* 1: 5–47.

Halliday, M. A. K. and Hasan, Ruqaiya. 1976. *Cohesion in English*. London: Longman.

Hare, Brian, Brown, Michele, Williamson, Christina, and Tomasello, Michael. 2002. "The domestication of social cognition in dogs." *Science* 298: 1634–1636.

Harris, Roy. 2003. *Saussure and His Interpreters*, 2nd edn. Edinburgh University Press.

Harris, Roy and Taylor, Talbot J. 1989. *Landmarks in Linguistic Thought: The Western tradition from Socrates to Saussure*. London: Routledge.

Haslam, Michael, Hernandez-Aguilar, Adriana, Ling, Victoria, Carvalho, Susana, de la Torre, Ignacio, DeStefano, April, Du, Andrew, Hardy, Bruce, Harris, Jack, Marchant, Linda, Matsuzawa, Tetsuro, McGrew, William, Mercader, Julio, Mora, Rafael, Petraglia, Michael, Roche, Hélène, Visalberghi, Elisabetta, and Warren, Rebecca. 2009. "Primate archaeology." *Nature* 460: 339–344.

Hasson, U., Nir, Y., Levy, I., Fuhrmann, G., and Malach, R. 2004. "Intersubject synchronization of cortical activity during natural vision." *Science* 303: 1634–1640.

Hauser, M., Chomsky, N., and Fitch, W. T. 2002. "The language faculty: What is it, who has it, and how did it evolve?" *Science* 298: 1569–1579.

Henderson, E. (ed.) 1971. *The Indispensable Foundation: A Selection from the Writings of Henry Sweet*. London: Oxford University Press.

Hendrick, Roberta, Masek, Carrie, and Miller, Mary Frances (eds.) 1981. *Papers from the Seventeenth Regional Meeting of the Chicago Linguistic Society* (CLS 17), Chicago Linguistic Society (http://humanities.uchicago.edu/orgs/cls/).

Herder J. G. 1986 [1772]. *Essay on the Origin of Language*. J. H. Moran and A. Gode (trans.). University of Chicago Press.

Hewes, Gordon W. 1973. "Primate communication and the gestural origins of language." *Current Anthropology* 14: 5–24.

Hockett, Charles F. and Altmann, Stuart A. 1968. "A note on design features," in Sebeok (ed.), pp. 61–72.

Holzhaider, Jennifer C., Hunt, Gavin R., and Gray, Russell D. 2010. "The development of pandanus tool manufacture in wild New Caledonian crows." *Behaviour* 147: 553–586.

Hopkins, William D. and Cantero, Monica. 2003. "From hand to mouth in the evolution of language: the influence of vocal behavior on lateralized hand use in manual gestures by chimpanzees (*Pan troglodytes*)." *Developmental Science* 6: 55–61.

Horwitz, Barry, Amunts, Katrin, Bhattacharyya, Rajan, Patkin, Debra, Jeffries, Keith, Zilles, Karl, and Braun. Allen R. 2003. "Activation of Broca's area during the production of spoken and signed language: a combined cytoarchitectonic mapping and PET analysis." *Neuropsychologia*, 41: 868–1876

Hrdy, Sarah Blaffer. 2009. *Mothers and Others: The Evolutionary Origins of Mutual Understanding.* Cambridge, MA: Harvard University Press.

HUGO Pan-Asian SNP Consortium. 2009. "Mapping human genetic diversity in Asia." *Science* 326: 1541–1545.

Hurford, James R. 2007. *The Origins of Meaning.* Oxford University Press.

Hurley, Susan. 1998. *Consciousness in Action.* Cambridge, MA: Harvard University Press.

Huttenlocher, Peter R. and Dabholkar, Arun S. 1997. "Regional differences in synaptogenesis in human cerebral cortex." *Journal of Comparative Neurology* 387:167–178.

Imai, Michita. In Progress. "Utterance generation based on Growth Point." Dept. of Computer Science. Keio University, Tokyo.

Ishino, Mika. 2007. Metaphor and metonymy in gesture and discourse. Unpublished Ph.D. dissertation, University of Chicago.

Iverson, Jana M. and Goldin-Meadow, Susan. 1997. "What's communication got to do with it? Gesture in congenitally blind children." *Developmental Psychology* 33: 453–467.

Iverson, J. M., Caprici, O., Longbardi, E. and Cacelli, M. C. 1999. "Gesturing in mother-child interactions." *Cognitive Development* 14: 57–75.

Jackendoff, Ray. 2002. *Foundations of Language: Brain, Meaning, Grammar, Evolution.* Oxford University Press.

    2007. *Language, Consciousness, Culture.* Cambridge, MA: MIT Press.

Jakobson, R. 1960. "Concluding statement: Linguistics and poetics," in Sebeok (ed.), pp. 350–377.

James, William. 1890. *The Principles of Psychology.* New York: Holt.

Jarvella, R. J. and Klein, W. (eds.) 1982. *Speech, Place, and Action.* Chichester: John Wiley & Sons Ltd.

Johansson, Petter, Hall, Lars, Sikström, Sverker, and Olsson, Andreas. 2005. "Failure to detect mismatches between intention and outcome in a simple decision task." *Science* 210: 116–119.

Karmiloff-Smith, Annette. 1979. "Micro- and macrodevelopmental changes in language acquisition and other representational systems." *Cognitive Science* 3: 91–118.

Kelso, J. A. Scott. 1995. *Dynamic Patterns: The Self-organization of Brain and Behavior.* Cambridge, MA: MIT Press.

Kendon, Adam. 1980. "Gesticulation and speech: Two aspects of the process of utterance," in Key (ed.), pp. 207–227.

    1988a. *Sign Languages of Aboriginal Australia: Cultural, Semiotic and Communicative Perspectives.* Cambridge University Press.

    1988b. "How gestures can become like words," in Poyatos (ed.). 131–141.

    1991. "Some considerations for a theory of language origins." *Man* 26: 199–221.

    2004. *Gesture: Visible Action As Utterance.* Cambridge University Press.

2008a. "Some reflections on the relationship between 'gesture' and 'sign.'" *Gesture* 8: 348–366.

2008b. "Review of Call and Tomasello (eds.), 'The gestural communication of apes and monkeys'." *Gesture* 8: 375–385.

2009. "Manual actions, speech and the nature of language." In Gambarara and Givigliano (eds.), pp. 19–33.

2010. "Accounting for forelimb actions as a component of utterance: An evolutionary approach." Plenary Lecture. International Society for Gesture Studies, Frankfurt/Oder, July 25, 2010.

Key, M. R. (ed.) 1980. *The Relationship of Verbal and Nonverbal Communication.* The Hague: Mouton and Co.

Kimbara, Irene. 2006. "On gestural mimicry." *Gesture* 6: 39–61.

King, Elaine. 2006. "Supporting gestures: breathing in piano performance," in Gritten and King, pp. 142–164.

Kingston, J. and Beckman, M. E. (eds.) 1990. *Papers in Laboratory Phonology I: Between the Grammar and Physics of Speech.* Cambridge University Press.

Kinzler, K. D. and Dautel, J. 2012. "Children's essentialist reasoning about language and race." *Developmental Science* 15: 131–138.

Kita, Sotaro. 1990. *The Temporal Relationship between Gesture and Speech: A Study of Japanese-English Bilinguals.* Unpublished M.A. thesis. Department of Linguistics, University of Chicago.

1997. "Two dimensional semantic analysis of Japanese mimetics." *Linguistics* 15: 379–415.

2000. "How representational gestures help speaking," in McNeill (ed.), pp. 162–185.

(ed.) 2003. *Pointing: Where Language, Culture, and Cognition Meet.* 2003. Mahwah, NJ: Erlbaum.

Kita, Sotaro and Özyürek, Asli. 2003. "What does cross-linguistic variation in semantic coordination of speech and gesture reveal? Evidence for an interface representation of spatial thinking and speaking." *Journal of Memory and Language* 48: 16–32.

Kita, Sotaro, Ösyürek, Asli, Allen, Shanley, Ishizuka, Tomoko and Fujii, Mihoko. Submitted. "The role of iconicity in symbolic development: Children's preference for sound symbolic words and their early couplings with iconic gestures."

Klima, Edward and Bellugi, Ursula. 1979. *The Signs of Language.* Cambridge, MA: Harvard University Press.

Konopkla, Genevieve, Bomar, Jamee M., Winden, Kellen, Coppola, Giovanni, Jonsson, Zophonias O., Gao, Fuying, Peng, Sophia, Preuss, Todd M., Wohlschlegel, James A., and Geschwind, Daniel H. 2009. "Human-specific transcriptional regulation of CNS development genes by FOXP2." *Nature* 462: 213–218.

Krause, Johannes, Fu, Qiaomei, Good, Jeffrey M., Viola, Bence, Shunkov, Michael V., Derevianko, Anatoli P. and Pääbo, Svante. 2010. "The complete mitochondrial

DNA genome of an unknown hominin from southern Siberia." *Nature* 464: 894–897.

Krauss, R. M., Morrel-Samuels, P., and Colasante, C. 1991. "Do conversational gestures communicate?" *Journal of Personality and Social Psychology*. 61: 743–754.

Krauss, Robert M., Chen, Yihsiu, and Gottesman, Rebecca F. 2000. "Lexical gestures and lexical access: a process model," in McNeill (ed.), pp. 261–283.

Lakoff, George and Johnson, Mark. 1980. *Metaphors We Live By*. University of Chicago Press.

Langacker, Ronald W. 2000. *Grammar and Conceptualization*. Berlin: Mouton.

LeBaron, Curtis and Streeck, Jürgen. 2000. "Gestures, knowledge, and the world," in McNeill (ed.), pp. 118–138.

Lenneberg, Eric H. 1967. *The Biological Foundations of Language*. New York: Wiley.

Levelt, W., Richardson, G. and LaHeij, W. 1982. "Pointing and voicing in deictic expressions." *Journal of Memory and Language* 24: 133–164.

Levelt, Willem J. M. 1989. *Speaking: From Intention to Articulation*. Cambridge: MIT Press/Bradford Books.

Levelt, Willem, Roelofs, Ardi, and Meyer, Antje S. 1999. "A theory of lexical access in speech production." *Behavioral and Brain Sciences* 22: 1–75.

Levitin, Daniel J. and Menon, Vinod. 2003. "Musical structure is processed in 'language' areas of the brain: a possible role for Brodmann Area 47 in temporal coherence." *Neuroimage* 20: 2142–2152.

Levy, Elena T. 2008. "Pre-construction of third-person elicited narratives: Relationships between short- and long-term language change." *Narrative Inquiry* 18: 274–298.

2009–10. "The mediation of coherent discourse by kinesthetic reenactment: A case study of an autistic adolescent, Part II." *Imagination, Cognition and Personality* 29: 41–70.

2011a. "Constructing and pre-constructing coherent accounts of the social world." *Narrative Inquiry* 21:1

2011b. "A new study of the co-emergence of speech and gestures: Towards an embodied account of early narrative development." Poster presented at the 2011 *Language Fest*, University of Connecticut, Storrs, CT.

Levy, Elena T. and McNeill, David. Manuscript. "Gesture and the Absence of Gesture: Some Relationships Between Onto- and Microgenetic Change."

Liberman, A. M. 1996. *Speech: A Special Code*. Cambridge, MA: MIT Press.

Liddell, Scott K. 2003. *Grammar, Gesture, and Meaning in American Sign Language*. Cambridge University Press.

Liebal, K., Bressem, J., and Müller, C. 2010. "Recurrent forms and contexts: Families of gestures in non-human primates." Conference of the *International Society of Gesture Studies*, Panel 13: Towards a grammar of gesture: Evolution, brain and linguistic structures, Frankfurt/Oder, Germany.

Lieberman, Philip. 1998. *Eve Spoke*. New York: Norton.

2002. "On the nature and evolution of the neural bases of human language." *Yearbook of Physical Anthropology* 45: 36–62.

2006. *Toward an Evolutionary Biology of Language*. Cambridge, MA: Harvard University Press.

Lieven, Elena, Salomo, Dorothé, and Tomasello, Michael. 2009. "Two-year-old children's production of multiword utterances: A usage-based analysis." *Cognitive Linguistics*. 20: 461–507.

Liu, Xiling, Somel, Mehmet, Tang, Lin, Yan, Zheng, Jiang, Xi, Guo, Song, Yuan, Yuan, He, Liu, Oleksiak, Anna, Zhang, Yan, Li, Na, Hu, Yuhui, Chen, Wei, Qiu, Zilong, Pääbo, Svante and Khaitovich, Philipp. 2012 (published online, February 2). "Extension of cortical synaptic development distinguishes humans from chimpanzees and macaques." *Genome Research* (accessed 02/06/12).

MacNeilage, P. F., and Davis, B. L. 2005. "The frame/content theory of evolution of speech: A comparison with a gestural-origins alternative." *Interaction Studies* 6: 173–199.

MacNeilage, Peter F. 2008. *The Origin of Speech*. Oxford University Press.

Maestrpieri, Dario. 2007. *Macachiavellian Intelligence: How Rhesus Macaques and Humans Have Conquered the World*. University of Chicago Press.

Mampe, Birgit, Friederici, Angela D., Christophe, Anne, and Wermke, Kathleen. 2009. "Newborns' cry melody is shaped by their native language." *Current Biology* 19:1–4.

Matsuzawa, T., Humie, T., and Sugiyama, Y. (eds.) 2011. *The Chimpanzees of Bossou and Nimba*. New York: Springer.

Mayberry, Rachel and Jaques, Joselynne. 2000. "Gesture production during stuttered speech: insights into the nature of gesture-speech integration," in McNeill (ed.), pp. 199–214.

McCullough, Karl-Erik. 2005. Using Gestures During Speaking: Self-Generating Indexical Fields. Unpublished Ph.D. Dissertation, Department of Linguistics, University of Chicago.

McNeill, David. 1974. "Sentence structure in chimpanzee communication," in Connolly and Bruner (eds.), pp. 75–94.

1985. "So you think gestures are nonverbal?" *Psychological Review* 92: 350–371.

1989. "A straight path – to where? Reply to Butterworth and Hadar." *Psychological Review* 96: 175–179.

1992. *Hand and Mind*. University of Chicago Press.

2000. "Catchments and contexts: non-modular factors in speech and gesture production," in McNeill (ed.), pp. 312–328.

(ed.) 2000. *Language and Gesture*. Cambridge University Press.

2003a. "Pointing and morality in Chicago," in Kita (ed.), pp. 293–306.

2003b. "Aspects of aspect." *Gesture* 3: 1–17.

2005. *Gesture and Thought*. University of Chicago Press.

2008. "Unexpected metaphors," in Cienki and Müller (eds.), pp. 155–170.

2009. "Imagery for speaking," in Guo, *et al.* (eds.). pp. 517–530.

2010. "Gesten der Macht und die Macht der Gesten," in Wulf and Fischer-Lichte (eds.), pp. 42–57.

McNeill, David, Bertenthal, Bennett, Cole, Jonathan, and Gallagher, Sahun. 2005. "Gesture-first, but no gestures? Comment on Michael Arbib's 'From monkey-like action recognition to human language: An evolutionary framework for neurolinguistics'." *Behavioral and Brain Science* 28: 138–139.

McNeill, David and Duncan, Susan D. 2000. "Growth points in thinking for speaking," in McNeill (ed.), pp. 141–161.

2010. "Gestures and growth points in three language disorders'," in Guendouzi, Loncke and Williams (eds.), pp. 663–685.

McNeill, David, Duncan, Susan D., Cole, Jonathan, Gallagher, Shaun, and Bertenthal, Bennett. 2008. "Growth points from the very beginning." *Interaction Studies* (special issue on proto-language, D. Bickerton and M. Arbib, eds.) 9: 117–132.

McNeill, David, Duncan, Susan, Franklin, Amy, Goss, James, Kimbara, Irene, Parrill, Fey, Welji, Haleema, Chen, Lei, Harper, Mary, Quek, Francis, Rose, Travis, and Tuttle, Ronald. 2010. "Mind merging," in Morsella (ed.), pp. 143–164.

McNeill, David and Levy, Elena. 1982. "Conceptual Representations in Language Activity and Gesture," in Jarvella and Klein (eds.), pp. 271–296.

McNeill, David and Pedelty, Laura. 1995. Right brain and gesture. In Emmorey and Reilly (eds.), pp. 63–85.

McNeill, David and Sowa, Claudia. 2011. "Birth of a morph," in Stam and Ishino, pp. 27–47.

McNeill, Randall L. B. 2010. "*Cum tacent, clamant*: the Pragmatics of Silence in Catullus." *Classical Philology* 105: 69–82.

Mead, George Herbert. 1974. *Mind, Self, and Society from the Standpoint of a Social Behaviorist* (C. W. Morris ed. and introduction). University of Chicago Press.

Meier, R. P., Cormier, K., and Quinto-Pozos, D. (eds.) 2002. *Modality and Structure in Signed and Spoken Language.* Cambridge University Press.

Mekel-Bobrow, Nitzan, Gilbert, Sandra L., Evans, Patrick D., Vallender, Eric J., Anderson, Jeffrey R., Hudson, Richard R., Tishkoff, Sarah A., and Lahn, Bruce T. 2005. "Ongoing adaptive evolution of *ASPN*, a brain size determinant in *Homo sapiens.*" *Science* 309: 1720–1722.

Menenti, Laura, Gierhan, Sarah M. E., Segaert, Katrien, and Hagoort, Peter. 2011. "Shared language: Overlap and segregation of the neuronal infrastructure for speaking and listening revealed by functional MRI." *Psychological Science* 22: 1173–1182.

Merleau-Ponty, Maurice. 1962. *Phenomenology of Perception* (C. Smith, trans.). London: Routledge.

Miller, George A. 1956. "The magical number seven, plus or minus two: Some limits on our capacity for processing information." *Psychological Review* 63: 81–97.

Mithen, Steven. 2006. *The Singing Neanderthals: The Origins of Music, Language, Mind, and Body.* Cambridge, MA: Harvard University Press.

Mittelberg, Irene. 2008. "Peircean semiotics meets conceptual metaphor: Iconic modes in gestural representations of grammar," in Cienki and Müller (eds.), *Metaphor and Gesture*, pp. 115–154.

  2009. "Open and closed class systems in coverbal gestures: A first approach." Abstract posted on the International Cognitive Linguistics Conference website, 03/20/09.

Montaigne, Michel de. 1958. *The Complete Essays of Montaigne* (D. Frame, trans.). Stanford University Press.

Morrel-Samuels, P. and Krauss, R. M. 1992. "Word familiarity predicts temporal asynchrony of hand gestures and speech." *Journal of Experimental Psychology: Learning, Memory, and Cognition.* 18: 615–622.

Morris, Desmond, Collett, Peter, Marsh, Peter, and O'Shaughnessy, Marie. 1979. *Gestures: Their Origins and Distribution.* New York: Stein & Day.

Morsella, E. (ed.) 2010. *Expressing Oneself/Expressing One's Self: Communication, Language, Cognition, and Identity.* London: Taylor and Francis.

Morton, John, Marcus, Steve and Frankis, Clive. 1976. "Perceptual centers." *Psychological Review* 83: 105–108.

Mufwene, Salikoko. Ms. 2009. "'Protolanguage' and the evolution of linguistic diversity." Department of Linguistics, University of Chicago.

Müller, Cornelia. 1998. "Iconicity and gesture," in Santi, Guaïtella, Cavé and Konopezynski (eds.), pp, 321–328.

  2008. *Metaphors - Dead and Alive, Sleeping and Waking. A Dynamic View.* University of Chicago Press.

Murray, L., Fiori-Cowley, A., Hooper, R., and Cooper, P. J. 1996. "The impact of postnatal depression and associated adversity on early mother–infant interactions and later infant outcome." *Child Development* 67: 2512–2526

Nelson, Katherine (ed.) 1989. *Narratives from the Crib.* Cambridge, MA: Harvard University Press.

Nelson, K. and Levy, E. 1987. "Development of referential cohesion in a child's monologues," in Steele and Threadgold (eds.), pp. 119–136.

Nishitani, Nobuyuki and Hari, Riitta. 2000. "Temporal dynamics of cortical representation for action." *Proceedings of the National Academy of Sciences* 97: 913–918.

Nishitani, Nobuyuki, Schürmann, Martin, Amunts, Katrin and Hari, Riitta. 2005. "Broca's region: from action to language." *Physiology* 20: 60–69.

Nobe, Shuichi. 1996. Representational gestures, cognitive rhythms, and acoustic aspects of speech: a network/threshold model of gesture production. Unpublished Ph.D. Dissertation, University of Chicago.

  2000. "Where do *most* spontaneous representational gestures actually occur with respect to speech?," in McNeill (ed.), pp. 186–198.

O'Regan, J. Kevin and Noë, Alva. 2001. "A sensorimotor account of vision and visual consciousness." *Behavioral and Brain Sciences* 24: 939–973.

Oberauer, Klaus. 2005. "Access to information in working memory: Exploring the focus of attention." *Journal of Experimental Psychology: Learning, Memory, and Cognition.* 31: 714–728.

Okrent, A. 2002. "A modality-free notion of gesture and how it can help us with the morpheme vs. gesture question in sign language linguistics," in Meier, Cormier and Quinto-Pozos (eds.), pp. 175–198.

Ortony, A. (ed.) 1979. *Metaphor and Thought.* Cambridge University Press.

Ouattara, A., Karim, Lemasson, Alban, and Zuberbühler, Klaus. 2009. "Campbell's monkeys concatenate vocalizations into context-specific call sequences." *Proceedings of the National Academy of Sciences* 106: 22026–22031.

Özçaliskan, Şeyda and Goldin-Meadow, Susan. 2009. "When gesture-speech combinations do and do not index linguistic change." *Language and Cognitive Processes* 24: 190–217.

Özyürek, Asli. 2000. "The influence of addressee location on spatial language and representational gestures of direction," in McNeill (ed.), pp. 64–83.

Pagel, Mark, Atkinson, Quentin D., and Meade, Andrew. 2007. "Frequency of word-use predicts rates of lexical evolution throughout Indo-European history." *Nature* 449: 717–720.

Park-Doob, Mischa Alan. 2010. Gesturing Through Time: Holds and Intermodal Timing in the Stream of Speech. Ph.D. dissertation, University of California, Berkeley.

Paraldé, Meaghan V. and Iverson, Jana M. 2011. "The interplay between language, gesture, and affect during communicative transition: A dynamic systems approach." *Developmental Psychology* 47: 820–833.

Parrill, Fey. 2007. "Metagesture: An analysis of theoretical discourse about multimodal language," in Duncan, Cassell and Levy (eds.), pp. 83–80.

2008. "Subjects in the hands of speakers: An experimental study of syntactic subject and speech-gesture integration." *Cognitive Linguistics* 19(2): 283–299.

2011. "The relation between the encoding of motion event information and viewpoint in English-accompanying gestures." *Gesture* 11: 61–80.

Parrill, Fey and Sweetser, Eve. 2004. "What we mean by meaning: Conceptual integration in gesture analysis and transcription." *Gesture* 4: 197–219.

Paule, Merle G., Bushnell, Philip J., Maurissen, Jacques P. J., Wenger, Galen R., Buccafusco, Jerry J., Chelonis. John J., and Elliot, Rebecca. 1998. "Symposium overview: The use of delayed matching-to-sample procedures in studies of short-term memory in animals and humans." *Neurotoxicology and Teratology.* 20(5): 493–502.

Payrató, Lluis. 1993. "A pragmatic view on autonomous gestures: A first repertoire of Catalan emblems." *Journal of Pragmatics* 20: 193–216.

Peça, João, Feliciano, Cátia, Ting, Jonatham T., Wang, Wengting, Wells, Michael F., Venkatraman, Talaignair N., Lascola, Chrisopher D., Fu, Zhanyan, and Feng,

Guoping. 2011. "*Shank3* mutant mice display autistic-like behaviours and striatal dysfunction." *Nature* 472: 437–442.

Peña, Marcela, Bonatti, Luca L., Nespor, Marina, and Mehler, Jacques. 2002. "Signal-driven computations in speech processing." *Science* 298: 604–607.

Peña, Marcela, Maki, Atsushi, Kovacić, Damir, Dehaene-Lambertz, Ghislaine, Koizumi, Hideaki, Bouquet, Furio, and Mehler, Jacques. 2003. "Sounds and silence: An optical topography study of language recognition at birth." *Proceedings of the National Academy of Sciences USA.* 100:11702–11705.

Petitmengin, Claire. 2007. "Towards the source of thoughts: The gestural and transmodal dimension of lived experience." *Journal of Consciousness Studies* 14: 54–82.

Pika, Simone and Bugnyar, Thomas. 2011. "The use of referential gestures in ravens (Corvus corax) in the wild." *Nature Communications* 29 November 2011.

Pinker, Steven. 1994. *The Language Instinct.* New York: Harper Perennial.

Pollick, Amy S. 2006. Gestures and Multimodal Signaling in Bonobos and Chimpanzees. Unpublished Ph.D. dissertation, Emory University.

Poyatos, F. (ed.) 1988. *Cross-Cultural Perspectives in Nonverbal Communication.* Toronto: Hogrefe.

Quaeghebeur, Liesbet. 2010. *A Philosophy of Everyday, Face-to-Face Conversation.* University of Antwerp.

Quaeghebeur, Liesbet and Reynaert, Peter. 2010. "Does the need for linguistic expression constitute a problem to be solved?" *Phenomenology and the Cognitive Sciences* 9: 15–36.

Ramachandran, Vilayanur and Blakeslee, Sandra. 1998. *Phantoms in the Brain: Probing the Mysteries of the Human Mind.* New York: William Morrow.

Reddy, Michael J. 1979. "The conduit metaphor: a case of frame conflict in our language about language," in Ortony (ed.), pp. 284–297.

Rhodes, Richard A. and Lawler, John M. 1981. "Athematic metaphors," in Hendrick *et al.* (eds.), pp. 318–342.

Richards, I. A. 1936. *The Philosophy of Rhetoric.* New York: Oxford University Press.

Rieber, Robert W. and Carton, Aaron S. (eds.) 1987. *The Collected Works of L. S. Vygotsky. Volume I: Problems of General Psychology. Including the Volume "Thinking and Speech"* (intro. and trans. by Norris Minick). New York: Plenum.

Rizzolatti, Giacomo and Arbib, Michael. 1998. "Language within our grasp." *Trends in Neurosciences,* 21: 188–194.

Rizzolatti, Giacomo, Fadiga, Luciano, Gallese, Vittorio, and Fogassi, Leonardo. 1996. "Premotor cortex and the recognition of motor actions." *Cognitive Brain Research* 3: 131–141.

Rossini, Nicla. 2012. *Language "In Action": Reinterpreting Gesture as Language.* Amsterdam: IOS Press.

Rowe, Meredith and Goldin-Meadow, Susan. 2009. "Differences in early gesture explain SES disparities in child vocabulary size at school entry." *Science* 323: 951–953.

Rozzi, Fernando V. Ramirez and de Castro, José Maria Bermudez. 2004. "Surprisingly rapid growth in Neanderthals." *Nature* 428: 936–939.

Sahin, Ned T., Pinker, Steven, Cash, Sydney S., Schomer, Donald, and Halgren, Erik. 2009. "Sequential processing of lexical, grammatical and phonological information within Broca's Area." *Science* 326: 445–449.

Sandler, Wendy. 1993. "Hand in hand: The roles of the non-dominant hand in sign language phonology." *The Linguistic Review* 10: 337–390.

Sandler, Wendy and Lillo-Martin, Diane. 2006. *Sign Language and Linguistic Universals*. Cambridge University Press.

Santi, S., Guaïtella, I., Cavé C., and Konopezynski, G. (eds.) 1998. *Oralité et Gestualité: Communication Multimodale, Interaction*. Paris: L'Harmattan.

Sapir, Edward 1921. *Language: An Introduction to the Study of Speech*. New York: Harcourt, Brace & World.

  1929. "A study in phonetic symbolism." *Journal of Experimental Psychology* 12: 225–239.

Saussure, Ferdinand de. 1959. *Course in General Linguistics* (Charles Bally and Albert Sechehaye, eds., Wade Baskin, trans.). New York: The Philosophical Library.

Savage-Rumbaugh, E. Sue. 1986. *Ape Language: From conditioned response to symbol*. New York: Columbia University Press.

Savage-Rumbaugh, E. Sue, Shanker, Stuart G., and Taylor, Talbot J. 1998. *Apes, Language, and the Human Mind*. New York: Oxford University Press.

Sawyer, R. K. (ed.) 1997. *Creativity in Performance*. Greenwich, CT: Ablex.

Schegloff, Emanuel A. 1984. "On some gestures' relation to talk," in Atkinson and Heritage (eds.), pp. 266–298.

Schiffrin, D. (ed.) 1984. *Meaning, Form, and Use in Context: Linguistic Applications*. Washington, DC: Georgetown University Press.

Schrier, A. M. and Stolnitz, F. (eds.) 1971. *Behavior of Nonhuman Primates, vol. IV*. New York: Academic Press.

Science Magazine. 2008. "Report on a conference on primate behavior and human universals." 25 Jan. 318: 404–405.

Scott, G. R. and Gibert, L. 2009. "The oldest hand-axes in Europe." *Nature* 461: 82–85.

Sebeok, T. (ed.). 1960. *Style in Language*. Cambridge, MA: MIT Press.

  (ed.). 1968. *Animal communication: Techniques of Study and Results of Research*. Bloomington, IN: Indiana University Press.

Sekine, Kazuki. 2009a. "Changes in frame of reference use across the preschool years: A longitudinal study of the gestures and speech produced during route descriptions." *Language and Cognitive Processes* 24: 218–238.

  2009b. "Creating context: a function of gesture." Seminar at the University of Chicago, Jan. 21, 2009.

Senghas, Ann. 2003. "Intergenerational influence and ontogenetic development in the emergence of spatial grammar in Nicaraguan Sign Language." *Cognitive Development* 18: 511–531.

Senghas, Ann and Coppola, Marie. 2001. "Children creating language: How Nicaraguan Sign Language acquired a spatial grammar." *Psychological Science* 12:323–328.

Severance, Elizabeth and Washburn, Margaret F. 1907. "The loss of associative power in words after long fixation." *American Journal of Psychology* 18: 182–186.

Silverstein, Michael. 1984. "On the pragmatic 'poetry' of prose: parallelism, repetition, and cohesive structure," in Schiffrin, D. (ed.).

1997. "The improvisational performance of culture in realtime discursive practice," in Sawyer (ed.), pp. 265–312.

2003. "Indexical order and the dialectics of sociolinguistic life." *Language & Communication* 23: 193–229.

Simon, Herbert A. 1968. *The Sciences of the Artificial.* Cambridge, MA: MIT Press.

Sinclair-de Zwart, Hermine. 1967. *Acquisition du langage et développement de la pensée.* Paris: Dunod

Skipper, Jeremy I., Goldin-Meadow, Susan, Nusbaum, Howard C., and Small, Steven L. 2007. "Speech associated gestures, Broca's area, and the human mirror system." *Brain and Language* 101: 260–277.

Slobin, Dan I. 1987. 'Thinking for Speaking', in *Berkeley Linguistic Society, Proceedings of the 13th Annual Meeting,* pp. 435–445.

2009. "Review of M. Bowerman and P. Brown (eds.), 'Crosslinguistic perspectives on argument structure: Implications for learnability'." *Journal of Child Language.* 36: 697–704.

Soproni, Krisztina, Miklósi, A., and Topál, Jósef. 2002. "Dogs' (*Canis familiaris*) responsiveness to human pointing gestures." *Journal of Comparative Psychology* 116: 27–34.

Sowa, Timo, Kopp, Stefan, Duncan, Susan, McNeill, David, and Wachsmuth, Ipke. 2008. "Implementing a non-modular theory of language production in an embodied conversational agent," in Wachsmuth *et al.* (eds.), pp. 425–450.

Sparhawk, Carol M. 1978. "Contrastive-identificational features of Persian gestures." *Semiotica* 24: 49–86.

Stam, Gale and Ishino, Mika (eds.) 2011. *Integrating Gestures: The Interdisciplinary Nature of Gesture.* Amsterdam/Philadelphia: John Benjamins.

Steele, Ross and Threadgold, Terry (eds.) 1987. *Language Topics – Essays in Honor of Michael Halliday, Vol. I.* Amsterdam: Benjamins.

Stefanini, Silvia, Caselli, Maria Cristina, and Volterra, Virginia. 2007. "Spoken and gestural production in a naming task by young children with Down syndrome." *Brain and Language.* 101: 208–221.

Streeck, Jürgen. 2010. *Gesturecraft: The Manu-facture of Meaning.* Amsterdam/Philadelphia: John Benjamins.

Supalla, T. 1982. "Structure and acquisition of verbs of motion and location in American Sign Language." Unpublished Ph.D. Dissertation, University of California at San Diego.

Sweet, Henry. 1971/1900. "The history of language," in Henderson (ed.), pp. 1–24.

Sweetser, Eve. 2007. "Compositionality in gesture: Structural real-space blends." Paper presented at the meeting of the International Society for Gesture Studies, Evanston, IL.

Talmy, Leonard. 2000. *Toward a Cognitive Semantics. Vol. II: Typology and Process in Concept Structuring*. Cambridge, MA: The MIT Press.

Thomason, Sarah. 1997. "On mechanisms of interference." In Eliasson and Jahr (eds), pp. 181–207.

   2011. "Does language contact simplify grammars? (No.)" Talk given at the University of Chicago, April 12, 2011.

Tomasello, Michael. 1999. *The Cultural Origins of Human Cognition*. Cambridge, MA: Harvard University Press.

   2008. *Origins of Human Communication*. Cambridge, MA: MIT Press.

   2009. *Why We Cooperate*. Cambridge, MA: MIT.

Tomasello, Michael and Slobin, D. (eds.) 2005. *Beyond Nature-Nurture: Essays in Honor of Elizabeth Bates*. Mahway, NJ: Erlbaum.

Tomasello, Michael and Call, Josep. 2007. "Ape gestures and the origins of language," in Call and Tomasello (eds.). pp. 221–235.

Trudgill, Peter. 2011. *Investigations in Sociohistorical Linguistics: Stories of Colonization and Contact*. Cambridge University Press.

Tsohatzidis, S. L. (ed.) 1990. *Meanings and Prototypes: Studies in Linguistic Categorization*. London: Routledge.

Tuite, Kevin. 1993. "The production of gesture." *Semiotica* 93: 83–105.

van Eijck, Jan and Visser, Albert, 2010. 'Dynamic semantics,' in Zalta (ed.), http://plato.stanford.edu/archives/fall2010/entries/dynamic-semantics/ (accessed 22 April 2011).

Vasta, Ross (ed.) 1990. *Annals of Child Development*, vol. 7. London: Jessica Kingsley Publishers.

Voineagu, Irina, Wang, Xinchen, Johnston, Patrick, Lowe, Jennifer K., Tian, Yuan, Horvath, Steve, Mill, Jonathan, Cantor, Rita M., Blencowe, Benjamin J., and Geschwind, Daniel H. 2011. "Transcriptomic analysis of autistic brain reveals convergent molecular pathology." *Nature*, published online 25 May 2011.   www.nature.com.proxy.uchicago.edu/nature/journal/vaop/ncurrent/full/nature10110.html (accessed 26 May 2011).

Volterra, Virgina, Caselli, Mari Cristina, Caprici, Olga, and Pizzuto, Elena. 2005. "Gesture and the emergence and development of language," in Tomasello and Slobin (eds.), pp. 3–40.

Vonk, J. and Shackelford, T. K. (eds.) 2012. *The Oxford Handbook of Comparative Evolutionary Psychology*. Oxford University Press.

Vosniadou, Stella. 1987. "Children and metaphors." *Child Development* 58: 870–885.

Vygotsky, Lev S. 1987. *Thought and Language.* Edited and translated by E. Hanfmann and G. Vakar (revised and edited by A. Kozulin). Cambridge: MIT Press.

Wachsmuth, Ipke, Lenzen, Manuela, and Knoblich, Guenther (eds.). 2008. *Embodied Communication in Humans and Machines.* Oxford University Press.

Weir, Ruth H. 1962. *Language in the Crib.* Janua Linguarum, Series major, 14. The Hague: Mouton.

Werner, Heinz and Kaplan, Bernard. 1963. *Symbol Formation.* New York: John Wiley & Sons Ltd. [reprinted in 1984 by Erlbaum].

Wertsch, James V. (ed.) 1985. *Culture Communication, and Cognition: Vygotskian Perspectives.* Cambridge University Press.

Whorf, Bejamin Lee. 1956. *Language, Thought, and Reality. Selected Writings of Benjamin Lee Whorf.* J. B. Carroll (ed.). Cambridge, MA: The MIT Press.

Willems, Roel M., Labruna, Ludovica, D'Esposito, Mark D., Ivry, Richard, and Casasanto, Daniel. 2011. "A functional role for the motor system in language understanding: Evidence from theta-burst transcranial magnetic stimulation." *Psychological Science* 22: 849–854.

Wimmer, Heinz and Perner, Josef. 1983. "Beliefs about beliefs: Representation and constraining function of wrong beliefs in young children's understanding of deception." *Cognition* 13: 103–128.

Woll, Bencie. 2005/2006. "Do mouths sign? Do hands speak?," in Botha, Rudie, and de Swart, Henriette (eds.).

Wrangham, Richard W. 2001. "Out of the pan, into the fire: How our ancestors' evolution depended on what they ate," in de Waal (ed.), pp. 119–143.

Wulf, Christoph and Fischer-Lichte, Erika (eds.). 2010. *Gesten.* Munich: Wilhelm Fink.

Wundt, Wilhelm. 1970. "The psychology of the sentence," in Blumenthal (ed. and trans.), pp. 20–33.

Wynn, Thomas and Coolidge, Frederick. 2008. "Why not cognition?" *Current Anthropology* 49: 895–897.

2011. *How to Think Like a Neandertal.* Oxford University Press.

Xu, Jiang, Gannon, Patrick J., Emmorey, Karen, Smith, Jason F., and Braun, Allen R. 2009. "Symbolic gestures and spoken language are processed by a common neural system." *Proceedings of the National Academy of Sciences* 106: 2064–2069.

Zalta, Edward N. (ed.) 2010. *The Stanford Encyclopedia of Philosophy (Fall Edition),* http://plato.stanford.edu/archives/fall2010/entries/dynamic-semantics/ (Accessed 22 April 2011).

Zbikowski, Lawrence M. 2011. "Musical Gesture and Musical Grammar: A Cognitive Approach," in Gritten and King (eds.), pp. 83–98.

Zinchenko, V. P. 1985. "Vygotsky's ideas about units for the analysis of mind," in Wertsch, James (ed.), pp. 94–118.

Index

Yorkshire Dales

*A photographic journey around a unique area
of natural beauty*

Dave Coates

MYRIAD BOOKS

Swaledale

Swaledale is the most northerly of the main dales. This dale is famous for its spring meadows and the wonderful array of field barns. The glacial action that formed the dale has left the farmers with areas of good bottom land, such as those at Gunnerside and Muker. Over the years, this land has been turned into patterns of fields bounded by the famous drystone walls, which now reach up the sides of the fells. There is an intimate quality about the dale because it is fairly narrow so the fellsides are never far away.

Barns and meadows of Gunnerside Bottoms (below)

Without any doubt one of the visitor's favourite places in Swaledale – and there are many – is Gunnerside Bottoms. This is a fertile stretch of old glacial flood plain that has been turned into a patchwork quilt of fields. Each field is bordered by drystone walls and many have their own traditional field barn. It is seen here at its best in evening light, in early June when the meadows are in full flower.

Storm clouds gathering over the meadows

Even on a spring morning the weather can change and give an oppressive feeling to the landscape. Here, in early morning in late May, the sun shines in from the east while threatening storm clouds gather from the west. The result is a landscape of beauty and drama.

Open stile leading through the meadows

A number of footpaths thread through this maze of fields and barns. Access to the fields is usually by means of simple gate stiles like this one. But watch out for the gate closing behind you – some of them have quite powerful return springs which have resulted in many a hapless walker getting a sharp rap on the ankles as the gate swings closed after them!

Oxnop Ghyll and its meadow land

Small tributary dales leading away from the main dales often have their own visual treats for the visitor who has time to wander off the beaten track. Oxnop Ghyll is no exception. Here the meadows fill the foreground, while the farmstead nestles in a dip under the lea of the fellside. The farm has been sited here not just for shelter but also to be near a source of running water from the stream behind.

Field patterns of Gunnerside

There often seems to be little reason for the random and crooked shapes of the fields. But what has resulted is a scene of real beauty – a wonderful example of how a combination of the landscape and livestock farming has created a scene of real beauty.

Gill Head towards Satron Side

This is the view from the road to Askrigg in Wensleydale as it winds up Oxnop Ghyll. The undulating and rolling fells of Swaledale are clearly visible. In the foreground, the farmstead with its fields stands on a high point but is sheltered by a stand of mature trees. In the middle distance is Satron Side and in the far distance the heather-covered moors are on the other side of Swaledale.

Heather moors with Calver Hill behind

After the meadows have been cut, the display of colour in the Dale moves upwards away from the fields as the heather carpets the fells in a purple haze. In the foreground are the moors near Surrender Bridge and Calver Hill is in the distance.

Oxnop Scar, towards Muker

If you take the gated and little used road along the eastern side of Oxnop Ghyll you will enjoy this magnificent view. On the right are the limestone crags of Oxnop Scar with the contrasting screes of shale below. The light and shade caused by passing clouds helps to emphasise features in the landscape. In the distance is Swaledale and beyond it Swinner Gill and the Kisdon Fells.

Muker with Kisdon Fell behind

The land around Muker in Swaledale can rival even the famous Gunnerside for the beauty of its spring meadows. This photograph is taken from Muker Side looking into the dale; the village of Muker lies to the left of the picture. The view is of a broad sweep of glorious spring meadows stretching out across the valley floor and up the lower slopes of the surrounding fells. The scattering of farmsteads and field barns complements the rest of the scene.

Upper Swaledale from Buttertubbs Pass

The dale has many moods and this photograph of the upper dale, taken from the Hawes to Thwaite road in winter, looks down and across a dale overshadowed by lowering skies. But even on the most cloudy of days, small breaks in the cloud allow the sun to light up the surrounding fells like a patchwork quilt.

Swaledale above Gunnerside

This photograph of Swaledale just above Gunnerside was taken on a lovely November morning. The full clarity of early light brings out the autumn colours and highlights the barns and farms dotted across the fellside.

Evening sunlight near Angram

In the hills above Thwaite, close to the little hamlet of Angram, sheep graze in the meadow as the shadow of the evening sun extends across them. The typical stone-built barn, with its faded red paintwork and the fellside beyond, provides a perfect counterpoint. Despite the beauty of the scene more practical thoughts often occur when you look at a scene such as this. How, for example, did the farmstead on the distant fell ever manage to provide anyone with a living?

Field barns near Thwaite

These field barns stand in the warm winter sun like sentries at the foot of the fellside. Simply constructed, the barns were very effective for the purpose for which they were built. The lower floor was usually a shelter for animals, normally sheep or cattle; the upper floor was used to store winter fodder.

East Gill

East Gill falls are located at the foot of East Stonesdale and close to the intersection of the two most famous long-distance walks in the north of England: the Pennine Way and the Coast to Coast walk. On its way to join the Swale in less than a couple of hundred yards, they carry East Gill over this lovely tiered limestone formation, producing a wonderful tumbling flow of water as it cascades downwards.

Wain Wath Falls

The area around Keld has a plethora of stunning waterfalls. The Wain Wath Falls are more familiar to most visitors because they are visible from the West Stonesdale road. The falls are made even more attractive by their dramatic setting beneath the rugged limestone crags of Cotterby Scar. In this picture, the patterns of foam that had formed into spectacular swirls after tumbling over the falls are particularly striking.

Morning light

Wain Wath Falls is really a line of several individual smaller falls all lined up along the same outcrop of rock. This picture, taken in the early morning light, takes advantage of this by concentrating on just three sections of the falls. The warm sunlit rocks in the foreground add a touch of contrast and depth to the rest of the scene.

Birkdale Beck and Whitsundale Beck

This junction of these two streams could rightly be called the source of the Swale, for it is at this point that Birkdale Beck flowing in from the right of the picture joins Whitsundale Beck and becomes the River Swale itself.

The infant Swale flows toward Keld

The infant River Swale is seen here winding its way down the dale and past Cotterby Scar under an early autumn sky. The grasses have all gone to seed, changing the summer green of the fields to yellow with the odd tree also beginning to turn in colour.

Birkdale and High Bridge

This picture serves as a reminder of how hard the climate in the high dales can be. With High Bridge in the foreground, the view takes you up into the far reaches of Birkdale right at the head of Swaledale. The fact that this picture was taken on a late spring bank holiday Monday, with snow still dusting the far fells, speaks volumes about the Yorkshire Dales.

Wensleydale

Wensleydale runs parallel to Swaledale just over the fell and to the south. But it is a dale of completely different character to its near neighbour since it is on a much larger scale. For most of its length, Wensleydale is the broadest of the Yorkshire Dales and is not as intimate as its partner to the north. Wander about Wensleydale, however, and you will find so much to enjoy, often tucked away in corners and in the tributary dales which are so common. Above all, the dale has a rich vein of waterfalls created by the waters of the River Ure and its tributaries, tumbling down over the limestone steps created by the Yoredale Series limestone. This dale is less remote and has a rich history – its abbeys and castles bear witness to this. But one thing Wensleydale does have in common with all of the Yorkshire Dales is its natural beauty, particularly its attractive meadow land, wild flowers and field barns.

Coverdale valley
Stretching away from the main dale near to Middleham is Coverdale, the first of many of Wensleydale's tributary dales. Coverdale quickly opens up into typical dales farmland with its meadows and barns set against a backdrop of less cultivated moorland. This scene is typical, with the cattle in the near meadow and the odd field ploughed up for cultivation. Beyond that are higher sheep meadows with fields surrounded by drystone walls and dotted with field barns.

Middleham Castle from the hill above
Middleham Castle, two miles south of Leyburn, was once the stronghold of the Warwick family and King Richard III during the Wars of the Roses. It stands defiantly against the ravages of time overlooking the lower part of Wensleydale. The buildings clustered at its base form part of the famous horse-racing stables of Middleham. They remind you of how many local homes would be clustered under the walls of the castle for protection in medieval times.

Castle Bolton
Castle Bolton stands proudly overlooking the dale. A loyalist stronghold in the civil war it was rendered almost indefensible by Cromwell after a prolonged siege. The building has been lovingly restored over recent years and is well worth a visit. Many rooms are still as they were when Mary Queen of Scots was imprisoned here. The re-planting of a medieval herb garden and maze add to the atmosphere of the castle.

Sheep and dales barn, early spring

In very early spring, the bracken on the fells still glows gold in the sunlight. This flock of expectant ewes is confined to the lower meadows for protection against the worst of the dales' weather and to be near to the shepherd as lambing time approaches. The scene must have remained essentially unchanged for centuries. The barn adds to this timeless quality, as the building would have been used for storing winter fodder before tractors were the norm in farming circles.

West Burton Falls

Wensleydale is a place of hidden nooks and crannies and Bishopdale is no exception. West Burton Falls are tucked away in a quiet little corner of the village of West Burton. Seen here on an October afternoon, Walden Beck appears almost graceful as it tumbles down out of the autumn woodland and into the little gladed pool. The dark still waters of the pool with the shimmering reflection of the trees only adds to the feeling of peace and beauty.

Autumn colours in Waldendale

Looking down the little dale of Waldendale and back into Bishopdale you can see that, in many places, its steep sides are wooded. In the late afternoon, just before the sun dips down behind the fell, the autumn colours of the trees are seen in all their glory. It is as if nature is trying to put on a last defiant show before the onset of winter.

Semer Water from the overlooking fells

Semer Water, a glacial lake, lies a hanging valley left over by the ice age and surrounded by limestone fells. Seen here from one of the limestone crags, the skyline is dominated by the dramatic form of Addlebrough standing like a sentinel on the side of the valley. In the distance beyond, the repetitive shape of Penhill is visible. The foreground fellside glows gold in the late spring with the dead grasses left over from the previous year.

Semer Water in winter

It is always fascinating to return to locations in differing seasons and on this occasion the contrast between spring and winter is stark but beautiful. The lake is frozen and the low sun shines off its surface creating patterns of its own. Clouds are racing over the fells, with the threat of more snow to come. Even the infant River Bain – at three miles in length, the shortest river in England – is still partly frozen over.

Thoralby village in winter

Bishopdale is a tributary valley more or less opposite Castle Bolton. Here, in the depths of winter, the landscape is covered with snow, revealing all the more graphically the drystone walls that border the fields of the dales. The scattering of trees stripped of their leaves stand even more starkly against the landscape with the little village of Thoralby nestling at the foot of the fell.

The Upper Falls in autumn

Aysgarth Falls is, without doubt, one of the "hot spots" of tourism in Wensleydale – and it is easy to see why. In the space of a couple of miles, the River Ure passes over a series of three major waterfalls created by the limestone landscape of the dale. The Upper Falls, pictured here in the autumn sunshine, provides a peaceful setting following a long dry summer. The autumn colours of the trees add to the apparent peace and beauty of the location.

Still waters of the Ure near Aysgarth

The river Ure flows peacefully less than a mile from the point at which it crashes over the famous Aysgarth Falls.

Middle falls in winter

Come back to Aysgarth Falls in a different season and the mood changes completely. In its winter colours, the landscape now takes on monochromatic tones with only the stone of the church and the slight peat staining in the water revealing that this is, in fact, a colour photograph.

Lower Falls in autumn

The Lower Falls are a closely-placed series of limestone ledges that combine to create the step-like nature of this waterfall. Like the neighbouring falls, the banks of the river are surrounded by trees. Here, in the autumn sunlight, the foliage helps to make a near perfect scene with the water making its way over each limestone ledge in graceful steps. Spreading away from the base of the falls is a whole series of smaller ridges over which the water then passes.

Hardraw Force

Hardaw Force is one of those "must visit" locations. The fall, which at 100ft (30m) is the highest free-falling waterfall in England, is at the head of a small gorge behind the village of Hardraw and is reached through the local Green Dragon Inn. If there is any sunlight, the spray from the crashing waters invariably creates a rainbow, especially around the middle of the day when the sun is at the correct angle.

Sunlit barn with Addlebrough

The contrast between this sunlit barn and meadow in the foreground and the distant sight of Addlebrough in shadow makes for a strikingly simple picture which catches the mood of a glorious dales evening. The blue-grey of the high clouds above only seems to add to this mood.

Hawes

The dale between Aysgarth and Hawes is a patchwork quilt of small communities, farmsteads, barns and drystone walls interspersed with tr scattered along the river bank or field margins. This view, in the evening light, across the dale to Hawes, is typical of the landscape of Wensleyda

...ging valley of Cotterdale

...oraine land left by the ice age means you actually climb up
...the main dale before entering the valley. Beyond the
...e is a small flood plain of good bottom land that supports
...all farming community of the dale. Hidden away from casual
...t remains a small, but very real, cameo of life in the dales.

...ter frosts

...ter the landscape changes in colour and mood. Instead of the
...and yellows of summer and autumn, the browns of dead
...tion dominate the scene. The path which leads into
...dale displays these seasonal changes.

Askrigg

Askrigg nestles into the northern flank of the dale. The town was once the main
centre of the upper dale, since it lies close to the old Roman roads that lead either
over Stake Pass to Ilkley or further west over Cam Fell. When the turnpike roads
opened, trade and commerce went to Hawes instead. Askrigg achieved fame when it
became the location for filming the television series *All Creatures Great and Small*,
inspired by the Yorkshire vet James Herriot. Here the rooftops of the houses that line
the narrow winding main street glisten in the winter light as the residents stoke up
their fires against the cold.

Wharfedale

Wharfedale starts in the high fells and flows eastwards, as if to run parallel to and south of Wensleydale. However, the glacier that formed the dale came up against the huge mass of the fells of Buckden Pike and Great Whernside. This forced it to make a right turn and flow southwards so that Wharfedale now emerges to the south of the national park. Like Swaledale it is a narrow dale and has an intimate quality with the fells close by at all times. Wharfedale's landscape has been greatly affected by the Craven Fault, which thrust huge sections of great slab limestone to the surface and this is at its most spectacular at Kilnsey Crag.

Burnsall village

The well-loved village of Burnsall with its five-arched bridge is situated in the middle of the dale. It is alm a crossroads between the gritstone that lies downstream and the limestone country above.

Bolton Priory in autumn light

We start our journey at Bolton Abbey – or Bolton Priory as it is more properly known. Viewed from the shelf of wooded hillside over the river, the autumn colours of the trees add a touch of magic to an already beautiful landscape. Located on a bend in the river the old abbey buildings occupy a prime position beside the River Wharfe. The abbey and its grounds, which extend for 30,000 acres across both sides of the dale, are owned and maintained by the Duke of Devonshire.

The Strid

Deep in the gorge is the feature that gives this area its name. The Strid – or stride – is little more than a crack in the rock bed of the gorge through which all the waters of the River Wharfe have to squeeze. It is a place where nature has produced dramatic beauty. But it is also a place that can lead the unwary to tragedy – the sides of the gorge are slippery and the force of the water while exhilarating is unforgiving.

River Wharfe and Strid Wood

In this photograph of Strid Wood the River Wharfe is emerging from the gorge, with the trees all around at their very best in autumn colour. The rapid-like waters of the river tumble in a mix of white and deep blue as they pass over the rock-strewn river bed.

Littondale from Arncliffe Cote

Littondale reaches into the high fells of the dales and the River Skirfare flows down it eventually joining the River Wharfe between Conistone Pie and Kilnsey Crag. The dale has its own distinct style of small villages separated by the usual patchwork quilt of fields bounded by drystone walls and scattered with field barns. Seen here from the side of Arncliffe Cote, on the old monk's road, the dale stretches out before you with the limestone crags and heather of Old Cote Moor.

19

Conistone limestone pavement

Make the effort to climb the crag above the Dales Way and you will discover this wonderful limestone pavement laid out before you with the occasional isolated tree dotted around. Limestone pavements were created during the Ice Age, when glaciers scraped the earth from the underlying limestone. Over the millennia, since the glaciers receded, the chemicals in snow and rainwater have worked away at the limestone to produce the wonderful pattern of "grikes" – gaps or fissures – in the surface of the pavement.

Conistone Pie

Conistone Pie is a picturesque feature, an isolated circular plinth of limestone which stands like a sentinel overlooking Wharfedale. The cairn on the top helps to enhance the name by which it is popularly known. That this solitary piece of limestone got left behind by the power of the glacier is almost unbelievable. Thankfully, like many other unusual features of the limestone dales, it is there for us to enjoy.

Cupola smelting works

The tributary valley of Hebden Gill winds away from the main valley and up into the hills behind Grasssington. The industrial past comes to life here in the form of the Cupola Smelting Works. A network of tunnels leads across the moors to chimneys like this one which has been carefully preserved. The idea was to let the gasses from the smelting process pass up the tunnels to cool and deposit the lead in them on the tunnel walls. Children were then sent along the tunnels to recover the precious metal.

The upper dale from Conistone Pie

Across the dale from Kilnsey is one of the best-loved spots in the dales. Under the lea of Conistone Pie is a glorious picnic place, located close to the Dales Way, from which there is a wonderful view of Upper Wharfedale. Old Cote Moor, on the left, gives way to Upper Wharfedale itself and, on the right, the mass of Buckden Pike rises above the eastern side of the dale.

ards Starbotton from Goat Scar Crag

iew from Goat Scar Crag gives a panoramic view of the upper dale. It takes you all the way up to Buckden and beyond to Langstrothdale Chase. this perspective, the whole of the glacial valley is laid out before you. Field barns, originally built to store fodder and give shelter to livestock, are across the valley bottom with fields bounded by drystone walls.

Hubberholme church

The little church at Hubberholme has to be high on any list of places to visit in Wharfedale. This early English place of worship is seen here in late winter with its graveyard a carpet of snowdrops. Wander inside to appreciate the original architecture and one of the few minstrel's roods that remain in an English church. In complete contrast, but blending in with the building, are the modern oak pews each with a little carved mouse on them depicting their maker: the famous furniture-maker, "Mousey" Thompson of Kilburn.

Langstrothdale and Hubberholme from the old Roman Road

The old Roman road linking the settlements of Ilkley and Bainbridge climbs north out of Wharfedale from Buckden village. Seen from the Roman road above Buckden, in the early autumn sunshine, one can clearly see the parish church of Hubberholme nestling among the trees at the foot of Langstrothdale Chase. The chase and its principal village of Buckden both got their names during the period after the Norman invasion of Britain when this part of the dale was a deer-hunting estate. Nowadays, the chase and the village are a centre for tourism in the dale.

gstrothdale in
umn

...trothdale is far more
...ate than the larger
... With the autumn
...rs falling more
...gly on the fellsides
...the trees, there is real
...y here. The wildness
... high fells is never
...ay yet, on a fine
...ke this with the
... flowing gently by,
...an be at peace with
...orld.

...er Wharefdale

...iver Wharfe in
...trothdale is barely
...than a small stream
...vends its way down
...ale over a bed of
...tone. The drystone
...on the far side are
...ently set back to
... the route of the
...Way to pass along
...verbank itself.

Malham and the Three Peaks

Towards the southern end of the Yorkshire Dales is one the most impressive features of its landscape, Malham Cove. It is perhaps the most magnificent manifestation the Craven Fault, the presence of which has done so much to create the unique landscape of the dales. We start here before moving across the moors to Upper Ribblesdale and around the Three Peaks of Pen-y-ghent (2,277ft/694m), Ingleborough (2,372ft/723m) and Whernside (2,415ft/ 736m). The limestone features and the results of glacial action really stand out; some the finest examples in Britain are to be found around Ingleborough and Crummackdale.

The outstanding geology of this area is due to the massive limestone slabs which were forced to the surface during the last ice age. Limestone is usually a dull, white colour since it is formed from the remains of millions of tiny sea-dwelling animals over the millennia. This helps to make it stand out dramatically among the dark colouring of the surrounding dales. The most impressive limestone features occur in crags such as Malham Cove or in large, flat areas called pavements. The pavements are worn down by the effects of wind and rain into "clints", or flat areas, and "grikes", which are fissures or gaps in the rock. Because limestone is easily eroded by chemicals in the air and water it is quickly weathered into unusual and dramatic shapes. Limestone is also porous, so surface water often disappears suddenly into sink holes such as those found above Malham.

Warrendale Knotts

The crags of Warrendale Knotts stand guard over the old green road below, well to the west of Malham Moor and on the fells overlooking Ribblesdale. They are more rounded than the cliffs of Malham or Kilnsey, with large amounts of loose stone screes.

Malham Cove

Before the permafrost thawed at the end of the last ice age, this massive 260ft (80m) limestone cliff was in all probability a gigantic waterfall. Today we have been left with one of the most dramatic features of the Yorkshire Dales limestone landscape, created by the Craven Fault which formed the limestone uplands.

dale Scar

to Malham Cove, Gordale Scar is an equally impressive sight. Created over nds of years by vast torrents of water that poured down from the fell, we w left with an awe-inspiring gorge with magnificent limestone crags and verhanging fells. Water still tumbles down through a stone archway and all at the head of the gorge. It is common for walkers to make their way side of the waterfall gradually climbing on to the moors beyond.

Pen-y-ghent from above the caves

Pen-y-ghent is also visible from the hills around Winskill. In the evening light of late summer the great bulk of the fell can be seen rising above the little farmsteads in Silverdale below. The course of a drystone wall can be traced climbing up the steep crags and over the summit itself. In times gone by, the boundaries of nearly all the parishes of the Dales were marked out by drystone walls.

Looking up Ribblesda[le] to Whernside

The great whale-shaped hump [of] Whernside at the head of Ribblesdale marks the skyline looking up the dale from the fellside above Horton in Ribblesdale. The combination o[f] little limestone outcrops, drysto[ne] walls and barns is typical of thi[s] part of the dale. At the top of Ribblesdale is Ribblehead, famo[us] for the Ribblehead Viaduct, wh[ere] the Settle to Carlisle railway lin[e] crosses the moor.

Ingleborough from th[e] Winskill Stones

Follow the track from Attermir[e] and Warrendale Knotts northw[ard] and you will eventually overloo[k] Upper Ribblesdale near the Win[skill] Stones. Seen below in the foreground, they provide a stri[king] counterpoint to this view acros[s the] dale towards Ingleborough, wh[ich] is covered in snow on the dista[nt] skyline. The hamlet of Upper Winskill is in the middle distan[ce] and the scars from quarrying, n[ear] Helwith Bridge, are evident on [the] far fellside.

...leborough in low cloud

...early morning light and changeable weather often produce
...spheric landscapes. Here, the sky is full of drama with the light
...ing through the clouds which are swirling around the summit of
...borough. The fells in the middle distance are in deep shadow from
...louds overhead, but are in complete contrast to the tranquil spring
... with sheep and their lambs grazing contentedly in the foreground.

...estone pavement above the dry valley

...waters that once poured over Malham Cove go underground at the
...r sinks" leaving a "dry valley" between them and Malham Cove.
...ong lines of clints and grikes in this limestone pavement, which
...ooks the "dry valley", are displayed in a spectacular fashion in the
...fternoon light. In the distance, Dean Moor Hill (with the Pennine
...making its way around its flanks) lies to the left and Combe Hill and
...Vatlowes to the centre and right of the skyline.

...enscar and Ingleborough

...r the lea of the northern face on Ingleborough lies Ravenscar, a series
...estone pavements that stretch out along a plateau of land under the
... lonely thistle flowers defiantly from one of the grikes, surrounded
... broad clints that are so typical of Ravenscar.

Twin Pecca Falls

The waterfalls in the two valleys which begin at Ingleton are some of the finest in the dales. As you follow the course of the River Twiss, one of the first waterfalls that you come to after crossing Pecca Bridge is the Twin Pecca falls, pictured here. In a series of steps, the water tumbles 98ft (30m) over the rock formations surrounded by the high sides of the valley which almost form a gorge around the river.

Dentdale from Deepdale

Take the road up Kingsdale from Ingleton and, once over the watershed, you will discover this panoramic view down Deepdale and into Dentdale. On the left of the picture the Howgill Fells can be seen in the distance. On this fine late June day, the freshly cut meadows add a variety of colours to a green and fertile landscape.

Drumlins near Ribblehead

The glorious late evening light shows off the undulating terrain at the head of Ribblesdale to its best effect. Known as drumlins, these rolling lines of hillocks are formed of boulder clay rocks and pebbles, and were created by glacial action. The sunlight has picked out the gable ends of the barns and the lines of drystone walls as they seem to wander over the rolling landscape.

Cottongrass *(Cyperaceae eriophorum)* and meadows

High on the fells at the head of Dentdale is this attractive view across wild and uncultivated moorland. In the foreground is a mass of cottongrass, blowing gently in the summer breeze. The contrast between the cultivated fields on the distant fellside and the wild moorland landscape below is unusual.

Roadside flowers

At this time of year the road verges along the valley in Dentdale are covered in a rich variety of wild flowers. In this quiet lane with the old barn as a backdrop you will find common vetch, red campion, dog roses, meadow cranesbill and many more.

Dent Town

The village of Dent Town is the main centre and for many the chief attraction in Dentdale. It is a few miles south-east of the market town of Sedbergh. With its narrow but well-maintained cobbled streets lined with period buildings, this little gem is the quintessential place to stop and browse. Here the freshly whitewashed row of shops and cottages takes you back to a former age.

Crummackdale

Tucked away between Ribblesdale and Ingleborough is a little dale that epitomises all that is best about the limestone dales of Yorkshire. Crummackdale is not a big place – barely five miles long – but its small scale is more than compensated for by the views. From the fells around Crummackdale, you can enjoy some of the finest limestone scenery to be found anywhere. To enjoy it though, you will have to walk because roads are – thankfully perhaps – very scarce.

Limestone view to Pen-y-ghent

In this view, again with a glorious sky overhead, we can see across the head of the dale, with Moughton Scar in the middle distance and the great massive form of Pen-y-ghent standing proud on the skyline. It is difficult to believe that this landscape was created over 300 million years ago at the bottom of a tropical sea.

Limestone arch

This photograph of a limestone arch is taken from a low position to get a good view of its base. The plinth stone is perched so finely that you would not think it could withstand the power of the elements, especially in winter, but it does.

The lone tree

An impression of the vast panoramas to be seen on this route can be gained from this view of the upper reaches of the dale, which are bounded by the massive Moughton Scars. Taken from the western ridge this lone tree seems to emphasise the sheer grandeur of Crummackdale

The limestone pavement from Sulber Gate

At the head of the dale you come to Sulber Gate, from where you can look down on the almost unbelievable view of what is one of the most sensational of all the limestone pavements in the Yorkshire Dales. Literally stretching for miles, the pavement continues right on to the top of Moughton Fell itself. To the right, Crummackdale leads away southwards and, in the distance, some 20 miles away and well into Lancashire, is the unmistakeable shape of Pendle Hill.

Evening sky over Moughton

Between Moughton Scar and Moughton Fell you come to an old packhorse route which leads you back down into the dale, across limestone meadows and eventually back to your starting point. This photograph, taken from the track, shows the mass of Moughton Fell combined with the lonely tree and a wonderful evening sky. Crummackdale is a place which draws visitors back time and time again. It is the essence of what the limestone dales are about on a grand but also intimate scale.

First published in 2009 by Myriad Books Limited
35 Bishopsthorpe Road, London SE26 4PA

Photographs and text copyright © Dave Coates

Dave Coates has asserted his right under the Copyright, Designs and
Patents Act, 1988, to be identified as the author of this work

ISBN 1 84746 241 3

Designed by Jerry Goldie

Printed in China